Epistemic Explanations

Epistemic Explanations develops an improved virtue epistemology and uses it to explain several epistemic phenomena. Part I lays out a telic virtue epistemology that accommodates varieties of knowledge and understanding particularly pertinent to the humanities. Part II develops an epistemology of suspension of judgment, by relating it to degrees of confidence and to inquiry. Part III develops a substantially improved telic virtue epistemology by appeal to default assumptions important in domains of human performance generally, and in our intellectual lives as a special case. This reconfigures earlier virtue epistemology, which now seems a first approximation. This part also introduces a metaphysical hierarchy of epistemic categories and defends in particular a category of secure knowledge.

Born in Cuba, **Ernest Sosa** immigrated to the USA as a teenager. After his BA from the University of Miami, and his PhD from the University of Pittsburgh, he has taught at Brown University and then at Rutgers, each for decades. During that time he has had numerous dissertation students who have attained distinction. He was a President of the American Philosophical Association (Eastern) and was elected to the American Academy of Arts and Sciences. In 1980 he inaugurated the virtue theoretic approach in epistemology, which he has developed through a half dozen books, many published articles, and replies in many author/critic sessions and books. He has given several distinguished lectures, including the Locke and the Carus Lectures, and has received several prizes. The APA has established a prize lectureship and a fellowship in his honor for excellence in epistemology.

About the front cover:

Calligraphy by Miley Mi . The Classical Chinese character for knowledge is on the left and consists of two parts: to the left within the character is ARROW and to its right is MOUTH. On our cover, to the right of that whole character is the character for wisdom, which puts SUN beneath arrow and mouth. In these two whole characters, the virtue epistemologist might see: "from the mouth come assertions aimed at truth, which can attain the success of knowledge in the way an arrow aimed at a target can attain success. And such an assertion can attain a further success of wisdom when guided in proper conditions provided by sunlight."

Epistemic Explanations

A Theory of Telic Normativity, and What It Explains

ERNEST SOSA
Rutgers University

Great Clarendon Street, Oxford, OX2 6DP,
United Kingdom

Oxford University Press is a department of the University of Oxford. It furthers the University's objective of excellence in research, scholarship, and education by publishing worldwide. Oxford is a registered trade mark of Oxford University Press in the UK and certain other countries

First published 2021
First published in paperback 2024

Published in the United States of America by Oxford University Press
198 Madison Avenue, New York, NY 10016, United States of America

British Library Cataloguing in Publication Data
Data available

Library of Congress Cataloging in Publication Data
Data available

ISBN 978-0-19-885646-7 (Hbk.)
ISBN 978-0-19-890100-6 (Pbk.)

DOI: 10.1093/oso/9780198856467.001.0001

Acknowledgments

My earlier books have drawn from previously published articles or from lecture series. This book has reversed direction, as it was conceived whole, divided into its four parts. Only subsequently have a couple of its chapters overlapped substantially with journal articles. Chapter 3 overlaps with "Suspension as Spandrel," *Episteme* (2019): 357–368. Chapter 9 overlaps with "Reflection and Security," *Episteme* (2019): 474–489. Chapter 11 overlaps with "Intuitions and Foundations: the Relevance of Moore and Wittgenstein," in *The A Priori in Philosophy*, ed. by Albert Casullo and Joshua C. Thurow (Oxford University Press, 2013).

I have benefited from presenting this material in seminars and workshops at Rutgers over several years, receiving helpful feedback in that connection from Bob Beddor, D Black, Laura Callahan, Chris Copan, Megan Feeney, Will Fleisher, Carolina Flores, Danny Forman, Georgi Gardiner, Igal Kvart, James McIntyre, Andrew Moon, Paul Pietroski, and Caroline von Klemperer. In that connection, and also more recently, discussion with Matt McGrath and Chris Willard-Kyle has been helpful, especially on the nature and epistemology of suspension. Discussion with Stephen Grimm has long been helpful, including in connection with several events organized by him at Fordham. Finally, I am also grateful for the epistemological work and input of many friends and interlocutors, over many years, including Robert Audi, Guy Axtell, Jason Baehr, Heather Battaly, Matt Benton, Sven Bernecker, Paul Boghossian, Rodrigo Borges, Bob Brandom, Bill Brewer, Brit Brogaard, Fernando Broncano, Fernando Broncano-Berrocal, Jessica Brown, Otavio Bueno, Tyler Burge, Al Casullo, Leo Cheung, Matthew Chrisman, David Christensen, Eli Chudnoff, E.J. Coffman, Stewart Cohen, Annalisa Coliva, Juan Colomina-Alminana, Juan Comesaña, Earl

Conee, Josep Corbi, Alberto Cordero, Charles Cote-Bouchard, Jonathan Dancy, Marian David, Claudio de Almeida, Mike DePaul, Keith DeRose, Kate Devitt, Imogen Dickie, Jose Diez Calzada, Pascal Engel, Angeles Eraña, Jesús Ezquerro, Jeremy Fantl, Richard Feldman, Miguel Angel Fernandez, Dick Foley, Bryan Frances, Lizzie Fricker, Miranda Fricker, Jane Friedman, Richard Fumerton, Manuel García-Carpintero, Angel Garcia Rodriguez, Claudia Lorena García, Tamar Gendler, Brie Gertler, Hans-Johann Glock, Sandy Goldberg, Alan Goldman, Alvin Goldman, Thomas Grundmann, Anil Gupta, Michael Hannon, John Hawthorne, Allan Hazlett, David Henderson, Stephen Hetherington, Chris Hill, Eli Hirsch, Frank Hoffman, Terry Horgan, Joachim Horvath, Paul Horwich, Robert Howell, Yong Huang, Michael Huemer, Bruce Hunter, Guillermo Hurtado, Alex Jackson, Carrie Jenkins Ichikawa, Jonathan Jenkins Ichikawa, Frank Jackson, Bredo Johnsen, Mark Kaplan, Jason Kawall, Tom Kelly, Andrea Kern, Jens Kipper, Peter Klein, Hilary Kornblith, Saul Kripke, Jonathan Kvanvig, Jennifer Lackey, Maria Lasonen-Aarnio, Adam Leite, Keith Lehrer, Noah Lemos, Clayton Littlejohn, Manolo Liz, Kirk Ludwig, Michael Lynch, Jack Lyons, Susanna Mantel, Peter Markie, John McDowell, Aidan McGlynn, Brian McLaughlin, Guido Melchior, Anne Meylan, Michael Mi, Alan Millar, Jennifer Nado, Jesús Navarro, Martine Nida-Rümelin, Michael O'Rourke, Michael Pace, Carlotta Pavese, Chris Peacocke, Carlos Pereda, David Perez Chico, Manuel Perez Otero, Christian Piller, Alvin Plantinga, Joelle Proust, Jim Pryor, Peter Railton, Baron Reed, João Carlos Salles, Carolina Sartorio, Jonathan Schaffer, Josh Schechter, Susanna Schellenberg, Fred Schmitt, Eric Schwitzgebel, Daniele Sgaravatti, Joseph Shieber, Susanna Siegel, Nico Silins, Waldomiro Silva Filho, Brian Skyrms, Michael Slote, Martin Smith, Jason Stanley, Pedro Stepanenko, Matthias Steup, Stephen Stich, Joshua Thurow, Claudine Tiercelin, Josefa Toribio, Nick Treanor, Cheng-Hung Tsai, John Turri, Luis Valdés Villanueva, Margarita Valdés, Jim Van Cleve, Jesús Vega, Enrique Villanueva, Brian Weatherson, Ralph Wedgwood, Michael Williams, Tim Williamson, Nick Wolterstorff, Crispin Wright, Linda Zagzebski, and José Zalabardo.

I was much saddened by the passing of Tony Brueckner, Jaegwon Kim, Adam Morton, and Barry Stroud, with all of whom I discussed epistemology very helpfully for many years.

Large chunks of this text have been presented at various venues, where critical discussion and formal commentaries have led to much improvement. This includes the *Episteme* conference organized by Jennifer Lackey in honor of my work and held in Tenerife in 2019, with proceedings later in the journal; four lectures at the Urbino summer school in epistemology, organized by Adriano Angelucci and Daniele Sgaravatti; the 2020 conference in my honor in La Laguna, organized by Margarita Vazquez and David Perez Chico, and whose proceedings will appear in a volume edited by Perez Chico and Modesto Gomez Alonso; lectures in Paris organized by Joelle Proust at the Jean Nicod, by Pascal Engel at the Ecole Normal Superiore, by Claudine Tiercelin at the College de France, and by Jean-Baptiste Rauzy at the Sorbonne; the 2020 conference held at Fudan University in Shanghai, whose proceedings will appear in a book, *Ernest Sosa Encounters Chinese Philosophy*, edited by the organizer, Yong Huang, and published by Bloomsbury Press; and a series of three lectures at UC-Irvine, organized by Duncan Pritchard, with comments by Pritchard and by Annalisa Coliva.

I am *especially* grateful for repeated interaction on ideas in this book, in depth and over a span of recent years, with Adam Carter, Modesto Gomez Alonso, Peter J. Graham, John Greco, Chris Kelp, Matt McGrath, Lisa Miracchi, Ram Neta, Duncan Pritchard, Blake Roeber, Mona Simion, David Sosa, Kurt Sylvan, and Chris Willard-Kyle.

Contents

IV. A HISTORICAL ANTECEDENT

Preface

This book develops an improved virtue epistemology and uses it to explain several epistemic phenomena.

Part I takes up a sort of firsthand knowledge and understanding particularly suitable for the humanities, and lays out a telic virtue epistemology that accommodates such knowledge alongside other varieties.

Chapter 1 takes up that distinctive sort of understanding, and proposes a virtue-theoretic account of its normative standing. The widespread desirability of such understanding holds two lessons concerning humanistic issues, including many in philosophy: first, one about the place of disagreement over such issues; second, one about the epistemic standards appropriate for them.

Chapter 2 lays out a telic virtue epistemology that accommodates such knowledge and understanding. Based on that telic account, the chapter also distinguishes two sides of epistemology: the theory of knowledge ("gnoseology," for short) on one side, and intellectual ethics on the other.

Part II develops an epistemology of suspension.

Chapter 3 explains what it is to suspend judgment, and how such suspension attains normative status. Problems are raised for a competing view, strict evidentialism, and virtue-theoretic solutions are offered for those problems.

Chapter 4 refocuses on suspension, on degrees of confidence, and on inquiry; along with their explanatory interrelations.

Chapter 5 takes up when and how suspension is epistemically apt.

Chapter 6 explores varieties of suspension and the relation of proper suspension to being in a position to know.

Part III develops a substantially improved telic virtue epistemology.

Chapter 7 introduces a distinctive idea of default assumptions, and explains how that idea reconfigures earlier virtue epistemology.

That earlier virtue epistemology now seems a first approximation whose insights require appeal to default assumptions, as is next shown more fully, in Chapter 8.

Chapter 9 introduces a metaphysical hierarchy of epistemic categories, and defends in particular a category of secure knowledge.

Chapter 10 explains how our expanded view makes room for a sort of "epistemic justification" constitutive of knowledge.

Part IV is about the Moore–Wittgenstein episode in twentieth-century epistemology.

Chapter 11 considers Wittgenstein's *On Certainty* response to Moore's epistemology, and places it in a broader epistemological context, by relation to Part III, and to Chapter 7 in particular.

PART I

INSIGHT AND UNDERSTANDING, AND TWO SIDES OF EPISTEMOLOGY

1
Insight and Understanding

Let us explore a particular sort of understanding, understanding why, and a related sort of *knowledge why—firsthand* knowledge why—and the place of this in the humanities, including philosophy.

We shall focus on one dimension of the humanities, not the whole, and on the humanistic side of philosophy, though there's a lot more to philosophy than that.

I'll be arguing for the importance of *firsthand intuitive insight.* And that in turn will bear interestingly on two questions in the epistemology of the humanities, including philosophy.

First question: Given that firsthand intuitive insight has special value and standing in the humanities, how is the epistemic standing of our own beliefs affected when we encounter the disagreement of others?

Second, if firsthand intuitive insight *is* shown to have such special standing and value, how if at all does this affect what epistemological standards are properly operative in humanistic domains?

Eventually, we will come to these two questions about the humanities, one about the place of disagreement, and the other about the proper epistemic standards. But first we take up the place and value of intuitive insight.

1. Of the varieties of understanding, one has special importance for our project, namely *understanding why*, *understanding why it is so that p.* Such *understanding why* is correlated with *knowing* why, and both come in degrees of quality, as in the following example.

Suppose a woman contracts an infection, which we attribute to the germs on her airplane tray table. Suppose she *did* pick up germs on those surfaces and transferred them to her nose or eyes. But what if the germs would not have affected anyone with normal defenses? Suppose

Epistemic Explanations: A Theory of Telic Normativity, and What it Explains. Ernest Sosa, Oxford University Press (2021). © Ernest Sosa. DOI: 10.1093/oso/9780198856467.003.0001

they would have come *nowhere near* doing so. Our woman acquires the infection *in part* because of the germs but mainly because her defenses are *very much* lowered (by her cancer treatment).

Suppose contact with the germs was indeed essentially involved in how and why the woman was infected. If so, we do have *some* knowledge of why she got infected. And so we do gain *some* understanding of why it happened. She was infected at least in part because of her contact with the germs. But our understanding in that case falls short. We have *some* understanding without understanding fully. Just as you might have *some* justification for a certain belief without being justified outright in holding that belief, so you might have some understanding of a certain phenomenon without understanding it well enough to really understand it outright.

2. We would like to understand a distinction between questions properly settled through epistemic deference, and questions that require or invite firsthand assessment, beyond sheer deference.

Many questions call just for information. Take utilitarian questions, whether financial, legal, or medical. Answering such questions has a practical value fully realized with no need for deeper understanding. By contrast, humanistic questions hold scant practical value, at least in the short term.

Although we focus on humanistic questions, we'll consider an account that extends to many questions in the liberal arts more generally; in fact, we begin with an example in geometry, a discipline not usually placed in the humanities.

A young teenager still innocent of plane geometry is told by his teacher that the Pythagorean Theorem is true. The teacher lays out the theorem (not any proof, just the theorem), and affirms it to be true. A smart kid with a good memory, the student thereby knows through deference the truth of the theorem. But he falls short in his understanding of why the theorem is true, lacking as he does an adequate grasp of any proof.

It does not help if the student accepts by sheer deference the conditional that conjoins in its antecedent all the premises of some proof, and contains the theorem itself as its consequent, along with accepting by deference *also* the truth of the antecedent. He still does not grasp the truth of that conjunction well enough firsthand. He accepts it just through deference to the teacher.

That is why he falls short in his understanding of the truth of that theorem. The desired level of understanding requires insight of one's own into the premises and into the immediate inferences that constitute a proof.[1]

3. Nevertheless, although an insightful proof would constitute a higher attainment, deference to the geometry teacher *can* still enable knowledge of the theorem's truth, even absent understanding.

Compare also humanistic domains such as art and its appreciation, the nature and content of morality, and many issues in philosophy. In these domains, knowledge through deference seems again *available.*

Prima facie, someone trustworthy might answer aptly some normative yes/no question, which provides some secondhand knowledge to their hearers. Many others might then add their powerful support, with no dissent in view, enhancing the quality of that secondhand knowledge. So, what distinguishes moral, aesthetic, and other humanistic domains is *not* that secondhand knowledge is there *unavailable*, but rather that *firsthand* knowledge *is both available and particularly desirable.* What is further available in those domains, *and* particularly desirable, is also knowledge, firsthand knowledge, attained when the thinker gets it right sufficiently through firsthand competence.

4. Why might normative humanistic questions invite, reward, and even require understanding, and not just information?

Here is one reason: Because anyone who navigates uncritically, on mere instinct or tribal mores, or on mere deference, neglects their rational standing.[2] But why do we prioritize *firsthand* knowledge as we

[1] And it is not just understanding-why and knowledge-why that admit our distinction between a grasp that is merely deferential and one that is firsthand. Expressionless and in a flat voice, you may tell me you have a headache, and I may thus acquire deferential knowledge of your headache. But your firsthand knowledge has higher quality, is more certain.

[2] Any proper human life will include a set of values—prudential, political, moral, aesthetic—supported by a humanly relevant outlook on oneself and the environing world. Such a view would then contain degrees of the coherent generality that underwrite corresponding degrees of understanding.

so often do? Because it is so often through such knowledge that you flourish as a *rational* animal. Practical, utilitarian questions are properly answered with mere information acquired through sheer deference. But deeper choices require rational guidance beyond deference.

5. That is the high road, which I am myself willing to take, but there is also a less lofty route.

Suppose human flourishing does not *require* that we prioritize firsthand thought. Suppose instead that each of us has leeway on how much of that to go in for. That is bound to depend on one's specific situation, interests, and abilities.

A life of tilling the land is far removed from the Aristotelian life of pure contemplation. But no one is to blame for a life of hard labor if they have no choice all things considered. Of course such a life can be admirable, even if deprived of much rational attainment.

We need not even agree with Aristotle's hierarchical claims. Suppose we recognize the widest range of proper life plans, and we put them *all on the same level*, or anyhow we omit any hierarchy. Suppose we just focus on lives that *do* make room for intrinsically motivated desire to understand. For *such* lives, our distinction between the utilitarian and the humanistic *still* comes to the fore.

That distinction then has extremely broad application. It is not restricted to highbrow interests in the fine arts, the humanities, and pure philosophy. On the contrary, firsthand judgment is apposite in athletic stadiums and arenas as well as in symphony halls and museums, in barroom arguments as well as in seminar dialectic. It may be *even more jarring* to *just defer* in lowbrow venues.

On this more democratic, less prescriptive approach, when is firsthand judgment preferable to mere deference? This now depends on the agent's desire for understanding, whether highbrow or lowbrow; and it depends also on whether such understanding requires firsthand insight. So, we are still left with an interesting question to consider: Just when is a desire for outright understanding satisfiable only through firsthand insight?

6. *When and why* does outright understanding require a firsthand approach? According to our account, you understand well enough why

p if, and only if, you *know well enough why p*, which requires knowing, for some fact, *that p because of that fact*. That is a minimum *necessary* condition.

Even when that is not *sufficient*, however, what is required in addition may just be more of the same. That is suggested already by our case of infection caused by germs on a tray table, where we learn that the woman's defenses are low. More generally, what is needed for enhanced understanding may be just *more knowledge*, more propositional knowledge that is properly interrelated.

We thus face the following challenge.

Suppose you know why it is so that p. Might you not know this simply because you know, about some rich and deep enough set of facts, that it is *because of those facts* that it comes about that p? Is such rich and deep enough knowledge attainable only through a firsthand approach?

Not clearly. Why can't it be attained through deference to testimony *that p because q, r, s,...?* Such testimony might be provided through a textbook or through a treatise. And this now threatens to drive a wedge between two things that seemed to be bound together: namely, the desirability of going beyond testimonial deference, and the thirst for understanding, with the latter explaining the former. It has become less clear why we need to go beyond deference. How is this challenge to be met?

7. Here first is a concession. We need not insist that, *on any possible question*, outright understanding requires firsthand access, beyond deference. In order to understand better why the woman got infected, for example, I need to know *also* that her defenses were extremely low. Her infection is more fully explained when we attribute it not only to the germs but also, and mainly, to the lowered defenses. But this further fact is one available through testimonial deference.

So much for our concession. Not all important questions call for thoroughly *firsthand* understanding and knowledge-why. On many questions a deep, full explanation might amount to a rich enough set of facts, whose grasp through deference enhances understanding.

However, questions in the humanities might still require a particularly large and salient element of direct rational appreciation. If so, why might this be so?

8. Why might a question call for *much* more than deference? Because it might call for a kind of rational understanding.

Consider first the aesthetic assessment of an artwork. Is it original, arresting, elegant? Let's focus here just on whether it is (artistically, not just financially) *successful*. If it is indeed successful, there will be *reasons* why that is so, reasons that will form the ground of its success, in virtue of which the work attains that success.

And there is then a notable distinction between the following two cases:

> In the *first* case one knows through sheer deference about the success of a certain artwork (identified just as the seventh on a certain list).
>
> In the *second* case one spots at least implicitly the reasons why the work is successful, so that one's knowledge of its success is based on those grounding reasons (even if this basing remains implicit).

In the latter case, one has firsthand knowledge of the work's success along with understanding its success by knowing why it is successful, through insight into the grounds for that success. Here firsthand humanistic knowledge comes with understanding attained through insightful rational explanation. One experiences the work in the relevant way—be it a piece of music, a painting, or a novel—and one discerns the reasons for the work's success through firsthand experience.

9. *Objection*

Not so fast! Suppose a critic explains that the work has features F1, F2,...Fn, and that these are the features that make it successful. Would that not enable one to know why the work is successful?

Reply

Yes, if the critic is reliable enough, then deferring to their testimony may enable us to know that much. But one might still fall short significantly in one's understanding. Recall the student who knows the Pythagorean theorem to be true, and also knows to some extent *why* it is true, but *only* by deferring *throughout* to the teacher.

10. Our point about aesthetic judgment applies also to moral judgment.

An adolescent may defer to a parent's moral advice, for example, with no proper firsthand appreciation of the features that make the recommended action right, nor of the fact that they do so. The mother may say: "Tommy, you must apologize." She may have seen the whole action and may be sensitive to various features of the case that she is unable to specify fully in an English formulation. She may have seen the level of grief in the eyes of the friend at being bullied by Tommy. The behavior was not terrible, but it was definitely bad enough to require an apology. Tommy may just defer to the mother and go ahead with his apology. But even later that day he may fail to appreciate on his own when an apology is required.

In that case, the child gains from the mother *some* understanding of why he must apologize. She tells him that it's because of the bullying and the grief that it caused. And Tommy does sincerely defer. But his secondhand knowledge falls short. It manifests insufficient appreciation of the behavior that matters, and of the relevant level of upset. He takes it entirely on deferential trust that his behavior and the upset that it caused were bad enough to require apology. And this gives only truncated understanding.

11. The Pythagorean example is comparable in its own way. Also comparable in a different way is a tourist's deference to a museum guide who attributes a painting's success to how the pastel colors contrast with the darker reds. The tourist gains some appreciation and understanding of why the painting is successful. But what if *he is color blind*? In that case, the tourist falls short in his understanding, even as he views the painting firsthand.

Understanding through firsthand knowledge is salient for normative issues generally, and for moral issues more specifically. It is salient in the humanities generally, where we should and do often prioritize firsthand, nondeferential judgment.

12. Something similar applies to another side of the humanities, namely metaphysics.

Suppose the topic of social construction comes up in bar-room conversation and someone points out that we are sitting on bar stools, artifacts composed of disks attached to legs. But she then adds that this observation is partial and superficial. What matters more deeply is that such items are given a certain purpose by the culture, one that their physical constitution enables them to serve. Bar stools are constructed by carpenters, true enough, but more deeply they are socially constructed. If that function were not conventionally assigned to objects so shaped, they might constitute side tables rather than stools. From there we might turn to more gripping issues of gender, or race, or the nature of persons, or justice, or knowledge, as Socrates might have done. (Recall the *Euthyphro* on the direction of grounding. Does it go from god-love to goodness, or from goodness to god-love?)

Through reflection we might attain a kind of firsthand insight as to what grounds various phenomena of great human interest. What we need is insight into thought experiments that will reveal the relevant metaphysical *by-relations*, the metaphysical basis, so that the phenomenon of interest comes to be *thereby*. Of course, if such subject matter eludes one's grasp, or its subtlety leaves one bored or impatient, then one may forego such insight, and that is fine. Such metaphysics is not for everyone, nor is philosophy, nor the humanities.

Such issues of social construction illustrate a sort of understanding that some of us do find enlightening.

Humanistic understanding can thus be desirable for at least two sorts of reasons. First, it can be required for the understanding of values and choices that should guide a rational animal. Second, it can also be desirable just for its own sake, for the satisfaction of our curiosity. This latter is crucial in the humanities, and in the liberal arts more generally, as with geometry.

It remains only to draw some lessons about the proper epistemology for the liberal arts, including the humanities, and philosophy more specifically.

13. *First lesson*

Note first the intimate connection between testimony and disagreement, which holds a lesson about disagreement.

There is a notorious problem of disagreement in the humanities, philosophy being no exception. How can we claim to know much at all in fields with so much disagreement? Faced with that, should we just suspend on all disputed issues? Not if we downgrade deference, for this now has an interesting implication.

Once we properly aim for firsthand knowledge in pursuit of understanding, while bracketing secondhand information, *we can properly discount disagreement*. Disagreement must be discounted along with testimony, *disagreement being a special case of testimony*. In any such domain we properly aim for aptness of judgment *unaided* by deference. More generally, we aim for aptness of judgment *unaffected* by sheer deference.

In any case, we cannot have it both ways. Where deference is optional and best avoided, there disagreement does *not* after all render our judgments so problematic.

Firsthand knowledge in pursuit of understanding requires that you reach your answer through competence seated in yourself, not through sheer deference to others. The *mere* fact that someone else holds a contrary opinion need not move you to revise, not in the slightest.[3] It may instead prompt just an exchange of views. But even when engaged in such exchange, you may still aim to judge autonomously.

That makes for a hopeful epistemology of the humanities, including issues of aesthetic and moral interpretation and appreciation, and issues of armchair philosophy more generally.

Humanistic disciplines tend to be organized differently from what is familiar and important in the sciences. A lot of humanistic inquiry tends to be individual, with no deference to others. In philosophy the attitude is pervasive. Everything is subject to critical scrutiny. Nothing significant is accepted through sheer deference. That's how it is, and plausibly how it should be, which fits our discussion of the main role of testimony in philosophy. The interesting implication is that disagreement should not be as troubling in the humanities as it is often taken to be. In philosophy specifically, we should not be so much moved by disagreement, since we

[3] Except when "in my opinion no one holds any opinion contrary to my own," and such cases.

should rarely be moved to assign much weight to *the sheer say-so* of someone else, no matter how well placed. We can be moved to reconsider, yes. We can even be *obliged* to reconsider, on pain of negligence; but not to revise, not in the slightest. Note the distinction that matters here: *reconsidering* is to be distinguished from *revising*. You can do the former seriously, without doing the latter, without being moved in the slightest by the sheer say-so of someone else.

That view of humanistic accomplishment, in philosophy specifically, aligns well with Descartes's *Meditations*. These are a record of the author's meditations, but they also serve, and are surely meant to serve, as a script for the reader's own performance. A main aim of the work is the enlightenment of the reader, not through deference to the author but through guidance to firsthand insight and understanding.

A geometry teacher might also aim to provide a script meant to aid students attain their own insight into a proof of the theorem. In providing such guidance, she goes beyond merely presenting the abstract structure whose necessary truth underlies the soundness and validity of the argument. Rather, the teacher presents a script for a student's own performance through inferences by natural deduction. The student would be guided to the insights required, tied together by immediate inferences in proper sequence. By following that script properly, the student can attain firsthand insight into the truth of the Pythagorean theorem. In this respect, the cases are identical, even if Cartesian reflection is conducted in the first person, unlike geometry.

Correct judgment deriving from firsthand competence can of course depend on the conduit to reasons provided by testimony. That is how you can properly depend on guidance by Descartes, or by a geometry teacher. Having been made aware of good available reasoning, you can then make it your own, so that the success of your judgment is then a firsthand success. And the accomplishment will then depend not at all on *sheer* deference to someone else.

14. *Objection*

We are assuming that in humanistic domains we aim to answer our questions and to get it right in so doing. How then can we coherently have this aim while refusing to defer to others recognized as *more reliable* than we are?

Reply

That is a good question, but it has a good answer, by analogy with the case of archery, our model of evaluable performance.

As an archer, I would normally want to hit my target through first-hand competence. This might be in the sport of archery or as a hunter in the woods. When I allow a coach to guide my hands, by contrast, the desire for firsthand performance is suppressed. Not so when I perform as a competitor or a hunter. There I dispense with external aids. I cannot defer to a coach's direct guidance as I draw my bow and prepare to shoot. And this is so even if I still very much want to hit the target and know perfectly well that I could do so *much* more reliably with the coach's help!

In many domains agents aim for *firsthand* success attained aptly, through competence. Often, external aids that would boost competence must be shunned. Many are forbidden formally, as are performance enhancing drugs. An artist who performs on the stage with a coach at their elbow would ridiculously violate the conventions of artistic performance. Even when there are no laws, rules, or conventions that prohibit such aids, moreover, performers still aim for fully apt firsthand success.

15. The point is brought home by a striking example.

Of two aficionados addicted to the *NY Times* crossword puzzle, one tries to solve the puzzle with no external aids, and often succeeds. Another always waits for the answer to be published the next day, then dutifully fills it in, and gets the solution exactly right.

Why does that seem so foolish? Because the whole point of a crossword puzzle is to give you the amusement that goes with a challenge that can be met but not too easily, one that calls on your own resources and engages your attention pleasurably.

Both agents want equally to get it right, yet one of them foolishly neglects the proper objective. Truth *is* a part of the objective, but *only a part*. Attaining the truth by just copying the right answer is not in the right spirit. Rather, your aim must be not just success but *firsthand* success.

In *that* specific respect humanist judgments are like crossword solutions. Indeed, given our broad understanding of humanist questions, crossword puzzles constitute a light humanistic domain, where it is preferable and generally preferred to reach one's answers firsthand, not just through deference.

We saw earlier how humanist value judgments properly engage one's own autonomous competence. Proper deliberation uses testimony *only* as a conduit to reasons *which can then be accessed firsthand*, adopted as one's own, and deployed through firsthand reasoning. Testimony can play *that* role of conduit perfectly well, since the recipient need give no weight to the word of the testifier as such.

16. This last point gains further importance when we move beyond the evaluative side of the humanities, as with many questions in philosophy. If our aim as philosopher were only correctness no matter how attained, then deference would tend to be required. Suppose I am convinced that my opponent is a more gifted, skillful philosopher, more likely to have the right answer. If then my sole aim on that question is to answer it correctly, I am best advised to defer.

By contrast, if my aim is to attain a correct answer, *and to do so firsthand*, I must *not* defer to the opponent's say-so, *simply as such*. But is one not acting *incompetently* by failing to give proper weight to a source recognized as most likely to be correct? And so, is one not *obliged* to yield through deference to such a superior opponent?

No, one is no more bound to yield deferentially when one aims to hit the mark of truth firsthand, than one is bound to yield deferentially to a coach's hands in an endeavor to hit a bullseye.

17. *Second lesson*

A further lesson concerns how standards differ substantially across epistemic domains. Doctors and lawyers are socially bound to issue their expert opinions based on due care and diligence. Scientists must abide by social rules binding on communities of collective inquiry. High standards of reliability apply, since members of the community must be able to defer to the reported results of experts. Negligence may even call for a lawsuit.

Even everyday practice imposes social standards for information storage. Violators incur disapproval, blame, and loss of trust.

But humanistic domains seem interestingly, importantly different.

Suppose others are neither expecting nor expected to rely on you for their opinions in a certain domain. Suppose in that domain there is pressure to avoid *mere* deference, and to form one's views *firsthand*. We are thus pressured to go beyond sheer deference, even in some cases where deference is not disallowed, and *even* in cases where deference is *required*. How can this be so?

Here it is crucial to note that through a single doing one can make more than one attempt. Thus, one might flip a light switch in an endeavor to illuminate a room, and *also* in an endeavor to alert someone outside. Similarly, through a single affirmation, whether public or to oneself, one might endeavor to get it right on a certain question, perhaps by sheer deference, while *also* endeavoring to get it right *firsthand*. Here one makes two attempts through one doing, and the doing is also overdetermined, since one bases one's affirmation on deference and *also* on separately sufficient reasons that one deploys firsthand (without the aid of deference in *that* deployment). Such doubling up is not impossible, as we have seen, and need not even be rare in intellectual endeavor.

Faced with a weighty moral decision, we may do our best to arrive at a correct firsthand judgment while also giving due weight to the say-so of a trustworthy authority. The issue may indeed be important enough that we are morally *required* to give due weight to that authority and even to defer.

Again, we might aim to simply get it right, and endeavor to do so deferentially, i.e. by giving substantial weight to the sheer say-so of an authority, while *at the same time, with the very same affirmation*, we might or might not *also* endeavor to get it right firsthand.

However, we might *alternatively* just refuse to defer even when we know that we are thereby rejecting a more reliable way to answer our question. We might prefer instead to leave the question open until we can address it through our own resources. This I take to be a quite proper and common attitude to humanistic questions of art appreciation, moral assessment, and other philosophical insight.[4]

[4] There is moreover a *further* objective that matters greatly in these domains: namely, discovery, originality. One aims not only to reach the truth firsthand, through one's own insight or reasoning. That much one can do, as we have seen, even while concurrently also deferring on the very same question. What one *cannot* do while also deferring is to *discover* that truth. However, discovery seems ambiguous. In a weaker sense it is possible for one to discover anew, for oneself, what had also been discovered previously by someone else. In a stronger sense, that cannot possibly happen. One cannot discover a truth that had already been discovered by

All of that being so, your firsthand judgments in humanistic domains need not be so reliable. At least that is so from a social point of view, from the perspective of social norms on responsible judgment. In such domains you are not so concerned with others in your distinctively desirable and responsible judgments, since others are not supposed to give much weight to your say-so in forming *their* judgments. The *reasons* you can provide might matter greatly, but you are just a conduit to those reasons, which others will need to assess and apply firsthand. Others must assess firsthand the soundness of any arguments you may present. Your say-so will carry zero weight as such. So, your judgment can still be competent enough while less reliable. Such domains thus tolerate more risk. And that is why intellectual performance is subject to less stringent social standards of reliability in philosophy, and in the humanities.

18. *Summing up*

We have explored a particular sort of understanding, understanding why, and a particular sort of knowledge why—*firsthand* knowledge why, especially through intuitive insight—and its place in the humanities including philosophy.

I have argued for the special importance of firsthand intuitive insight on many questions in the humanities, and for implications concerning two things: concerning, first, disagreement, and concerning, second, the applicable epistemic standards of reliability.

someone else. Even if one had no awareness of the prior discovery by someone else, that still rules out the possibility that one also discover that truth at the later time. (This is a rough, generic distinction, which allows nuances.)

2

Gnoseology and Intellectual Ethics

A telic virtue epistemology (TVE) was presupposed in our treatment of insight and understanding.[1] What follows lays out the main elements of that telic theory, and locates its place in epistemology broadly understood.[2]

A. A Virtue Epistemology

1. All achievements are bound to be attempts that succeed, but the converse is false. Success by luck rather than competence need not be achievement. However, a successful performance *can* be an achievement though still lucky. And this is no less true for epistemic achievements. In particular, there are many ways to be lucky in affirming correctly while still achieving epistemic success, thereby knowing the truth of what you affirm. You might be lucky to be alive, for example, having barely escaped a bolt of lightning. You might be lucky to retain the proper use of your faculties, as you drink by luck from the one safe glass out of many before you. You can still achieve knowledge through the exercise of faculties retained by luck.

For telic virtue epistemology, the luck that blocks knowledge on a given question is luck that clashes with the subject's getting it right through competence on that question,[3] a clash that is not distinctive of the epistemic domain. *Achievement*, whether epistemic or of any other

[1] The opening section of this chapter is for the convenience of readers unfamiliar with the framework and terminology of TVE. But the rest of the chapter goes generally beyond earlier presentations, especially so in sections B and F.

[2] Its place is in a subdomain titled "gnoseology" for referential convenience. We shall consider particulars of that domain in due course, and reflect, in section G, on its place in a broader epistemology.

[3] This is a first approximation.

Epistemic Explanations: A Theory of Telic Normativity, and What it Explains. Ernest Sosa, Oxford University Press (2021). © Ernest Sosa. DOI: 10.1093/oso/9780198856467.003.0002

sort, is blocked by *such* luck. An attempt constitutes an achievement only if it succeeds sufficiently through competence.[4]

2. Achievement requires success that is *apt*: through competence rather than luck. This emerges from a review of telic theory's five main phenomena: *attempt, success, competence, aptness, achievement.*

If an archer shoots at a certain target, we can assess that shot in various respects. First, does it *succeed*? Does it hit the target? Second, how competent is the shot? The arrow may exit the bow with an orientation and speed that would normally take it straight to the bullseye. Even if a gust diverts it, the shot might still be competent. It can be *adroit* without being *accurate*. And it can be accurate by luck, without being adroit. But even a shot that is both accurate and adroit might still underperform. An arrow adroitly released from a bow may be headed straight to the bullseye when a gust diverts it so that it would now miss the target narrowly, except that a second gust eases it back on course. The archer succeeds in that attempt to hit the target, and the shot is also competent, as the arrow leaves the bow perfectly directed and with the right speed. But the shot is accurate because of the lucky second gust, with a distinctive luck that repels competence. It does not manifest the competence required for the success to be creditable to the agent, not even partially (as when the agent joins with others in a collective success).

When generalized to all attempts, of whatever sort, that is an account of the telic normativity of attempts as attempts, in terms of their accuracy, adroitness, and aptness.

3. You earn *telic* credit when a success is thus "creditable" to you—*attributable* to you as agent—without necessarily importing any more substantive axiological standing. A shot might be a "perfect" murder, including its excellence *as a shot*, and *thus* creditable to its agent, while constituting an abominable crime, to the agent's moral *dis*credit.

[4] Thus the apt title of John Greco's *Achieving Knowledge*.

4. If a driver is both skillful and in good shape, does that make him competent to drive safely on a given road? Yes, if the road is in appropriate condition. But what if the road is then covered with ice? In acknowledging that this deprives the driver of *complete* competence to drive safely on that road, we recognize varieties of competence. The complete competence requires not only that the agent be sufficiently skilled and in proper shape; the situation needs to be favorable as well.

Similarly, might an archer be skillful and in fine shape while lacking the complete competence required for success through competence, because spoiler wind is too likely? Suppose that, although high wind is *very* likely, in fact no gust intervenes, and the arrow goes straight to the bullseye, just as it would normally do, given its orientation and speed off the bow. How does the high likelihood of spoiler gusts bear on the quality of that shot? Does it put the archer in an *in*appropriate situation? Does he thereby lack the *complete* competence required for apt success?

Surely that archer deserves a high measure of credit for the shot's success so long as the arrow is *in fact* unaffected by wind on its way to the target, no matter how likely a spoiler gust may have been.

The "situation" required for such credit turns out not to be a *modal* property of the spatiotemporal volume involved. Success in hitting the target across the relevant space is quite unlikely at that time, despite our archer's excellent skill and shape. What makes success so unlikely is the high risk (by hypothesis) of a spoiler gust. However, so long as no spoiler gust *in fact* comes along, our archer enjoys the competence required for highly creditable, apt success, with a competence and aptness unaffected by the unfavorable modal situation.

Surprisingly, aptness depends not on a modally safe situation but on an *actually* favorable situation, no matter how accidentally it may be favorable. Beyond this, the Situation need only combine with the agent's Skill and Shape to make *that particular* SSS combination likely enough to yield success.[5]

Apt performance, including apt epistemic performance, is not dependent on how safely one *possesses* relevant competence. This applies to all three sorts of competence: first, the (innermost) skill; second, the

[5] Still in first approximation, to be superseded in Part III.

skill plus the required inner shape; third, the skill and shape, in turn, plus the required situation. None of these varieties of competence need be *safely* in place. The safety that *does* seem required for apt performance, including apt judgment and belief, is rather the SSS-relative safety constituted by the fact that one is (actually, however luckily) sufficiently SSS-competent, so that, if one tried *when thus SSS-competent*, one would likely enough succeed.[6]

Whether lucky or not, *possession* of each pertinent S facilitates corresponding competence. However, in other ways luck does clash with competence. How much a success is by *credit-reducing* luck depends on how little it is due to competence. *Excess of such luck* aligns with *deficiency of corresponding competence*, which reduces or blocks relevant "credit" to the agent for the success of their attempt.

5. We have seen how archery provides an example of a telic triple-A normativity constituted by our five main ideas, those of *attempt*, *success*, *competence*, *aptness*, and *achievement*. And our archery example also shows how achievement comes in degrees within at least two dimensions. One dimension is that of the apt shot, accurate *because* adroit. The other dimension is that of the *fully* apt shot, where the agent aims not just at accuracy but at aptness, and succeeds through competence in this more complex endeavor.

As Diana surveys a landscape in search of game, she may see prey in the distance (in good light and calm wind). If the prey is beyond her range, then her shot would be poorly selected. But if the prey is within her range, then her shot might be well selected, one she'd be well advised to take, given her aim to hunt well. If a shot is too risky, it is ill advised. A shot can attain quality *in being well selected*. A well selected shot can thus rate higher *in that specific regard* than one that falls short through pertinent negligence or recklessness. This involves a view of the "shot" as an attempt, whose being "well selected" is constituted by the intentional aiming to hit the pertinent target. Such an aiming is surely assessable by reference to how likely it is to succeed (relative to one's

[6] To continue with our first approximation. The account will be supplemented in Part III through the (Cartesian) supplementary notion of *security*.

possession of the pertinent competence, including the pertinent skill, shape, and situation), so as to avoid recklessness, and also assessable by reference to how negligent (or not) it may be.

A dimension of second-order evaluation of Diana's shot thus involves more than its aptness, its success through (first-order) competence. Also relevant is whether the attempt is well selected so as to avoid recklessness, and even negligence.

That is so even if the dimension of interest to us is that of creditability, independent of moral concerns such as whether the act is a murder, and independent of the admirability that involves degree of difficulty. An instance of absolutely certain knowledge, of the highest degree of relevant epistemic quality, need involve no difficulty *at all*. Think of the *cogito*! Not much of an "achievement," that one, but still a minimal one, nonetheless. Or, rather, not much of an achievement *in respect of the minimal difficulty overcome*. But still an achievement that reaches epistemic heights, nonetheless. How so?

When successfully enough guided that way, an attempt rises to the level of the *fully apt*. Nothing short of this will suffice for *achievement full well*. If an attempt succeeds aptly without being fully apt, there is an element of relevant luck in its success. Its aptness is not secured through the guidance of the agent's second-order competence. It is thus lucky that the agent succeeds aptly. And this sort of luck reduces or blocks credit to the agent for their success, as it reduces or blocks credit to the agent for the aptness of their success.[7]

[7] So, the "virtue" of our telic virtue epistemology is aim-relative (wherefore its "telic" character). Telic assessment need not import any moral or prudential or aesthetic assessment of the aim. Telic excellence allows awful aims, as in a "perfect" murder. Such telic assessment is the sort of "gnoseological" assessment that telic virtue epistemology applies to our beliefs as instances of knowledge.

It may be thought that we have no real option but to affirm alethically on any given question if one's total pertinent evidence is on balance weighty enough. Accordingly, it may be added, we have no option but to *both* sustain that question *and* to answer it in the affirmative.

Not so. That overlooks our option to *give up* the question through the operation of a mechanism that might well remain implicit and subconscious. That mechanism might involve giving up the question in aid of mental health and social interaction, which may be quite appropriate ethically (as a kind of mirror opposite of the implicit bias that operates similarly).

True, we may quite often be morally bound to inquire into certain questions, and it is easy to come up with powerful examples, as in "Is that child in the water crying for help?" But it is not so easy to come up with similar examples that are distinctively intellectual or epistemic. At a

6. Narrowing our focus from virtue theory in general, here is a main thesis of telic virtue *epistemology*:

> that the normativity of *knowledge* is a special case of such *telic normativity.*

Knowledge is then a central sort of epistemic achievement. Here we find the traditional issues of skepticism, and other issues of the nature, scope, and value of knowledge.

Telic "normativity" has thus its own distinctive character. It involves the assessment of attempts as attempts. Such assessment is relative to the aims of a given agent. The apex of such normativity is the fully "creditable" attempt, whose success is fully *attributable* to the agent. This sort of assessment is sealed off from more substantive axiological or deontic assessment.

Gettiered thinkers may now be seen to fall short either because their pertinent belief falls short of aptness altogether, or because it falls short of *full* aptness.

B. Attempts and Aimings

1. The main phenomenon of telic normativity is that of an attempt. What is an attempt? How might you attempt to attain an objective?

In two ways at least.

> First, you might make an attempt by implementing means aimed at the objective targeted, where the means are

minimum, we have vastly greater freedom if we select topics and questions based on *purely intellectual* value or curiosity.

In any case, telic virtue epistemology is an account in gnoseology, not in intellectual ethics. Gnoseological assessment does not concern why or how well we opt to take up and sustain a question. Gnoseological assessment presupposes a thinker who takes up a given question, no matter why or how well they have chosen to ponder that question. And the virtue of such epistemology is the broader "virtue" (arete) present even in a sharp knife excellently suited to its proper function, so that it will perform well if used for its proper use, for cutting well (however awful the broader aim may be, as when the agent is a murderer rather than a surgeon). It is such broader "virtue"—the sort pertinent to *adroitness* or *competence*—that suits you to attain the distinctive gnoseological aim of answering knowledgeably a question taken up (however silly or inappropriate that question may be).

preliminary, and viewed as such. The attempt is then the taking of such means, so aimed. This is to *instrumentally* attempt, to take preliminary means, viewed as auxiliary in that way. For example, you might thus aim to reach a *position to know*, to gain the SSS profile required for complete competence to attain that objective.

Second, you might make an attempt by implementing means aimed at the objective, where the means are constitutive, or at least grounding, and viewed as such. The attempt is then the taking of such means, so aimed. This is to *constitutively* attempt, or at least to attempt through means *whereby* you would succeed, thus *grounding* your success.

2. In *functional* epistemic performance, including functional belief, the agent aims at truth and aptness of representation, but does so only implicitly and teleologically, as when our perceptual systems aim at correctly representing our surroundings.[8]

Here, however, we shall focus not on functional, subconscious representation, but mainly on judgment, and on judgmental belief, where the agent aims *with conscious intention* to get it aptly right on a given question. What is involved in this?[9]

3. Sayings include utterances of declarative sentences by actors on a stage. When an actress says, "I am the queen," she does not really say *that* she is the queen. If Queen Elizabeth is in the audience, she would be wrong to object: "No, she isn't!" Play-acting is pretense, and pretend affirmations are not the genuine article. Only some sayings of declarative sentences are *affirmations*, genuine sayings of the form *that* p. And only some affirmations are *alethic* affirmations, in the endeavor to get it

[8] It may be objected that you do not aim in virtue of your perceptual system doing so. But that does seem a natural way of thinking and speaking. When a thermostat is said to monitor the temperature in a room, it would seem implausibly artificial to object that "the *thermostat* does not monitor; only its built-in thermometer does so!"

[9] Although our focus is mainly on conscious judgment, the structure of our telic account is surely replicable for functional representations. All we need for the replication is that, in representing, the representer have an aim, and exercise a competence. But the aim might be just functionally teleological, as would then be the competence for its part.

right on a given question (whatever else one may also be endeavoring to bring about thereby).[10]

An alethic affirmation might be just a guess, as when a contestant tries to affirm the correct answer to a quiz show question. But an oncologist would aim not just to guess but to affirm competently, indeed *aptly*. Only an alethic affirmation can amount to a judgment, which it can do only if it aims not just at truth but also at aptness. This yields the following hierarchy.

> Saying of "p"
>
> Affirmation: saying that p
>
> Alethic affirmation: endeavor (attempt) to get it right by affirming that p
>
> Judgment: endeavor (attempt) to get it right *aptly* by alethically affirming that p

These can all be public, in outer speech, or private, in silent soliloquy. They are commonly and generally free acts.

Objection: It's not clear that judgment can be defined in terms of the endeavor to get it right aptly by alethically affirming that p. After all, conjecturing is distinct from judging and yet when conjecturing that p one will aim to get it right aptly by alethically affirming that p.

Reply: Yes, good point; so far our picture is a first approximation. A fuller development, would distinguish varieties of judgment (as we began to do in Chapter 1 by distinguishing judgments that are firsthand from those that are just deferential). There are of course varieties of *expert* judgment more ambitious than ordinary judgment.

What is more, even an "educated guess" might count as a sort of judgment, since one does then affirm in an attempt to affirm with alethic

[10] True, there is something that the actress playing the queen is doing right when she says, "I am the queen," which the actor playing the jester would not get right by voicing that same sentence. The "jester" would pretend incorrectly, would not speak his lines correctly. The "queen" would at least pretend correctly, would speak her lines as expected. But her pretend assertion that she is the queen would not be a real assertion, one subject to correction by Queen Elizabeth as she sits in the audience (not even to correction by the Queen in the privacy of her own mind).

aptness. The educated guess is an attempt to affirm with some significant degree of aptness, constituted by some significant degree of competence. It is thus not a sheer guess. Conjectures are *educated* guesses.

Bottom line: Judgment that p can be defined as endeavor to get it right aptly (aptly outright, aptly full stop) by alethically affirming that p; *but* we must recognize the varieties of judgment determined by the degree and the sort of aptness aimed for. *Firsthand* judgment we encountered in Chapter 1, and we've also distinguished between the minimal or zero aptness in the aim of a quiz show contestant and the degrees aimed for by expert oncologists.

C. Judgments

1. A judgment that p is a constitutive attempt to get it right aptly by alethically affirming that p. We then take means viewed as constitutive of getting it right *aptly*; we aim to get it right through competence and not just by luck. Such judgment thus aims at knowledge of a sort, at animal knowledge. It aims at knowledgeable judgment.

A dispositional correlate of that is then constituted by *judgmental belief*, not judgment. This belief, a knowledgeable belief, will constitute knowledge of a sort, of a judgmental sort. Such belief is a state, not an act, and yet it can be agential, in the way of a policy. When we sustain a policy we act as agents, as diachronic agents. The sustaining of the policy is extended, not instantaneous as is an act. But the sustaining of the policy can of course be in pursuit of an aim. And so aims can be pursued through extended agential states, such as sustained policies, as when we sustain our driving policies with the aim of driving safely and controlling risk.

Beliefs I would argue can be like that. Judgmental beliefs are like that. We adopt the policy of systematically responding to the question <p?> with the judgment that p: that is, with the alethic affirmation that p, in the attempt to get it right aptly on the question posed. (Analogously, there is the sustained functional policy, sustained not with conscious intention, but with teleological aiming, to respond to the question <p?> with the *representation* that p, aimed (with teleological functionality) at getting it right aptly through our representational attempt, an attempt that can and normally will figure in then ongoing functional reasoning.) Also there is the policy of holding that representation type <p> in readiness for use as a premise in practical reasoning, on whether to ø, and in theoretical reasoning, on whether p.

2. By contrast, inquiry aims not constitutively but *instrumentally* at attaining such knowledge. Once we affirm alethically, however, in the endeavor to do so aptly (once we judge), this would not constitute further inquiry. Inquiry aims rather at putting us *in a position* to know. For example, inquiry aims to gather relevant evidence, so as to give us a basis for competent alethic affirmation, and even for apt alethic affirmation. So, inquiry on whether p would implement preliminary, rather than constitutive means to the end of apt alethic affirmation on that question, apt affirmation that tries to get it right on whether p.

Varieties of inquiry will be defined by corresponding varieties of judgment. A minimal inquiry may conclude with an appropriate conjecture, for example, which was its objective, even while inquiry still continues vigorously in pursuit of a more substantial ordinary judgment that will meet a higher standard. Going beyond mere conjecture, an oncologist may appropriately judge that a patient has cancer, may so judge in dinner conversation with her partner, even while still vigorously pursuing workday inquiry aimed at expert judgment.

Ordinary-grade inquiry thus goes beyond conjectural inquiry, but itself falls short of expert inquiry.

What inquiry you should pursue on a given question is a matter of intellectual ethics and not of gnoseology. And that may well depend on the practical situation of the agent. Thus the quiz show contestant is perfectly well justified in conjecturing (in *affirming in the endeavor to get it right*, even while in no position to know), while the oncologist would invite a lawsuit if they issued a diagnosis based on mere conjecture.

Telic *gnoseological* assessment would be unaffected by practical considerations. The assessment of a thinker's attempt to judge with success would depend on the particular sort of judgment that is under assessment. In dinner conversation, again, the oncologist might conjecture with no flaw or fault in speaking privately to their spouse. That intellectual performance is not appropriately assessed by the professional standards proper to medical practice. Nor is the pertinent inquiry properly assessed by the standards of expertise.

The varieties of judgment thus determine corresponding varieties of proper inquiry.

D. Representations

1. Closely related to the concept of judgment is another main concept of epistemic telic normativity. I mean the concept of representation. Affirmations are a species of representations, *explicit* representations, with several varieties.

Affirming that one is the queen is saying *that* one is the queen, which requires more than just saying 'I am the queen' as this could be by an actress on the stage. *Alethic* affirmation requires a saying that p in the endeavor to say what is true.

Judgment requires aiming not only at truth but also at aptness (like the oncologist, unlike the contestant).

2. Functional alethic representations are implicit representations teleologically aimed at truth, at representing correctly, and also at corresponding aptness, where the correctness is not guess-like, but judgment-like, aimed at representing not only correctly but competently, and aptly.[11]

3. Representations come in various forms: explicit, implicit, verbal, public, private, conceptual, nonconceptual. They are all episodic, not just dispositional, have truth-evaluable content (truth-evaluable at least contextually), and often constitute reasoning that leads to and explains conduct, reasoning that can be consciously, deliberatively intentional, or alternatively can be functionally teleological.

[11] Compare the instinctive sphex with the plover who ostensibly opts deliberatively, or quasi-deliberatively, from a much broader fan of options, including the broken wing ruse against potential predators of her nest. Only the latter begins to approach truth-directed representations that might explain behavior when combined with antecedent goals in a kind of practical *reasoning*.

E. Conscious Judgments

1. In what follows the conscious judgment is front and center, as implicit representations are left in the background. What is the judgment itself? We could conceive of it as the affirmation, but in TVE we focus on the whole attempt, not just on the affirmation, nor even just on the alethic affirmation. We focus on the *attempt* itself to get it right aptly, and not just on the affirmation *whereby* the thinker attempts to attain that outcome.

Our "alethic affirmation that p" is the attempt to get it right on whether p by affirming that p. So, the alethic affirmation is not just the affirmation with the property of being aimed at truth. It is rather the attempt itself to get it right by affirming that p.

2. In our telic framework, judgments are thus attempts that attain to fully apt reflective knowledge if all goes well. Success, adroitness, aptness, and full aptness are then properties both of alethic affirmations (of attempts to get it right by affirming), and of judgments (of attempts to get it right *aptly* by alethically affirming).

F. The Swamping Problem for Reliabilism

1. According to generic process reliabilism, a belief is justified to the extent that the relevant process whence it derives is one that reliably enough yields belief that is true. A belief is here viewed as a *product* quite distinct from the process that produces that product. Thus, a belief can be viewed as a sort of map, one separable from the "cartographic" process that yields it.

A problem for such reliabilism is raised by Linda Zagzebski through her analogy with a good espresso produced by an espresso machine. The quality of that coffee is determined by how tasty it is, which is independent from the reliability of the process that produces it. A terrible espresso machine that normally produces undrinkable coffee may on occasion produce a delicious espresso, whose evaluation is hence unaffected by the reliability score of that process.

Similarly, goes the objection, the relevant epistemic quality of a belief is unaffected by the truth-reliability score of the epistemic process that yields that belief. The coffee-pertinent quality of a cup of coffee does not depend on the reliability of whatever process produces it. By analogy, then, the knowledge-pertinent quality of a belief does not depend on the reliability of whatever process produces that belief. Reliabilism is thus said to fail as an account of the knowledge-pertinent epistemic quality of beliefs.

Suppose we think of beliefs as maps that help us steer. If we wish to go to Larissa, an accurate map will serve us well. And the accuracy of a map could reach its highest level independently of the quality of the cartographic process that produces it. A map could reach the highest accuracy accidentally if the cartographer is just guessing. So, reliability seems as inessential to the accuracy of a map as it is to the quality of a cup of espresso. We can get to Larissa just as well by means of an accurate map that is unreliably produced as by an accurate map that is reliably produced. All that matters to the quality of a map as a guide to action is its degree of accuracy. What mainly matters is that it be accurate enough to guide us well enough to our destination.

Plato's *Meno* problem can be put thus in terms of beliefs as maps, but the problem clearly extends to beliefs as representations more generally.

And so the problem extends to affirmations generally, whether these take the form of vocalizations or that of inscriptions, or that of subconscious representations. Considered simply as maps to guide action, our affirmations are assessable without regard to our reliability as cartographers. If accurate enough, a map is a good enough map, regardless of how reliably it came to be that way, in line with Plato's point in the *Meno*.

Accuracy is the pertinent epistemic quality of maps, and the same would then seem to be true of beliefs considered simply as guides to steer by. The problem remains if we take the map to be a complex set of dispositions to guide behavior given a set of desires. If we think of that set of dispositions as just lodged in the agent however it may have got there, we will have another version of the same problem.

We thus have an ostensible problem for any account of a belief's justification in terms of how truth-reliable is the process that produces that belief. This is still a problem if we think of the justification of that belief in terms of how reliably it is put in place so as to guide action well. And it remains a problem even if we think of the pertinent desideratum for that belief as its degree of accuracy, never mind its navigational value. We can focus on that quality of a map, even when it is a map that locates Timbuktu, and we have no plans to go there, nor will or would we ever go there, nor to any other place located on that map. It can still count as a fine map because of its degree of accuracy. But this too is compatible with its having been produced by a terrible cartographic process. So, the analogy with the good espresso remains, and Zagzebski's objection is sustained.

2. In contrast to process reliabilism, telic virtue epistemology takes a different view of judgment and representation, and of belief more generally, whether judgmental or functional, conscious or subconscious. Our virtue epistemology takes representations, judgments, and beliefs to be not maps but *attempts*.[12] So, the right analogy is not to a product separable from the agent. In our view, the right analogy is rather to *the producing*, to the agent's *attempt to get it right* on a given question. Because of that, the reliabilism of telic virtue epistemology is not the reliabilism of process reliabilism. The telic focus is rather on *agency*, not on process. This enables us to reject the damaging analogies to maps and cups of coffee and their respective sorts of quality. The quality that matters to us is the quality of action, and thereby the quality of a very distinctive sort of products of agency.

Our focus is on *actions*, whether of praxis or of episteme. This imports a normativity that is telic, and undetachable from the agent and their

[12] The postulation of subconscious mental acts just comes along with the postulation of implicit reasoning in the explanation of much human and other animal conduct. Suppose we postulate such reasoning in explaining why someone reaches for a glass of water even when they engage consciously in no such reasoning, when instead they just "automatically" reach for the glass that is obviously in their field of vision. Such explanation would seem to require the agent's occurrent acceptance of premises that they do not accept *consciously*, and this acceptance would seem to count as an act, even while remaining subconscious. Out of the plethora of declarative "sentences" or representations stored in their "belief box," that particular one is then "activated" in an act-like way, so as to function as a premise of their (subconscious) reasoning on that occasion. And the like would seem to be required for folk explanation in animal ethology. (But this is just to hint briefly at a way of thinking about subconscious mental acts and their place in our rational economy.)

agency. For virtue epistemology, the epistemic normativity of belief is not detachable from its adroitness, from the degree of reliability of the competence that it manifests. Such normativity of belief is hence not detachable from reliability, in contrast to how the quality of a cup of coffee *is* detachable from the coffee machine and its operation. Our focus is the aimed øing of the agent who øs, the competence that is exercised in that øing, the success of the øing, the aptness of that success, etc.

So, the relevant analogues of the judgments and beliefs of our telic epistemology are not cups of coffee, nor maps. The relevant analogues would be performances of the barista or the cartographer, or even performances of the map user who plans an itinerary. The focus is not just on the map but on the cartographer's epistemic performance, and on the epistemic *use* of the map, whether consciously intentional and deliberative, or subconscious and functional.

The swamping problem turns out accordingly to be a problem not for reliabilism but for *process* reliabilism. The telic normativity of virtue reliabilism invokes not just processes but exercises of agency, with a focus on epistemic *competence* and its manifestations, which makes the swamping objection inapplicable to virtue epistemology.

G. Two Sides of Epistemology: Gnoseology and Intellectual Ethics

1. Consider some forms of doxastic assessment (assessment of judgment, belief, or suspension, as well as of degree of confidence):[13]

a. An athlete may do well through confidence that they will succeed, if this confidence will aid their success. Their confidence is an *athletic asset* and positively evaluable that way.
b. A patient may similarly do well through confidence that they will recover, which avoids the high stress that would in fact kill them. It is *medically beneficial* for them to sustain that high level of confidence, which is again a positive doxastic assessment. (This is

[13] This section develops ideas initially suggested in my *A Virtue Epistemology*, pp. 88–91.

of course essentially similar to case a above, but suggests also how extensively the phenomenon extends.)

c. You might harm someone close to you by doubting them in some practically important way, some way that hurts them deeply, reducing their self-confidence and ability to function well, so as to impede their flourishing. This might even be a moral failure on your part, as your relationship placed on you a moral demand not to harm them that way.

Nor would such assessment be appropriate only if your belief were under the sort of voluntary control that requires ability to choose directly through arbitrary choice. So much of what we do at nearly every turn is assessable with no such requirement, and requires only that the doing be rationally based, or perhaps just a manifestation of competence. Indeed, often enough just the *attributability* of the assessed doing suffices, as it is then a deed, and thus the agent's own doing. In no such case need the agent meet any requirement of direct arbitrary control.

d. It is not just athletic or medical success that is potentially boosted by self-confidence. Other important components of personal flourishing, in one's career or in one's personal life, can also be affected that way. So, one's self-confidence through confident belief in one's own competence can also be commendable *in that respect.*

e. A community or a political leader might attain important political objectives through mythology, as with Platonic "noble lies." And they might well be aided in that endeavor by their heightened confidence in the truth of those myths.

It is hard to be sure about specific cases, but all of these seem obviously possible.

2. It might be thought nonetheless that you cannot believe for any such pragmatic reason, that your belief cannot be rationally motivated in any such pragmatic way. And it seems *especially* doubtful that your *judgment* could be motivated by such reasons.

What then is a judgment, and why is it impossible to judge with such motivation, at least impossible to so judge properly?

3. Clearly one can *affirm* that p with pragmatic motivation. One might properly lie for advantage if one thereby saves a life. An affirmation is not necessarily a judgment, however, so that other essential components of judgment might still preclude *judging* for advantage.

It does seem initially plausible that potential advantages would be the wrong sorts of reasons for judgment. Judgment after all involves alethic affirmation at a minimum, affirmation aimed at truth. And even alethic affirmation seems *not possibly* motivated by advantage, or if possibly at least *not properly* motivated by advantage.

Really? Isn't the quiz show guess an alethic affirmation aimed at truth, and yet properly motivated by advantage, by the aim to win a prize? Yes, but a distinction shows why this misfires as an objection. The contestant affirms alethically and does so, not because of any disinterested curiosity, but only because the truth will win the money. Contestants conduct at least minimal inquiry, by scanning their memory banks in a desperate search for evidence. And here lies the crucial contrast.

If they are to proceed properly with their alethic project (success in which will win the prize), contestants must not deviate deplorably from that purely alethic inquiry. For example, they'd be ill advised to answer based just on what would please their partner sitting in the audience. This would allow *improper* pragmatic influence on their alethic+contestant project. (Their attempt to please the partner is at best irrelevant and possibly deleterious to their project of *answering the question correctly and thereby winning the prize*.)[14]

And that is indeed a sort of telic impropriety that would affect judgments and beliefs in cases 1a–e above.

[14] They might know that their partner would be pleased, and this might even be a reason why they would *still* give that answer if they lost interest in the prize. This would make their answer *motivationally* overdetermined. However, the aim to please the partner might still be quite irrelevant to the *telic* assessment of the attempt to get it right on their question. The aim to please would constitute a side attempt, subject to its own telic assessment, but it might well have no bearing at all on the quality of their attempt to get it right, or might even draw attention deplorably from the main objective.

So, there is a *sort* of motivation by advantage that is unproblematic (namely, the practical motivation of the professional who seeks the truth motivated by the aim to serve a client). But the sort of motivation by advantage that is problematic is quite different. It is not the motivation to attain the truth and *thereby* attain some practical aim or advantage. It is rather a sort of motivation to determine the *means* to getting it right on the question addressed. The problematic motivation is one that determines your means to answering the question correctly *and does so by the bearing of such means on some practically desired end unrelated to the correctness of your answer.*

4. Consider also what happens when we engage premises in pondering a question, so that we may reason our way to an answer. That question might hold riveting interest for us, greatly affecting our peace of mind. A negative answer would yield much harmful stress. So, one may greatly desire a positive answer to that question. In pursuit of *that* non-alethic objective, one may be highly motivated to accept premises favorable to that conclusion.

Such is the notorious wishful thinking of epistemic lore, of a sort broadly familiar in everyday life. A weighty reason why one accepts those premises may then be that they satisfy that practical requirement, in which case one's motivation for accepting them is not intellectually disinterested; it is not purely alethic.

5. Can one be motivated that way? Why not? What about the familiar implicit bias that too often motivates too many of us? Shall we say that this is not *rational* motivation, in the sense of "motivation by reasons *for which* we act"?

Well, the desire for the pragmatic good is apparently a *motive* for one's acceptance of the pragmatically conducive premises. It is a cause why one believes as one does. Is it not then a motivating reason, one that moves us (to some degree) to accept them?

If so, why can't it be a reason for which one might believe as one does? Because it would or should be disavowed once examined for probatory force? Well, is that not the fate of any fallacious inference? Are we to suppose that fallacious reasoning never involves improper, irrational basing on reasons?

Surely to commit a fallacy is to base one's conclusion incorrectly on a basis that is in that instance inadequate as a reason, and so it is to conclude "irrationally" to that extent. Why then should we not count implicit bias as just another instance of implicit irrationality, another case where we are motivated alright, motivated by reasons that move us to believe as we do, but move us irrationally, in an objectionable way?

6. In pondering that question we should distinguish as follows.

In a case of bias one might take the content of the offending reason to bear on the truth of the affirmation based on that reason. This might be so, for example, where one irrationally believes the race or gender of the target to bear on their competence. And here theoretical irrationality might of course reside in the insufficiency of one's basis for the connecting proposition (be it a generic; or a statistical or probabilistic generalization; or a universal claim). So, there is indeed irrationality in judgment biased against its target, irrationality that can be traced back to the irrationality of the thinker's acceptance of the connecting proposition.

However, that's not how it is in the case of wishful thinking. Here belief in the offending premises is not grounded thus in some prior irrational belief. It is grounded rather in the wishful thinker's pro-attitude to the truth of the conclusion. This is the desire (or hope, etc.) that leads the thinker to accept the premises or at least to believe them more confidently.[15]

Nevertheless, the thinker here does ostensibly have a reason for believing those premises in that way. He wants the conclusion to be true, and he thinks the truth of those premises will make it (sufficiently) more likely that it is true. And that is *why* he accepts those premises; that is by hypothesis his motive. He accepts those premises because that will lead to a pleasing outcome.

[15] Alternatively, it might be based rather on the *belief* that it would be good for the agent that the conclusion be true. I suppose it's an empirical open question exactly what happens in cases of that general sort. Maybe it's some of each: in some cases the basis is some pro-attitude, in others it is some belief. But even if all actual cases proceed via such a belief, it would still be irrational but possible reasoning to go from the belief that the conclusion would be good for the thinker to the premises from which the conclusion follows. And there would be a similar doubt whether actual thinkers could possibly base a belief on so improper a reason, whether the motivational reason takes the form of a pro-attitude or the form of a belief. Either way the irrationality is astounding, and one might still doubt that anyone could really believe in such a way.

Alternatively, the motive might be to have a more coherent body of beliefs that *includes* the desired belief. The thinker wants relief from lack of coherence but also wants to keep the desired belief in the conclusion.

Either way, why the reluctance to attribute a motivating rationale for judgment on those premises, for judgment and for judgmental belief? The rationale is bad, of course; no, it's horrendously, unbelievably bad. But research seems increasingly to show it to be at work, nonetheless. Since when is irrationality an insurmountable obstacle to human credulity? (And even if the research is eventually discredited, is it not plausible enough that we *could* be moved in that way.)

7. Granted, affirming that p for the sake of getting it right on whether p is different from affirming that p for the sake of some practical benefit. And clearly each of these two ways of affirming has its own distinctively relevant reasons. Is it not also plausible enough that one cannot properly switch those reasons? (Nor is this even clearly *possible*?)

However, our question is not whether one can affirm that p for practical reasons. That one can obviously do. Lies are public affirmations for practical reasons. Our question is rather whether one can *judge* whether p for practical reasons, and indeed whether one can so much as *affirm alethically* on whether p (positively or negatively) and do so for practical reasons, and properly so.

Well, we have seen already why the answer to those questions, exactly as phrased, is "Yes, of course!" Everyone does that daily, as we take up questions in pursuit of all manner of practical objectives.

A trickier question is whether one can determine, on the basis of practical reasons, the valence of one's answer to a whether question. And here again it seems *possible* for one to do so, as seems clear enough in the phenomenon of implicit bias. Implicit bias might even be defined as implicitly setting the valence of one's answer motivated by practical objectives, without proper regard to getting it right on that question, and even in complete disregard of that objective. (Additionally, implicit bias is plausibly at work in determining the degree and valence of one's *confidence* on the matter at hand, without proper regard to getting it right on that matter, and even in complete disregard of that objective.)

8. Let's suppose we are persuaded by that. How might that bear on whether or not we might proceed with a broader wisdom in cases where we proceed irrationally in a narrower epistemic sense, without proper *epistemic* circumspection?

Why, for example, is a father unwise to be slower to judge in the case of an accused daughter?

Note well, this is not *just* to wonder whether the father might not have a much broader fund of relevant knowledge about the daughter than does the prosecutor, broader knowledge that gives him a better basis for properly epistemic judgment.

No, the question is rather this: Why is the father prohibited from giving some weight to his loyalty to the daughter, to their special relationship, in determining whether and how to judge. This is not necessarily to think that his loyalty might affect what weight to give the evidence. Without necessarily affecting that, the question might remain: Should he give loyalty *more* weight in determining whether and how to judge?

But even that might be wrong-headed. Perhaps there is no all-purpose scale on which one can put evidential reasons and also practical reasons, such as reasons of loyalty, so that there is an objectively correct reckoning. Perhaps; still, might it not be that reasons of loyalty can be compared thoughtfully, whereby it becomes clear that loyalty to the daughter is more weighty than "loyalty" to a distant neighbor, while evidential reasons can also be compared, so that one can trust the advice of one's longtime doctor over that of a hawker on the web?

If reasons of loyalty can thus obviously be weighed against each other, as can evidential reasons, one might just wonder whether the demands of loyalty could not also trump those of evidence in this particular case. But trump in what way?

Various possibilities open before us: (a) Can loyalty trump evidence in determining whether to judge in the negative on the question of the daughter's guilt? (b) Can loyalty trump in determining whether to judge (at all, either positively or negatively) or to suspend (deliberatively, without abandoning the question)? (c) Can loyalty trump in determining whether to abandon the whole question?

9. It does seem possible, and even proper, for loyalty (and other practical considerations) to trump in determining whether to continue inquiry into a question, or to abandon it instead. What questions to take up, what questions to pursue, and how attentively and vigorously to do so, seem largely practical matters of intellectual ethics in the first place, and so matters on which all sorts of practical considerations can properly vie toward a rational decision.[16]

The more difficult issue is whether judgment itself can be properly affected by practical concerns. Again, this will of course depend on how we should conceive of judgment.

How plausible is it that one could attempt to answer a question correctly and could base *that* attempt on the basis that it would make some wished-for downstream conclusion more likely to be true? Even if this were metaphysically possible, is it really within the bounds of human ability and even competence.

In our telic view, a judgment is an attempt, an instrumentally ordered attempt. To judge that p, when one ponders whether p, is to attempt *constitutively* to get it aptly right on that question and to do so by affirming that p. If this is in one's power to do, attributably, as a deed, and not just as a *mere* doing not really one's own (as when one *does* fall on a rabbit upon being pushed unconscious off a cliff), is there then anything that blocks one's doing that whole thing, making that whole attempt, for some practical objective?

10. Again, our attempts are nearly always in pursuit of practical objectives. In performing epistemically, professionals perform dutifully for

[16] This raises an issue for the Pyrrhonians' guiding objective to suspend judgment on issues of objective values, so as to avoid the stressful worry as to whether one does or can attain such values. They find that suspension gives them the soothing calm of ataraxia. They discover this as inquirers into objective value. And it is a serendipitous turn of events, as is the foam caused by luck on a painted horse's mouth when the artist throws a sponge at the horse in frustration at his inability to create that effect. So, after that, they continue inquiry but now with the *explicit guiding aim* of attaining suspension. Thus their strategy of always seeking counterbalancing arguments that will protect them from assent, enabling suspension. It is by such counterbalancing that they always aim to attain the calm attendant on suspension. But now they need to face a fearsome issue: why continue to argue at all? Is there not an easier option that might import even greater calm with far less effort? I mean the option of simply *abandoning* the question in hand.

the sake of all sorts of practical objectives: Helping a client, say, or earning a fee, or attaining or protecting a professional reputation, etc. This all seems perfectly obvious, ordinary, and proper. And so it frequently goes for us all in an ordinary day.

However, the question is not whether we can judge for practical reasons, which we obviously can do. The question concerning judgment is again whether the "valence" of one's *judgment* (whether affirmative or negative) is ever properly affected by practical motivation, and similarly for the degree and valence of one's *confidence* on the question.

In our telic framework, a judgment is an attempt. Since attempts have constitutive aims, a telic assessment of judgments is hence automatically in place, an assessment not properly affected by extraneous objectives that the agent may *also* be pursuing through the same means. Here we are in the realm of *telic* assessment, and, in the case of judgment and judgmental belief, the aim determines how it would be proper to assess the pertinent attempts. For such assessment, the aim that matters is that of getting it right aptly with one's alethic affirmation. All such gnoseological assessment is then by reference to that aim, so that practical, extraneous aims are irrelevant.

Of course, extraneous aims may define attempts of their own, and these would be properly assessed by reference to *those* aims. But their assessment would remain irrelevant to gnoseology, the part of epistemology concerning truth-directed judgments and beliefs, and more specifically those that are *knowledge*-directed (those postulated by telic virtue epistemology, and detailed above).

11. It may well be thought that epistemic values—such as truth, justification, knowledge, and certainty—are just some of the values that one ought rationally to prize, and that loyalty, serenity, health, and athletic achievement are just additional values. Clashes might variously crisscross the epistemic/practical divide. For each clash, there will be degrees of the various values on each side of the divide, and the rational resolution of a clash will then depend on the respective weights.

That is a dubious approach, however, as may be seen if we reconsider the father–daughter example. Consider a case in which it is about as certain as could be that the daughter shoplifted, or that she was consumed by anger and envy at her elder sister's success. As the years go by, however, the pertinent facts lose any connection to the situation of the daughter, to her relation to the legal system or to her elder sister, etc.

Compare now two fathers. One lets bygones be bygones, and simply eases such beliefs out of his mind through some mechanism that aids mental health and better human relations. The other cannot help retaining the pertinent beliefs, which remain fresh and vivid not far from the surface of his consciousness. My own reaction to this may show a lack of integrity, but perhaps it shows rather an aversion to moralistic cant. In any case, to my mind it seems obvious how to think of this, all things considered. I say that the father might do well to move beyond bygones, and even beyond forgiveness. The best outcome might be a perfectly clean slate with no record whatsoever of the earlier faults.

That is to favor life over strict epistemology, or perhaps over epistemic hype. The truth is often worthless (as in counting the blades of grass), and it is too often worse than worthless.

However, that is not at all to favor life over gnoseology. There is simply no clash, nor even any tension here. Gnoseology is a domain of assessment that is sealed against practical incursions.[17] Truth, evidence, and knowledge are categories within that domain, and they are protected against practical incursion in the assessment of any thinker's intellectual or cognitive *telic* performance (in pondering how to answer a question alethically in pursuit of aptness).

What is more, it also seems implausible that we have two commensurable dimensions, so that we can just add up the rational weights and calculate our way to a rational decision. On this misguided approach, the more certain it is that the daughter was indeed guilty as charged, the worse it is for the father to ease that fact out of his mind.

On the contrary, such rational additivity seems implausible. Regardless of how certain the fact may be to the father, it may remain equally wise for him to usher it out of his mind. And this seems especially clear once

[17] Just as baseball is a domain where internal assessment is sealed against extraneous practical incursions, which is not to ignore or downplay the pragmatic basis for the standing of the domain itself in a particular community (as with American baseball) or in the human form of life (as with gnoseological performances).

the daughter's debt to society has been paid through proper punishment or compensation in the case of the shoplifting, or once the daughter has mellowed toward her sister with whom she now enjoys a warm and close relationship. What possible good could come of dwelling on those earlier unfortunate facts, or from retaining them in the father's memory close to the surface of consciousness, or even anywhere in its retrievable contents? Are we to suppose that there is some final or intrinsic good that resides in that retention, with a degree proportional to its degree of certainty (psychological or normative)?[18]

12. On the other hand, generalization is fraught in this complicated domain. In a particular case, family history might be prized and sustained through a wise assessment of its place and importance. True enough, but it could also be otherwise. In another case it might be the better part of wisdom just to move on, unburdened by the unpleasant and disturbing record.

That is why it seems possible to fetishize sheer truth or even certainty. All the same, knowledge is obviously a great human good, one essential to the flourishing of human beings and their communities, and not only because knowledge is power. Much knowledge does quite plausibly have a final or intrinsic value.

W. K. Clifford is surely right, moreover, to decry belief without proper regard for the pertinent evidence; and to deplore even belief through negligence in inquiry.[19]

Still, the preference for the one father over the other is in no conflict with such plausible views. There are indeed social norms such as one that opposes judging or believing contrary to what one knows deep

[18] The idea here is that gnoseological normativity is telic, and quite orthogonal to the normativity of ethics, including intellectual ethics, except only for the Cliffordian reasoning below, according to which gnoseological standing is itself an ethical requirement imposed by proper moral (social) norms. It is *not* that there is a consequentialist demand for true or knowledgeable belief, one to be weighed against other values in proper decision-making. That is quite misguided. The demands of gnoseology require a preset question that is properly entertained for all sorts of practical reasons. But the setting of the question may be extremely unwise, at an absolute minimum in standing, even when its gnoseological standing is at a maximum that rivals the *cogito*.

[19] See his "The Ethics of Belief," in T. Madigan, ed., *The Ethics of Belief and Other Essays* (Amherst, MA, Prometheus Books, 1999, pp. 70–96. (Originally published in 1877, in the journal *Contemporary Review*.)

down, or to what one is in a position to know, to what one could know if only one inquired properly. The favored father need not violate such Cliffordian wisdom. The favored father might just abandon the whole question, might ease it out of his mind. And this cannot possibly violate Clifford's advice, since to abandon a question is not to judge or believe on that question at all, nor even to suspend on it deliberatively.[20]

13. What about Clifford's further pronouncement that one should always proportion one's *confidence* to the evidence in one's possession? Is this not a requirement that the favored father would violate?

No, I cannot see that he would necessarily be guilty, since he might attain his wise aim by *relinquishing* the pertinent evidence along with the offending beliefs.

This begs for fuller development, which would go into what evidence is, and how it is possessed, and the extent to which a thinker might control its possession, and whether such control would require the radical freedom that is supposed to involve the agent's ability to arbitrarily determine their performance by sheer force of will.

For the present, I would suggest that a father might host a mechanism that removes from their memory anything that might count as evidence that the daughter had shoplifted. Such a mechanism might have a status quite like the status of mechanisms of improper bias. And such a fatherly mechanism might then be prized to an extent comparable to how deplorable are the instances of bias generally and properly condemned.

14. So we have seen reasons to distinguish the telic normativity of gnoseology from the broader epistemic normativity of intellectual ethics. The gnoseological normativity proper to the theory of knowledge is telic, and is thus protected against extraneous practical incursions in the ways we have noted. There is indeed a broader epistemic normativity, which does pertain to proper belief formation, via its obvious pertinence to what questions one should or should not take up and sustain. These latter are intensely practical matters properly affected by pragmatic

[20] The nature and normativity of such suspension will be taken up in the four chapters of Part II.

concerns of prudence and subject to moral demands and restrictions as well.

15. An important doubt lingers. True, if we define judgment as an attempt to get it right aptly, then the telic assessment of judgment is protected against direct pragmatic incursion. But is that not a purely verbal, Pyrrhic victory against pragmatism? The question will then remain in any particular case: *Why judge*? Why restrict your affirmations, and hence why restrict your reasoning, even your practical syllogisms, in a corresponding way? Why not quasi-judge, for example, where the attempt to get it right is *among* your objectives, but not necessarily primary, given other important pragmatic objectives that you may cherish. In this case, you would sustain the objective of getting it right (thus the "quasi"), but you would not necessarily give it priority; rather, you might allow it to be trumped by some conflicting cherished objective.

Even about the father, and about the family, why not go in for a bit of make-belief? Why not cultivate myths that will boost the self-esteem and the mutual esteem among them? What can be wrong with that, all things considered? Even if by and large we stick to judging and corresponding judgmental believing, why not also tolerate and even cultivate some quasi-judging and make-belief on certain issues important for social progress and welfare?

16. In my view, that is perfectly well taken. Why so much as take seriously the view, attributed to Kant, that we are never ever permitted to lie, not even about the location of a gun sought by a murderer? And the same seems about as plausible if what it would take to save the victim is that one sincerely affirm the lie even to oneself, since otherwise one might be too liable to give away the truth.[21]

[21] All hypothetical of course, despite how implausible it may seem that humans could affect their beliefs that way. We might still be able to affect our beliefs over time in ways that would be practically beneficial despite being gnoseologically questionable. And how important can it really be in any case whether the *way* praxis affects belief is indirect or direct? Surely, the more important issue is whether it can properly take place, even on purpose, and even if the purpose is teleological rather than consciously intentional; whether it can thus properly take place, however indirectly, and to what effect on the propriety of the belief thus affected.

Nevertheless, Clifford's view is still compelling. The social norms against lying and stealing have obvious exceptions, and it is not easy to formulate exceptionless norms. So, the social norms that favor judging over quasi-judging, and judgmental believing over make-belief would be hardly unusual in having exceptions.

17. Epistemologists have thus good reason to prize the distinctive department that we are calling gnoseology, or theory of knowledge. This department may be seen to have a kind of priority over the other side of epistemology, intellectual ethics. It has that priority in the importance of judgment and stored belief in accordance with the evidence: its importance socially, so that we can properly depend on each other for shared information; and its importance prudentially, in the face of an uncertain future where one may need to rely in unforeseen ways on stored beliefs.

Exceptions there may be, but if we're to coordinate on properly shared information, we must commit to basing our deliberations on shared knowledge. Plato's noble lies might exceptionally serve a community well, but the corresponding risk is the fake news that destroys democracy. So long as a community is not riven into enemy camps, so long as we want and need to collaborate with underlying respect, proper deliberative cooperation will generally require that we must still judge, rather than quasi-judge, and believe rather than make-believe. And what we need in order to understand these desiderata is a proper understanding of what this desirable judgment is and of how to assess it properly. That is why, despite the importance of a broader intellectual ethics and a theory of proper inquiry, there is also a prior gnoseology essential in defining those central objectives of intellectual ethics in general, and of proper inquiry in particular.

H. Appendix on Telic Normativity

This appendix supplements the account of telic normativity as a normativity of attempts structured in accordance with the AAA/SSS proposal.

This structure is specified through a crucial concept of agential competences relative to given domains of human agency, each normatively structured in accordance with its distinctive aims. There are numerous such domains in human life: games, sports, professions, scientific domains, artistic domains such as the performance arts, etc. Competences in such domains are agential dispositions to attain respective aims.

Three elements of competence can then be distinguished, when the aim relates the agent to some distal object or state of affairs. There is the Situational element involving a relation between the agent and the distal object or state of affairs. There is the Shape element involving a pertinent condition of the agent, one that is internal by involving no relation to anything distal. And there is, finally, the Skill element, again an internal condition that seats in the agent the disposition to succeed (upon trying) that constitutes the competence.

What is it for an agent to possess a human competence at a time? The theory of telic normativity considers this to be a phenomenon out in the world. The theory is about that phenomenon and not primarily about words, or semantics, or even concepts. Its objective is rather to understand that phenomenon in human, social reality. Such human competence is viewed as a key for understanding what constitutes human achievement, and in particular what constitutes human epistemic achievement, achievement of the specifically gnoseological sort, of the sort that constitutes human knowledge. Knowledge itself, then, *possessed* human knowledge more particularly, is viewed as itself an objective phenomenon, often enough one in social reality.

Very well, what then is that phenomenon of an agent's possessing a competence at a time? That is here viewed as a disposition to succeed when one tries, one with the triple-S structure sketched above, at least when the aim is distal. (So, we focus on this most complex case, though many competences have respective aims that are non-distal.)

What then is a (distal) skill? It is a condition, a state of the agent, one that seats a disposition to succeed reliably enough in that agent's attempts to attain the aim. *Any* attempts? No, a skill is determined as such by its seating a disposition to succeed reliably enough in an agent's attempts to attain the pertinent aim *when they try in certain preselected shape–situation pairs*. Failure when one is drunk or in the dark does not spoil (first-order) skill (though it may manifest higher-order incompetence to properly select one's attempts).

So, for the determination of a skill, for its social construction, we first need a preselection (by the pertinent community for that domain) of the relevant shape and situation parameters. It is attempts *within such parameters of shape and situation* that must succeed reliably *enough* in order for that *disposition* to ground a *skill*, an innermost *competence*, possessed by that agent.

For conventional dimensions, such as games, sports, and artistic performance domains, it is social convention that sets those settings of shape, situation, and sufficiency of success. (For more basic human competences, there would seem to be evolutionary settings that are not just conventional, but we leave that aside in this sketch.)

Next we turn to issues of suspension in epistemology, and in gnoseology more specifically, issues that soon come to the fore in traditional epistemology with its focus on knowledge and skepticism.

PART II

THE NATURE AND VARIETIES OF SUSPENSION

3
The Place of Suspension and Problems for Evidentialism

This chapter takes some first steps toward an epistemology of suspension within the framework of telic virtue epistemology.

A. The Place and Importance of Suspension

1. In the domain of action in general, not just epistemic action, we find a "forbearance" that amounts to *intentional omission*. Here two varieties can be distinguished through the following formulation:

> Forbearing from X'ing in the endeavor to attain an aim A.

Where might parentheses go into that formulation? Here are two options:

> *Narrow scope*: (Forbearing from X'ing) in the endeavor to attain a given aim A.
>
> *Broad scope*: Forbearing from (X'ing in the endeavor to attain a given aim A).

2. That distinction among forbearances enables us to zoom in on the suspension of judgment that is of main epistemic interest. But first consider how suspending comes in at least two varieties.

Epistemically idle suspending is intentional forbearing from judging (from both positive and negative judging) on a certain question <p?>, *without* doing this in pursuit of any ulterior epistemic objective concerning that question. By contrast, *epistemically aimed* suspending is

Epistemic Explanations: A Theory of Telic Normativity, and What it Explains. Ernest Sosa, Oxford University Press (2021). © Ernest Sosa. DOI: 10.1093/oso/9780198856467.003.0003

subordinate to a particular kind of intellectual attempt: namely, the endeavor to affirm alethically on the given question (positively or negatively) if and only if one's alethic affirmation would be competent and indeed *apt*.

One might intentionally omit endeavoring to attain a certain aim. Perhaps one intentionally ignores that aim, refusing to so much as consider it. One then broad-scope forbears *without* narrow-scope forbearing. Narrow-scope forbearing, relative to a given aim, requires that one endeavor to attain that aim.[1]

The suspending of main interest to us is a sort of forbearing, but it must be specifically *narrow* scope (narrow-scope intentional double omission of alethic affirmation, both positive and negative). And it must be epistemically aimed suspending. This is because the theory of knowledge *presupposes* a focus on *inquiry*, in the *broadest* sense, where the subject simply takes up a question, which you might do just casually and implicitly, as when you walk down the street while automatically monitoring your surroundings.

Judgmental knowledge involves judgment. You aim to get it right aptly on a given "whether" question <p?> by affirming alethically on that question (positively or negatively). To succeed (aptly) in this aim is to judge with (apt) success.

When we "consider" such a question, we may do so implicitly, as with our implicit monitoring in our walk down the street. Alternatively, we may focus consciously on our question, and ponder how to answer it, if at all. In this latter case, we may be led either to judge (positively or negatively) or else to suspend judgment, and these (judging and suspending) then share an aim: *to judge if and only if one would judge with*

[1] What "endeavor" requires on the present view is not just that one *adopt* the relevant aim. It requires further that one then *attempt to attain* it. On a given occasion you might *have* an aim A without then doing anything in the endeavor to attain it (well, other than just *having* that aim, and whatever this might necessarily involve). So, on that occasion you do not really *attempt* to attain your aim A, though you still *have* that aim. You do nothing in the endeavor to attain it. You do not then *try* to attain it, which *would* require that you do *something* in the endeavor to attain it. What then does inquiry require? Active inquiry requires endeavoring to find an answer to the question inquired into, but it does not require attempting to answer that question by actually affirming an answer, since one might then properly suspend instead. (Trying to find an answer to one's question, as one pores over documents, differs from actually *answering* the question, by affirming—positively or negatively—in the endeavor to get it right.)

success. Judgment, recall, aims not just at the truth of one's affirmation, but at its aptness. When one takes up a question, when one inquires seriously, as opposed to just guessing, one aims for alethic affirmation that will be apt, not *just* true (not just true and perhaps *in*apt).[2] One aims like the oncologist, not like the quiz show contestant.

When one faces *judgmentally* a question whether p, one deliberates on whether to judge (positively or negatively) or suspend (intentionally omitting judgment). Judgment on whether p would require aiming for *apt* alethic affirmation. So, competent pursuit of that aim would require aiming to affirm alethically only if one (likely enough) would so affirm aptly. One puts oneself in the appropriate shape and situation and approaches the question with the required skill so that one affirms alethically only if one there and then would do so aptly. Aiming to satisfy that conditional is inherent to a sort of serious inquiry defined in part by so aiming. And this is half of our biconditional objective: to alethically affirm (positively or negatively), on the question whether p, if and only if one would thereby affirm aptly. (In abbreviated form, the objective is: to affirm alethically re <p?> iff one's alethic affirmation would be apt.)

How is theory of knowledge related to theory of inquiry? Whether to take up a question, a concern central to the normativity and theory of inquiry is irrelevant to the normativity and theory of whether one knows through alethic affirmation on that question. One can know with great certainty and utmost epistemic standing truths whose utter triviality makes it inadvisable to inquire into them. The lowest justification of inquiry into a question leaves it possible that one attain the highest level of epistemic certainty for one's knowledge of the right answer to that question. It is hence important to distinguish between narrow-scope suspending and broad-scope suspending.

Why think that in such inquiry one must adopt the subsidiary aim to judge re <p?> *only if* one's judgment would succeed? If one judged when one's judgment would fail, then one would err in a way highlighted by Descartes, as a deeper error than mere falsity.[3] One of course errs when

[2] And the like holds as well when one just engages a question implicitly, without consciously intentional pondering.

[3] See the Appendix to this chapter.

one's alethic affirmation is false. But one is also in Cartesian error when one's alethic affirmation is true but inapt. Such affirmation is true by a sort of luck that blocks credit to the thinker. The attainment of truth is then not through competence but through that sort of epistemic luck. In proper inquiry we aim not just to attain apt alethic affirmation on the question addressed, whether p. We aim also for the avoidance of inaptness, of Cartesian error.[4] True, if we attain aptness, we thereby avoid inaptness. But one might avoid inaptness without attaining aptness. So, even when one *fails to attain* one's dominant aim of inquiry, one might *still attain* a subsidiary aim, namely avoiding inaptness, thus earning partial credit of a sort.

Unless aimed at least in part at avoiding inaptness, deliberation and its outcome would not be wholly competent. Unless one managed to avoid inaptness well enough, one's pursuit of aptness would fall short, so that any aptness one might attain would manifest insufficient competence. Unless one aims to affirm alethically *only if* one would do so aptly, and one properly guides oneself to do so, one's attainment of aptness is relevantly lucky. It is *in*sufficiently owed to competence.

So much for half of our subsidiary aim inherent in serious inquiry, according to which one is to judge *only if* one's judgment would succeed (one is to affirm alethically in the endeavor to so affirm aptly *only if* one would thereby succeed in that endeavor). What of the other half of our biconditional aim? Why think that in inquiry one must adopt the

[4] *Objection*: This does not generalize to performances in general. When playing a game of darts in which the first to hit the bullseye 20 times wins, I might be best advised to take many shots quickly, without regard for avoiding failure or inaptness. *Reply*: This objection prompts recognition that attempts can be nested. One attempts to hit the bullseye 20 times as quickly as possible, and in pursuit of that dominant objective one may make a series of quick attempts without trying for high competence or aptness with each attempt, but while trying to attain the *quick* 20-fold success with the highest available competence and aptness. So, the subsidiary attempt to hit the bullseye by shooting quickly properly reduces the degree of competence and aptness aimed for in that *particular* shot, for the sake of producing a *sequence* of shots that will thereby attain *its* success more competently and aptly. And this reveals a way in which an encompassing dominant attempt can trump a component subsidiary attempt, so as to lower the degree of aptness and competence properly aimed at in the latter. (Further afield, an extension of this point will also apply to the proper subordination of individual attempts in deference to important enough collective attempts, since humans are not only rational but also properly *political* animals.)

subsidiary aim to judge re <p?> *if* by so judging one would succeed? Well, isn't it inherent in inquiry that one should judge once one has put oneself in a condition wherein if one judged one would succeed? Isn't this just part of what it is to aim for the knowledge constituted by such judgmental success, by apt alethic affirmation?

3. A desirable level of human knowledge is the apt judgment, the *fully apt alethic affirmation*. Such knowledge constitutes a desirable sort of success in inquiry.[5] It thus provides a (main) norm of judgment, whether public or private. And it is thus not only a norm of *judgment*, but also a norm of *suspension*. The immediate aim that one promotes when one suspends properly is the aim of affirming alethically if and only if so affirming would be apt. This subsidiary aim is one that must be attained aptly if one is to attain aptly one's dominant aim. The subsidiary aim of proper suspension is that of affirming alethically if and only if one would thus affirm aptly. That objective is one properly pursued in suspending. And it is an aim subsidiary to hierarchically superior aims: that of apt alethic affirmation (animal knowledge), and that of apt judgment (knowledge full well).[6]

4. It may be argued that the proposal here over-intellectualizes the normativity of ordinary belief. However, the biconditional aim proposed as inherent to proper belief and proper suspension need not be a conscious aim.

Consider the *omissions* that might be made in functional, teleological pursuit of such an aim. Such omissions too can remain on a functional, teleological level.

Take for example the plover hen who seeks to protect her nest through her broken wing ruse. Her ostensible aim is to issue her ruse iff a predator gets too close. In cases where a predator is too far, her omission of

[5] And this is so whether the inquiry takes the form of conscious pondering or that of *implicit* functionally teleological "processing."

[6] More generally, achievement is the norm of attempt.

the ruse need not be owed to inattention, temporary blindness, or any other negligence or flaw. Rather, she may properly omit the ruse in pursuit of that biconditional aim. What is more, sometimes the plover hen can tell whether the nearing animal is likely to pose danger and she will then use the ruse if and only if she perceives real danger. If this sort of intellectual performance is not *functionally* beyond plovers, it is not plausibly beyond the subconscious functioning of humans.

5. Your lifetime record as an eye-exam subject may show it to have been no accident that you were so consistently right at a line with tiny letters where you thought you were just guessing. Yes, you were guessing at that line but your infallible success may show it not to have been a sheer guess. Both the eye-exam subject and the quiz-show contestant guess at the right answers. Neither is confident enough to aim for aptness.

What follows will focus mainly on achievement above that of the contestant's lucky guess and even above that of the eye-exam subject's reliably correct guess. Humans can of course attain such a functional level of knowledge, but we go beyond that through our conscious rationality and judgment.

We will focus on judgment, and hence on thinkers who aim for aptness and not just truth, *and who have a credal basis of sufficient confidence for their alethic affirmations.*

At a *merely* "animal" level, the eye-exam subject does epistemically well by getting it repeatedly right through a competence that operates with impressive subconscious, functional reliability. So, a sort of subcredal competence there provides a certain level of knowledge (in an ostensible guess aided by zero confidence). Yet this falls below the level of human judgment constituted by our rationally reflective faculties. Such *mere* animal knowledge thus falls below the reflective knowledge familiar to normal humans over a vast domain wherein we judge, share information, and coordinate action, through our remarkable ability to communicate.

6. *How is our epistemic hierarchy ordered?* Action hierarchies are normally ordered through a certain "by" relation. You may for example aim to alert a co-conspirator by illuminating a certain window, aim to do

this in turn by illuminating the room with that window, and aim to do *this*, in *its* turn, by flipping a certain light switch. How do you implement that plan? As follows: By flipping the switch, you thereby illuminate the room; by illuminating the room, you thereby illuminate the window; and by illuminating the window, you thereby alert the co-conspirator. And that is the hierarchical plan whereby you alert the co-conspirator.

That is *not* how our epistemic hierarchy need be ordered when we inquire. Suppose one has to *suspend* as one aims for this biconditional: *to affirm alethically (on the given question) if and only if one would so affirm aptly*. Suspending here is intentionally omitting alethic affirmation (whether positive or negative), in the endeavor to satisfy the two conditionals. If this is subordinate to knowing the answer to that question, it cannot be in the way familiar from ordinary action hierarchies. It can't be that by thus suspending one would *thereby* know the answer, either on the first order (with apt alethic affirmation, or "animal" knowledge) or on the second order (with apt judgment, or "reflective" knowledge full well). Such suspending can never constitute either apt affirmation or apt judgment. Instead it can be a sort of spandrel. It can be an inevitable byproduct of the serious pursuit of a dominant aim. That is what happens when suspending is the outcome of the inevitable pursuit of a subsidiary aim, one that must be pursued given one's primary aim. The subordinate epistemic aim must be *pursued*, for the sake of attaining a dominant aim, namely that of apt alethic affirmation.

Here next is an example that illuminates our unusual way in which an aim can be subordinate to a hierarchically dominant aim.

Suppose I play chess regularly with my young grandson, and I can see the fast improvement, but also the low confidence and the nervous anxiety. I continue to play so that (as I fully expect) he may start to win more and more of our matches and gain confidence and enjoyment in the game. Suppose that to be my master intention as we play our next game. I aim to lose by playing, confident that he is now the better player, so that by playing him I will likely further his winning. But I want the game to be real and fair, so I play to win, but with the overarching and guiding intention to lose. If I did not aim to lose I would not play, since I've been fearing that I might damage his fragile confidence and discourage him to the point of quitting the sport altogether.

I do try to win. And I might of course attain this aim aptly, through the exercise of competence. But I also aim to lose, and we can suppose that, if I attain *that* objective, I will do so competently. It will not be a fake loss. That is not what I want. Rather, I mean the loss to be a real loss. Although I really try to win, yet my *overarching* aim is to *really* lose, which requires that I seriously try to win. Paradoxically, it appears that one can appropriately and seriously aim *both* to win *and* to lose. How can this be?

How? In the way of our example, with one aim subordinate to the other. But this subordination is unusual. A more usual way in which one aim, A1, is subordinate to another, A2, is through one's *intention* to bring about the whole of the following: attaining A1, by attaining which one will, *thereby*, attain A2. In our unusual case, one aim is subordinate to another through one's aiming to attain the latter in part by *hosting* the former. Thus, it is not that I aim to lose to my grandson by winning. Rather, I aim to *really* lose to my grandson in part *by seriously aiming to win.*[7]

If it happens that I do win, this will be a sort of spandrel. In the circumstances it may be an inevitable consequence of my pursuit of an aim whose serious pursuit was required for the attainment of my dominant aim. And this is the sort of spandrel that suspension turns out to be when it occurs in the pursuit of an aim that must be pursued if one is to attain a certain dominant aim. Here one aims to affirm if and only if affirming would be apt (and otherwise to suspend). This subsidiary aim

[7] *Objection*: "Why not say instead that your aim is to win, though you hope to lose, or would prefer to lose? It is hard to see how one could aim both to win and to lose." *Reply*: Recall first how our reasoning has put in doubt the move from "aiming both to win and to lose" to "aiming to win and lose." Our reasoning would show that move to be invalid. Our chess example is one where the thinker/agent aims to win and to lose *without* aiming to win and lose. What would be incoherent is to aim to win and *by winning thereby lose*. That *would* be to aim to win and lose, and that is too absurd to countenance as an aim that a rational agent could possibly have. But that was not my situation in playing my grandson. I was aiming to lose. I was not just hoping to lose. I was actually trying to *bring about* my grandson's proper and serious win (or at least to contribute essentially toward that objective). Of course I realized that such a win would come about only through my seriously playing to win. But still it just seems right that I am playing seriously to win and doing so because I realize that only with such serious play would the win of my grandson be real, not fake. If I had thought that my serious play to win would actually succeed surely enough, I would *not* have played. I would have told my grandson that we should postpone our game and that he should play his playmate instead.

must be adopted when one pursues a dominant aim to affirm aptly on the question addressed.

In that way, knowledge is a main norm (a hierarchically dominant aim) not only of judgment (and assertion) but also of suspension.[8]

B. Suspension and Evidentialism

Epistemic negligence and recklessness are hard to square with evidentialist epistemology. These phenomena bear on epistemically justified suspension of judgment, and on epistemically justified judgment itself. They problematize evidentialism and favor an alternative *agential* framework.

1. Thinkers face a threefold range of options on any question <p?> that they may take up. Judgmentally they could affirm, deny, or suspend. Since to judgmentally deny <p> is just to judgmentally affirm <not-p>, thinkers also face the twofold choice between judging (positively or negatively) and suspending.

[8] In recent years Jane Friedman has published papers in which she develops a novel account of suspension, in relation to questions, beliefs, and inquiry. (In "Why Suspend Judging" (*Nous*, 2017), for example, and "Inquiry and Belief" (*Nous*, forthcoming).) Although not incompatible, our views are radically different. The main differences derive from the telic character of my own approach. We have seen how this opens up a view of epistemology as an account of one more domain of human endeavor. In this domain of epistemology there are several distinctive aims, so that an array of interrelated attempts unfolds, displaying crosscutting varieties. Some attempts are consciously intentional, while others are functionally teleological. For a second distinction, animal beliefs (mere alethic affirmations) fall hierarchically under reflective judgments, whose aim is not just truth but aptness, or truth through competence. Friedman relates suspension (as she views the phenomenon) to questions, to beliefs, and to inquiry. One important difference between our approaches derives from how telic threefold multiplicity falls into three categories: in how we can approach a question, in the sorts of objectives coordinate with any such approach, and in corresponding forms of inquiry. To take just one distinction, we may have a first-order conscious aim to answer a certain question correctly, as might a quiz show contestant; alternatively, we may aim to answer our question *aptly* (and not just correctly), as might an oncologist. But, again, that is just a partial account. In fact, there are, I believe, various constitutively different sorts of inquiry and suspension, corresponding to the varieties of epistemic aims. Each such aim will import various distinctive ways in which one can forbear from affirming. And suspension in all its varieties I take to be fundamentally a kind of intentional forbearing (or, more generally, a kind of *aimed* forbearing, including two quite distinct approaches to questions: first, involving consciously intentional aiming, and, second, involving just functionally teleological aiming).

2. Philosophical skeptics ostensibly follow reason in suspending, where (in first approximation) to suspend, on a "whether p" question, is to intentionally omit any judgment (whether positive or negative), on that question. But the relevant reason must be epistemic. You do not help a troubled skeptic to overcome their skepticism by threatening to shoot them unless they judge. That does provide a good reason to judge but not the right sort of reason. The reason it provides is pragmatic, not epistemic.

Pyrrhonian skeptics follow a set of interrelated principles concerning rational intellectual acts and attitudes. On one understanding, in terms of reasons, the simplest of them reads: *Insufficient reason to judge (positively or negatively) provides sufficient reason to suspend.* In order to be justified, epistemic acts and attitudes often need to be based on proper *reasons*. But how should we understand such *reasons* if they need to be epistemic, not just pragmatic?

3. Given the focus of epistemology on truth, on correct representation, our idea of "*epistemic* reason" is bound to be closely related to the truth/falsity dimension. We might thus understand that idea in terms of an evidencing or a probabilifying relation. And this fits a generic evidentialism formulable as follows.[9]

Evidentialism

> First comes the idea of what *would* justify you in judging that such and such if you *did* so judge. This is thought to be something in your intellectual possession on whose basis you could judge appropriately. This would be a balance of "evidence" that "evidences" the content of your judgment (with individual elements that evidence that judgment, *or its negation*, since negative evidence must also have its proper weight in the

[9] We focus here in the first instance on the act of judgment that p, but our account is extensible also to the ongoing state of believing that p, coordinate with a disposition to judge affirmatively upon considering whether p. And it is also extensible to a more general notion that includes truth-aimed functional belief.

pertinent total evidence). Thus, the first component of evidentialism is an account of *propositional* justification as follows.

(a) At t, S has *propositional* justification for judging that p iff, at t, S's total body of <p>-relevant evidence (sufficiently) evidences <p>.

Consider next a justified judgment that you've already made. What might make that judgment epistemically justified? This involves a second notion of justification, as follows.

(b) At t, S is *doxastically* justified in judging that p iff, at t, S's total body of <p>-relevant evidence both (sufficiently) evidences <p> and is a basis on which S judges (or judgmentally believes) that p.[10]

4. Problems for evidentialists.

It is hard to see how *suspending judgment* on a given question <p?> could ever be *based* on one's total evidence. *Judging* can plausibly be based on evidence if the evidence speaks sufficiently in favor of the content of your affirmation. But it is unclear how *suspending* could be *based*

[10] Alternatively, and to the same effect, we might require rather that the proposition "fit" the evidence, as do Earl Conee and Richard Feldman, the main champions of a broad evidentialism, in their canonical text. The most recent full-scale defense of such evidentialism is Kevin McCain's *Evidentialism and Epistemic Justification* (Routledge, 2014), an explanationist form of the doctrine that is detailed and sophisticated.

Problematic for that account is its treatment of suspension. A subject's *proper withholding at t on whether p* is defined as simply the failure of both <p> and <not-p> to fit that subject's total relevant evidence. However, suppose that <p> does fit your total relevant evidence although you have not yet had time to figure that out, and in any case you do not yet believe that p based on that possessed evidence. According to the definition, you are then at that time withholding *improperly*, but that seems questionable. Must you not withhold until you *do* properly believe? The fact that <p> fits your total relevant evidence seems insufficient to rule out your *properly* withholding, not while you are still deliberating.

Moreover, the view also seems subject to the problems attributed in our main text to the generic view. The book does contain a detailed, causal account of basing, in terms of interventionist causation. But one is said to be doxastically justified in believing that p if and only if <p> fits one's total relevant evidence (in an explanationist way), while one's belief is causally based on that evidence. And it is left open that one be quite *insensitive* to whether the hypothesis fits one's evidence (*in that explanationist way*). But it is hard to see how this can avoid the problem that one might be arriving at that hypothesis too much by luck. The hypothesis would fit one's evidence but one might not be properly sensitive to its doing so: i.e., one might not at all base one's belief on that further fact.

These are prima facie problems that any adequate evidentialism needs to confront.

on evidence in virtue of some relation between the evidence and the content of your suspending. Thus, you might have a slight balance of positive evidence in favor of a hypothesis. Your evidence might consist of perceptual data, testimony, remembered facts, etc. For example, the hypothesis might be that the temperature in Quito is now 70 degrees Fahrenheit. And your data might include reports to that effect from two obscure weather apps, and a contrary report from a third, more respectable app. But no such datum, whether positive or negative, could individually constitute a reason for *suspending* on that hypothesis. Nor could a combination of such data constitute a reason for suspension. You could not properly reason from the mere content of any such combination to suspending on that hypothesis.

Yet there must be something importantly in common between how *judging and suspending* are respectively justified. What needs to be justified on the given question is after all the *choice* between suspending, on one hand, and judging (positively or negatively), on the other. Whichever way the choice goes, its justification would involve a *comparison* between two incompatible options: judging and suspending. What matters is the *sufficiency or insufficiency* of your *total* relevant evidence. This is what the choice would be based on, presumably, so it would not be based *just* on the evidence, just on the *content* of your total evidence.

The choice between judging and suspending is often implicit. Still, whether you suspend properly is determined not just by the *total* evidence in your possession but also by whether that evidence is *sufficient* or *insufficient*. This being so, you must be adequately sensitive to such sufficiency or insufficiency not only when you suspend, but also when you judge (positively or negatively) rather than suspend. When doxastically justified in a "well formed" judgment, you must be guided to that judgment not only by the contents of your body of relevant total evidence E but also by the fact that E satisfies the following two conditions:

> first, that E be your *total* body of relevant evidence, that there be no *other* relevant evidence in your possession;
>
> second, that E be epistemically sufficient for judgment rather than suspension, that the balance of the contained evidence sufficiently favor judging as you do.

In other words, you must base your belief not only severally on the contents of your body of relevant evidence E. You must base it also on the fact that E satisfies those two conditions.[11]

A thinker who judges without adequately extensive basing would not succeed creditably. With no relevant change in their epistemic situation, such a thinker would be too liable to judge otherwise, a liability that precludes their judgment's manifesting proper competence.

Suppose, for example, you have in your possession a body of evidence E relevant to the question whether p. You consider whether to judge that p based on the contents of E. But you do not take into account whether that is your *total* body of relevant evidence, whether it is *all* of your evidence bearing on that question. Not even implicitly do you take that into account. Nor do you take into account whether you need to seek more evidence. Without taking any of that into account, without basing your judgment on those further factors, you judge that p just on the basis of E, just *severally* on the data contained in E.

According to our generic evidentialism, that is enough: you are thereby doxastically justified. But we have seen already why that is so problematic. In order to be fully justified, your act of judgment must be performed in part because of further factors not contained as evidence within your relevant evidential set. It also matters whether you are in possession of any further relevant evidence, and also whether you need to seek additional evidence. You must perform as you do on the basis not only of the relevant evidence severally, but also on your satisfaction of those further conditions.

5. I will argue that we should look to agency for a better understanding of the epistemic normativity that applies to judgment and belief, and for a better understanding of doxastic justification in particular.

As we have seen, you must be justified in *closing inquiry*. Or at least you must be justified in *willingly answering your question without awaiting any further evidence*, doing which seems compatible with remaining open to additional evidence, or even still seeking such evidence, with

[11] This just grants for the sake of argument the assumption that a well-formed judgment *would* need to be based (at least in part) on the total relevant evidence in the thinker's possession. Our question is whether, even granting this, we can accept the overall evidentialism.

willingness to revise in the light of any additional evidence that may come to light. (So, in that case you give an answer without awaiting what further inquiry might deliver, which does not mean that you close inquiry in the sense of *abandoning* further inquiry.) You must be *properly* satisfied that the evidence you take into account is your *total* evidence, which contains everything in your possession that bears on the question whether p. And you must also be satisfied that the evidence in your possession is sufficiently extensive as a basis for judgment. So, you quit depending on further inquiry at least for the sake of giving your answer at that time.

Here we have a *further*, distinct sort of sufficiency that is also required. You must take your evidence to be *sufficiently extensive*. You must do so at least implicitly, by assuming or taking it for granted that you need *not* seek any more data. Note how your thought must here ascend to the second order, by bringing within its scope (at least implicitly) considerations *about* your evidence, including its being *in your possession*, and *being on balance sufficiently extensive and strong*. Suppose that, on some question, you deliver your answer based on the evidence already in your possession, and on its sufficiency on balance, so that in a sense you "conclude" inquiry at least temporarily, for the sake of delivering your answer. Even once you've properly delivered your answer, you might still wish to make sure, or to make more sure, and you might thus *resume* inquiry to that end, without abandoning your answer.

A body of evidence is adequate for judgment on a given question only if the balance of the evidence (whether on the positive or the negative) is weighty enough to justify affirmation (positive or negative). And one must be able to properly judge even without further inquiry. One must avoid the *negligence* or *recklessness* of judging on a body of evidence prematurely. Such negligence or recklessness would preclude performance that is fully competent and apt.

6. Suppose you add in your head a column of equally long numerals, one that has an "area" constituted by its length times its width. Consider an ordering of such columns from area 2 to area 100. At some point we cross the threshold where your reliability falls too low, where you can no longer reliably enough calculate the sum through mental arithmetic. As we approach that threshold of insufficient reliability, suppose paper and pencil to be easily available, and even a calculator. To insist on mental arithmetic, while willfully ignoring easily available, more reliable methods, is to incur epistemic negligence or recklessness.

One way to see this is to consider a case where your evidence is just barely *sufficiently strong* support for your conclusion. So, in our case of counting, the evidence might consist of its seeming plausible enough to us that the column adds up to n. We can think of this as a case where we believe that the sum is n, and we do so based on that answer's seeming plausible enough. Some degree of that will presumably suffice, and we can assume that the evidence suffices, but only barely so (while taking into account whatever counter-evidence there may be). In this case there is plausibly negligence or even recklessness on our part. Why so? Because we are allowing an important element of risk into the attainment of our success, supposing we do attain success, and even *aptly* attain it. The element of risk resides in the fact that our *aptness* is then attained by luck rather than competence, even though we could so easily have attained aptness by competence rather than luck. We could have done so by employing a competence easily available to us, with the calculator so easily within reach.[12]

[12] *Objection*: "If no calculator had been in reach, you would not have been negligent, presumably, yet you still would not have known. So what work does the anti-negligence requirement do here?" *Reply*: I am suggesting that negligence *is* a failure of competence, that one proceeds inappropriately in performing as one does if one *should* have taken the steps by not taking which one is negligent. One is then to blame (in the negligence mode) for not having taken those steps. So, if there *is* no calculator available, nor any other such way of securely checking, then (by hypothesis) there is no available action by omitting which one incurs negligence. Accordingly, there is no failure of competence in view. (The matter turns on when other steps are or are not sufficiently available. So, we are in effect laying it down by hypothesis that the only way other good enough steps are sufficiently available in our example is through the calculator in reach.) Competent attainment of aptness requires availing yourself of sufficiently available means that would enable a more reliable assessment of your first-order aptness and competence. If there are no such means, then there is no such negligence, and no such incompetence. In such a circumstance, the agent might then be able to determine with sufficient competence that they are is a position to proceed competently enough on the first order. (This conception of competence, as requiring the avoidance of such negligence, would thus figure in the social standards by which epistemic communities determine sufficiency of competence; and that would include the case of humanity at large, as the standards imposed by humans as humans determines sufficiency for basic *human* knowledge, and thereby its scope and limits.)

7. Compare a practical example.

Suppose a small plane runs out of fuel and crashes just short of its destination. The pilot had not checked the fuel and took off anyhow, either negligently or recklessly. Despite his subsequent superb piloting, the pilot's performance is then seriously lacking. Moreover, the performance would still have been seriously lacking even if the plane had *not* run out of fuel.

Note also how that correlates with whether such success, if attained, would be excessively due to luck, which would reduce or preclude credit to the agent.

8. Suppose one is *insufficiently sensitive* to having met *all* of the relevant conditions on one's evidence or judgment. One's performance must be based on the relevant evidence in one's possession, on all of it. But it must also be based on its *sufficiency*, on the balance being sufficiently positive, and on one's having gathered *enough* evidence. And if this happens too much by luck or accident, one then falls short of a fully creditable performance in adopting one's attitude, *be it judgment or suspension.*

When you do meet all of those conditions, that is highly contingent and specific to the given case. If you do not at all base your judgment on whether you have met them, then even if you opt successfully by affirming, this is by luck in some measure, so that your success is not fully creditable to you. *Too easily*, perhaps, might you have affirmed despite failing to meet the required conditions.

C. The Bearing of Telic Normativity

We have seen how, despite its insights, evidentialism does not fully explain epistemic *gnoseological* normativity, the specific normativity that is pertinent to the theory of knowledge. So, we next consider an alternative framework that can accept those insights within their proper bounds, while also explaining how more broadly judgment and judgmental knowledge are agentially constituted, so that to judge is to act.[13] It is in

[13] The solution and its framework are extensible to belief and knowledge that are teleologically functional rather than judgmental. All we need for the extension is that the items under assessment be *aimings* that admit of success and competence, and thus admit of aptness. Such

this framework of agency that negligence and recklessness have their home.

We next review some elements of our epistemic telic normativity that deserve emphasis as we prepare to attack issues of philosophical skepticism.

1. What are one's options when one inquires into a given question as to whether p? If one rules out abandoning the question, one can opt either *to judge* (to *right then* affirm, positively or negatively, aiming for alethic aptness) or else *to suspend judgment* (i.e., to *right then* intentionally omit any such affirmation).

Your objective in affirming can vary, of course, even when you affirm to yourself, in the privacy of your own mind. You might aim to deceive, for example, or to shock, or to reassure yourself, and so on.

Are there objectives distinctive of epistemology? In epistemic performance, in inquiry, we narrow our focus to *alethic* affirmation, affirmation in the endeavor *to get it right*. And we focus more specifically on *judgment*, which we should distinguish as follows from just guessing.

An alethic affirmation aims simply to get it right on the question in hand. And we have seen how this can take either of two sharply contrasting forms. The "guess" of the quiz show contestant must be distinguished from the "judgment" of an oncologist. The contestant aims just at getting it right, even if it's just a guess, but the oncologist aims at *judging* right, through reliable competence.

2. Performance normativity concerns attempts, with their constitutive aims, as in the example of archery. That involves a sort of *telic* normativity, and not any substantive, absolute axiology. The assessment is telic assessment. In telic normativity, the aim is given. It is unassessed and unquestioned.

Here again is our main guiding proposal: *that the normativity of the theory of knowledge is telic*. How does suspension fit within this approach?

aimings can be the object of meta-aimings, ones that also admit of success and competence. And this would seem to be the case of any creature that can learn from experience, whether their aimings are consciously intentional or only functional.

D. Suspension and Epistemic Normativity

1. Telic normativity is a normativity of *attempts*, but isn't suspension a paradigm of something that is *not* an attempt? This ostensible problem, if real, has the following solution.

2. Diana's archery shots can be more or less well selected, by contrast with the shots of an Olympic archer. When she spots some prey Diana can properly aim as follows: *to make an attempt on that target if and only if the attempt would succeed aptly*. So, her forbearing is itself an attempt with an aim of its own. One can properly adopt such an aim in one's performance, and there are now two ways of falling short:

(a) One might *make* an attempt (on the target) when one *would not* succeed aptly.
(b) One might *fail* to make an attempt (on the target) when one *would* succeed aptly.

Either way lowers the quality of one's deliberation and choice on whether to attempt to E (to attain end E) by M'ing (by taking means M). One's deliberation would embrace a practical syllogism whose conclusion would be either an attempt or else an omission, intentionally either way. Both (a) and (b) would imply a failure on the part of the agent to attain their objective: the objective of making an attempt if and only if it would succeed aptly.

3. A proper performance will have its broader aim to make the pertinent attempt iff it would succeed aptly. There's no omitting the pursuit of that broader aim without leaving the relevant performance domain. Whether to engage in a certain domain is not generally a question *within* that domain.

Telic assessment within a domain assesses mainly the pursuit of aims proper to that domain. An exhausted tennis competitor *may* of course properly consider whether to default, but this is not a decision assessable *within* the sport. When you sense a heart attack in progress and quit for that reason, this is not a decision assessable by athletic criteria in the domain of tennis. Whether to keep on playing is not a tennis decision; it is a life decision.

4. Recall our case of a "perfect" murder, where we pass no comment on the value or normative standing of the end. The relevant comparison is with *forbearing*, which goes beyond simply not-attempting. Again, this forbearing is narrow scope and *shares* an aim with the corresponding positive attempt. They share the aim of making the relevant attempt if and only if that attempt would succeed aptly.

5. Suspending thus falls under our AAA (AccuracyAdroitnessAptness) telic normativity. The forbearing most relevant to theory of knowledge is narrow-scope forbearing. This is what constitutes *deliberative suspension* of judgment, which is an attempt in its own right, one that even shares with judging an epistemically distinctive aim, namely the aim of *affirming alethically (positively or negatively) iff that affirming would be apt (and otherwise suspend)*. By contrast, although *nondeliberative suspension* of judgment is also an intentional forbearing from alethic affirmation (both positive and negative), it derives rather from omitting inquiry into the pertinent question, from an intentional refusal to go into that question, whether the refusal is implicit or consciously explicit.

6. We can thus consider an account of doxastic justification that may improve on evidentialism. On this account, doxastically justified judgment is competent judgment, competent alethic affirmation aimed at truth *and* aptness. The competence exercised in a (thereby) competent judgment must be good *enough*. It must be a competence that would enable the epistemic agent to attain relevant epistemic aims with enough reliability. Salient among such overarching epistemic aims is, again, that of

> answering one's question aptly, with an apt alethic affirmation (positive or negative).

But doing so requires that one also adopt the following subordinate aim affirming alethically (positively or negatively) iff that affirming would be apt (and otherwise suspend).

Sometimes the exercise of an epistemic competence yields judgment, but sometimes it yields suspension. And both of these can be creditable epistemic attainments, even if suspension falls short of our dominant epistemic aims. Our dominant aims include not suspension but successful judgment (or *fully* apt alethic affirmation that *aptly* attains not only truth but also aptness of alethic affirmation).[14]

E. Skepticism

1. In thinking of judgments as we've been doing, we place them within the category of actions, under agential telic normativity.

Judgment is thus plausibly a special sort of affirmation, one that aims at truth (and competence, and aptness). What provides proper reason to M (to take means M) in attempting to attain end E is that M'ing would be a good (enough) means toward that attainment (or would be an essential part of such means, or the like). We thus focus on instrumental reasons of one or another sort, where it is by M'ing that one attempts to attain an end E. And that attempt (through the instrument of M'ing) is assessable positively depending on how likely it is to lead to one's attaining E.[15] Thus, one has (objective) reason to ingest an aspirin pill in the endeavor to relieve a headache depending on the likelihood that ingestion would bring about relief.

Similarly, if in judging one aims to affirm the truth, then one has better and better reason to affirm, the more and more likely it is that by so doing one will indeed affirm the truth (on the question pondered, whether p). Beyond that contained aim, moreover, fully proper inquiry

[14] Hence the distinctive way in which suspending is subordinate to knowing, so that (as proposed above) proper active suspending is an epistemic spandrel. It fulfills an aim that one must *host* in the endeavor to know the answer to one's question, even if it is not an aim whose *fulfillment* would enable attainment *thereby* of one's dominant epistemic aim.)

[15] Though a fuller treatment would take into account doings properly related to such means, as when M'ing is rather an *essential component* of such efficient means, so that it is *in part* by M'ing that one attempts to attain E.

requires also a dominant aim of answering one's question knowledgeably (aptly, with an apt affirmation, positive or negative).

How can judgment aim to affirm with alethic aptness, or even with alethic success, by affirming that p? It cannot be that this requires a prior belief that "by affirming that p one would affirm correctly (with truth)." For, this would be tantamount to the thinker's *already* believing that p. On this tack, a (judgmental) belief that p would require as a precondition that the thinker *already* believe that p. So that cannot be right; that tack is a blind alley.

Fortunately, there's another way in which one can affirm that p in the endeavor to affirm with truth and through competence. Compare one's intentionally *capturing a fox* (and not just one's intentionally capturing an animal that turns out to be a fox). One can do so by spotting a fox and then snaring it. Here it is a precondition that one already believe that the target, the thing to be captured, is a fox. One then goes about snaring that thing *in the prior belief that it is a suitable target, i.e., a fox.* Here 'intentionally øing an F' requires as part of one's øing procedure that one locate an F as an F. The intentional snaring of a fox involves: first, locating a fox *as a fox*; then, second, stalking it and attaining a position close enough to it that enables your action of lassoing it (while still taking it to be a fox) with your snare.

Alternatively one may capture a fox by trapping it, where one engages rather in a procedure that will reliably enough yield a trapped fox, where the procedure does not require any prior identification of the target *as a fox*. Intentionally trapping an F is attaining the outcome of *a trapped F*, which does not require that prior to the trapping one identify the item that will be successfully trapped as indeed an F (as snaring does require).

Snaring a fox requires that one go from a de dicto objective: I aim to bring it about that some fox or other is snared by me), through a de re objective: *through* my finding a particular fox that I then aim to snare).

By contrast, trapping a fox normally entirely skips that intermediate de re step. When I aim to trap a fox, I aim to bring it about that some fox or other is trapped by me, but normally there is no need at all for me to identify some particular fox that I then aim to trap. One can set one's trap and go to sleep and in the morning one may have intentionally brought it about that one trapped a fox, with no need for that intermediate de re step.

So, snaring as conceived above is identification dependent, in that there is that intermediate step where one must set one's sights on a particular fox to be then snared. By contrast, trapping as conceived above is not thus identification dependent. There is no such intermediate step that requires one's targeting a particular fox.

How does it go when we take up a question in the endeavor to affirm with alethic aptness, and where we are honest inquirers who do not *already* know the answer? In such a case we are trappers of the truth rather than snarers of the truth. We employ a competence whose employment does not require that one *already* believe where the truth lies on that question, does not require a prior identification of a proposition as both an answer to the question and also true.

We may thus employ (consciously or functionally) a method or procedure that will yield a correct answer reliably enough, but whose employment does not require that one have already spotted where the truth lies. We capture the fox of truth by trapping it, with no need to have already spotted it for trapping prior to the actual trapping.

2. Recall our contrast between the contestant aiming to get it right by luck, and the oncologist who wants an *apt* diagnosis, not just the truth by luck. Most often, and most importantly, our affirmations aim at aptness rather than mere truth. Given our fallibility, we should thus follow policies that tend to yield success. "Tend"? What does that mean? We want policies that would produce enough success (and little enough failure) in a sufficient spread of one's attempts, and in a high enough proportion. What we want, in a word, is competences, or policies that constitute competences.[16]

[16] A fuller treatment might make room for the nesting of attempts, and for how it is that high reliability in a nesting attempt can comport with low reliability in any one of the nested attempts. Relatedly, we would also want to allow cases where the nesting attempt is that of a group with which one identifies and as a member of which one acts with a *nested* attempt, as one does oneself M but in that special mode where one Ms *as a member of* G, and perhaps in a role that one plays because of one's station and its duties. (Thus, the harmonious singing of a choir nests the singing of each of the voices by the individual choristers. However beautiful *or*

3. This bears on Pyrrhonian skepticism. Why should it be thought that the stance of the Pyrrhonist must be granted any sort of default status? Why should we demand from the dogmatist any special effort to overcome that default status, while allowing the skeptic to sustain his position until the dogmatist manages to displace him? Why should the burden of argument, of reasoning, rest on the dogmatist? We have seen why suspension is a positive mental attitude of some sort, whether episodic or dispositional, or some of each. And we have seen why the propriety of suspension turns on the agent's proper assessment of the epistemic risks. As an agent you have an aim in suspending. How appropriately you suspend is hence *pro tanto* directly proportional to how competently you assess the pertinent risk. And I can see no reason to suppose a priori that *taking the risk to be too high* should be preferable by default over *taking the risk to be appropriate.*

4. The distinction between narrow-scope and broad-scope forbearing helps explain why the Pyrrhonian skeptic deserves no default standing that the dogmatist must work to defeat. *Broad*-scope forbearing is easily seen to have default standing as an *epistemically* unobjectionable stance, one that does not require epistemic argument in its defense. There are of course often stringent *practical* reasons why we seek answers to certain questions. That is obvious enough. But the practical pressure involved has no knowledge-constitutive epistemic implications. Broad-scope forbearing is not a standing *within* domains of inquiry, wherein it would be subject to the epistemic assessment of attempts that are potentially knowledge-constitutive.

We can of course assess an agent's inquiry in respect of epistemic goals and procedures. And this can be assessment in a broad sense; it can be assessment that is broad scope, even if restricted to intellectual ends. This broad assessment can involve wisdom and good judgment in the pursuit of knowledge. There's the choice of domain, in the light of one's capabilities, and within a domain there's the choice of particular projects of inquiry. And this is all obviously "epistemic" assessment, in a

not some such individual effort may be, it may still gain proper normative status because it is sung by its singer *as a member of the choir aiming on that occasion to sing harmoniously*.)

broad but perfectly good sense. Doing well epistemically in these ways has little bearing, however, on the narrower assessment of epistemic choices, such as whether to affirm alethically or suspend; and it is the latter assessment that bears on whether a judgment achieves the status of knowledge.

Is there a label for that distinctive sort of assessment? We are calling it "gnoseological," a shortened label for the distinctive department of epistemology that is the theory of *knowledge*. This is the department wherein we find the core issues of knowledge and skepticism in the history of epistemology, by contrast with the wisdom of inquiry, and with the intellectual ethics wherein we find issues of epistemic justice and epistemic vice, broadly conceived. This is not to denigrate the latter issues found in the overlap between epistemology and applied ethics. It is rather to state the fact that the issues of gnoseology have been the core issues of knowledge and skepticism especially prominent among the Pyrrhonian skeptics and in the history of the subject from Descartes to the present, including of course the long fascination with the Gettier problem.

That is not say that issues of a broader intellectual ethics have no place in the tradition. Descartes's attention to the rules for the direction of the mind is a counterexample, as is the attention to the will to believe by James and others. More recently such issues of applied ethics—of intellectual ethics—have attracted increasing attention and interest, deservedly so. But that is not because the core issues of the nature, extent, and normativity of knowledge have all been resolved by solid disciplinary consensus. Far from it, though this is nothing peculiar to epistemology by contrast with any other main philosophical subdiscipline.

What then is distinctive of the narrow epistemic assessment that we are calling "gnoseological," the sort that is particularly pertinent to our knowledge of fact. We have seen how this sort of assessment is *telic*, and *presupposes* a preset question taken up by the thinker. Here we abstract, more specifically, from whatever practical reasons may have led the inquirer to take up that question, even from whatever *intellectually* practical reasons may have been operative. Inquiry can be driven by idle curiosity, which is in no need of *any* supportive reasons, whether practical or otherwise (except of course for just the idle curiosity itself, but there need be no reason whatever for being curious about that particular question in the first place). Nor is there any general need to justify one's omitting inquiry, one's broad forbearance.

Here the following distinction is relevant:

a. There is no general need to justify one's omitting inquiry, to justify the broad forbearance that amounts to *not* entering a certain question.
b. There is no need to justify one's *generally* omitting inquiry, to justify one's *not* entering *any* question.

I have suggested only that 4a is true, without taking up the question whether 4b is true, nor does one need any justification for *not* taking up this latter question.

5. Can't the skeptic postulate Jamesian aims of avoiding error and attaining truth as fundamental in epistemology? Well, consider again our postulation of inquiry into a given question as a framework *required* for the epistemic assessment relevant to the theory of knowledge, to *gnoseology*. We have seen why a proper understanding of epistemology requires a distinction between gnoseology and intellectual ethics, where the latter includes theory of inquiry, with its distinctive normativity. An important sort of intellectual wisdom pertains to the pursuit of topics and questions, and to the proper allocation of resources, even when practical concerns are irrelevant, or treated as given without question. By contrast, knowledge-focused assessment is independent of such issues of intellectual ethics. Foolishness in the choice of topics and questions can be unbounded even when knowledge on such topics and questions reaches the zenith of certainty. Intellectual ethics must be kept apart from theory of knowledge if we are to avoid confusion.

6. Accordingly, the forbearance of special interest in theory of knowledge is narrow scope. It is this that properly constitutes epistemic, *deliberative* suspension of judgment. And now it is hard to see how the skeptic can have any default standing for his attitude of suspension on a

given question. The skeptic *shares* an objective with the dogmatist: that of judging (positively or negatively) on the given question iff the judgment would be apt (and would not incur excessive risk). The skeptic and the dogmatist on that question adopt incompatible attitudes. The skeptic narrow-scope forbears and the dogmatist narrow-scope judges. The skeptic *deliberatively* suspends while the dogmatist deliberatively judges. The very meaning of the Greek root for 'skeptic' is *inquirer*. In line with that, skeptical suspension does then seem to be deliberative. It is not the *nondeliberative* suspension of the intellectual slacker. But, on *the corresponding* disagreement, the disagreement between dogmatists and skeptics, both inquirers, what reason could there be for granting the skeptic any default advantage?

Since any instance of suspending would thus be subject to the telic assessment proper to attempts generally, we would need to ask whether it does or does not attain its aim, and how competently, how aptly: Does the attainment of the aim manifest the subject's pertinent competence? This applies to skeptics and their distinctive aim, no less than to any other agent pursuing whatever aim. As it turns out, skeptics do stick their necks out along with dogmatists.

Appendix

There's a history to this approach. At an epistemic juncture, the Cartesian objective, one highlighted by telic virtue epistemology, is that of making an alethic attempt if and only if it would be apt. This is to be distinguished from the Jamesian objective of attaining truth and avoiding falsehood. There is a distinctively Cartesian objective (like one found also in Aristotle, as we shall see below).

> If "...I simply refrain from making a judgment in cases where I do not perceive the truth with sufficient clarity and distinctness, then it is clear that I am behaving correctly and avoiding error [Latin *error*, French *erreur*]. But if in such cases I either affirm or deny, then I am not using my free will correctly. If I go for the alternative which is false, then obviously I shall be in error; if I take the other side, then it is by...chance [French *hasard*] that I arrive at the truth, and I shall still

> be at fault.... In this incorrect use of free will may be found the privation which constitutes the essence of error." (*Meditations*, IV.12)

> It is also certain that when we assent to some piece of reasoning when our perception of it is lacking, then either we go wrong, or, if we do stumble on the truth, it is by accident, so that we cannot be sure that we are not in error. (Principle 44 of the *Principles of Philosophy*)

In this respect, Descartes's epistemology is a special case of Aristotle's virtue ethics, as appears in the following passage (translations and glosses by Robert Bolton, unpublished).

> It is possible to produce something that is grammatical either by chance or under the supervision of another. To be proficient in grammar, then, one must both produce what is grammatical and produce it grammatically, that is, in accord with [kata=as an expression of] knowledge of grammar in oneself [not in some supervisor].
> (Aristotle, *Nicomachean Ethics* II 4, 1105a22–6)

This is in effect our concept of aptness. How crucial such a concept is to Aristotle's ethics may be seen in a further passage:

> human good proves to be an activity of soul [a successful one, presumably, given the importance of lucky externalities for Aristotelian flourishing] in accord with [kata=as an expression of] virtue and, if there are more virtues than one, in accord with [kata=as an expression of] the best and most complete. (*Nicomachean Ethics* I 7, 1098a16–17)

Since human good is what humans ought to pursue, the pursuit of interest to Aristotle is such activity of soul, that which constitutes human good, namely activity that attains desiderata, where the attainment is in accord with virtue. Aristotle is not in these passages so clearly and explicitly focused on the attainment of human good. Famously, however, he does postulate that flourishing is properly the main human end, and flourishing is activity of soul that succeeds in accord with virtue (spread over one's lifetime).

4
Suspension, Confidence, and Inquiry

Without taking back anything in Chapter 3, we now go on to distinguish various forms of suspension, aiming to deepen our understanding.

Here's the plan. We begin by reconsidering the nature and varieties of suspension of judgment, and then take up four questions: First, how is suspension related to degrees of confidence? Second, how is it related to instrumental means–end reasoning? Third, how is it related to inquiry? Fourth, when and how is suspension epistemically appropriate?

A. Suspension of Judgment: What It Is and Some Varieties

1. A dichotomy of ways to suspend has an important role in epistemology. Judgment might be suspended consciously on a given question either *deliberatively* or *non-deliberatively*. Let us take a closer look.

To judge on whether p is to judge either that p or that not-p. To suspend on that question is not just to omit judgment, to simply *not* judge (whether affirmatively or negatively). Rather, to suspend judgment on whether p requires that one *intentionally* omit judgment (or at least that one do so *attributably* to oneself as agent).

What is it to abstain? Is it simply to *not* vote either for or against? No, if one falls asleep, one does not abstain even if one votes neither for nor against. Is it then to *intentionally* vote neither for nor against? This is better but still not good enough. It overlooks that you can walk out of a meeting in disgust without abstaining. You do then intentionally omit voting either in favor or against, but no abstention would be counted on your behalf.

What abstaining requires is to intentionally omit voting while still participating in the vote, as one continues collaborating in the group's

Epistemic Explanations: A Theory of Telic Normativity, and What it Explains. Ernest Sosa, Oxford University Press (2021). © Ernest Sosa. DOI: 10.1093/oso/9780198856467.003.0004

attempt to reach a good decision. Shall the group proceed in the way proposed by the motion or not? In response the abstainers intentionally omit voting either way but they do so *in the endeavor to reach a correct decision by the group.*[1] So, they omit both an affirmative and a negative vote as a means to the following:

> to the group's acting on the motion *if and only if* so acting would succeed and would do so aptly, through sufficient deliberative competence.

The intentional omission of voting either pro or con might thus be either deliberative or non-deliberative. It is non-deliberative for those who leave the meeting in disgust. It is deliberative for those who continue to aim for a correct decision. Proceeding thus *in the endeavor to reach a proper decision*—if but only if it would attain proper (competent, apt) success—they may then abstain by voting *neither* pro *nor* con, intentionally so.

If correct, that suggests a model for epistemology generally. Thus, we can distinguish between two ways of intentionally omitting judgment: one might do so in the endeavor to judge successfully, or one might do so as one simply abandons the question.[2]

That aligns with our distinction between two parts of epistemology: namely, theory of knowledge (gnoseology, for short) vs. intellectual ethics (including theory of inquiry), a distinction invoked again in what follows next.

[1] Although abstention is normally performed through the performative 'I abstain', or through the raising of one's hand, this seems inessential. We can imagine a meeting that allows abstention through making it evident that one intentionally omits voting either for or against. Thus, the question might be posed sequentially to the members of the assembled group, with "abstention" constituted by an obvious intentional *nonresponse* to "For or against?" Of course, a nonresponse could always mislead, but that is always a risk, no matter how we allow abstention to be constituted.

[2] A careful reading of Sextus reveals a further possibility. One may inquire in the endeavor to suspend. That, it turns out, is the Pyrrhonist master goal. They find by accident that suspension brings ataraxia, and then adopt that as their explicit goal. And this reveals a further position in intellectual ethics, as one pragmatically seeks suspension for its practical benefits. That being so, the Pyrrhonists are surprisingly not really a part of the gnoseological tradition with its focus on assessments of endeavors to know (on presupposed questions taken up). They dismiss that endeavor, actually, and prefer to "inquire," to muster reasons, data, and arguments in an endeavor to sustain equipollence and thereby attain ataraxia.

2. The focus here is on the moment of the assessed performance, the moment of abstaining. What may or may not happen in the future is irrelevant to that assessment, as we here conceive of it. Of course, inquiry into a question might be ongoing. But our assessment of the thinker's performance assesses their performance *at a moment*. (Of course, one could also assess their diachronic performance over a stretch, but that is another matter; we here focus on what a thinker does at a given moment. Although we can generalize from the latter to assessing their performance at *every* moment in a stretch, or at most moments, etc., we here focus on the assessment of their performance at a given moment.)

The guiding objective for proper inquiry is presumably that of judging if and only if one is in a position to do so with success. And, as inquiry unfolds one may sustain that objective steadily. So, during a stretch of proper inquiry, one may well sustain the objective of judging if and only if one is well positioned to do so. Still, the following distinction needs to be made. At any given time t within that stretch, one can distinguish the following two objectives:

(a) the objective for the foreseeable stretch of inquiry (or, more generally, for an indeterminate future stretch) to judge at any given moment in that stretch iff one is well positioned to do so; and
(b) the objective right now, at a given moment t, to judge at this moment iff one is *then* well positioned to do so.

It is important to distinguish, for any given moment t, objective (a) from objective (b) in the mind of the thinker. It seems quite possible for either of these to be present without the other, but the objective that is crucial for the gnoseological assessment of the thinker's performance at a given moment t, is objective (b), or so I submit. Objective (a) has its own interest in the proper planning of inquiry, and is an assessment in intellectual ethics. But it will not necessarily bear directly on the gnoseological assessment of the thinker's performance at that very moment t, nor actually for any other moment in that later stretch. The assessment for any other moment will still focus on objective (b) specified for that other moment.

3. Animal versus reflective modes of suspension.

Recall the eye-exam subject whose lifelong medical record shows it to have been no accident that he would get it right at a line way down the chart where he thought he was just guessing. Neither the quiz show contestant nor this eye-exam subject engage in judgment; they aim not for aptness but for truth.[3]

The oncologist might be willing to guess at least to herself, or to her spouse in dinner conversation. So they might willingly affirm alethically, and might even attain aptness, as does the eye-exam subject even when they think it's a sheer guess. Despite actively guessing, however, the quiz show contestant and the eye-exam subject may still suspend *judgmentally*, unwilling as they are to try in their affirmation for *aptness* and not just truth. These are then ways in which one might attain *animal* knowledge even when one reflectively suspends.

Since our main interest here is oncologist-style judgments and not just contestant-style guesses, we focus on alethic affirmation aimed at aptness and not just at truth, and on the epistemic assessment of such attempts. Accordingly, the suspension of main interest here is judgmental suspension.

4. Confidence and judgment.

The eye-exam subject and the quiz show contestant share an attitude to their respective questions. Each of them guesses at the right answer. Each aims to get it right, but neither aims for aptness. This is because they each have a low opinion of their competence to answer correctly. And this of course aligns with their low confidence.

Still our two guessers differ importantly. The eye-exam subject attains a sort of knowledge, *sub-credal* knowledge, whereas the contestant does not attain even that low level of epistemic achievement.

Our scope in what follows is restricted to achievement above that of the contestant and also above that of the eye-exam subject. So, we focus on thinkers who do not just guess in *either* of those two ways.

[3] And there is a mode of suspension proper to their endeavor, since they could consciously and intentionally omit just alethic affirmation (both affirmative and negative), as opposed to intentionally omitting judgment.

We focus on judgment, and hence on thinkers who aim for aptness and not just truth, and rely on a credal basis of sufficient confidence for their alethic affirmations.

B. The Place of Confidence in Gnoseology (in the Theory of Knowledge)

1. How does confidence fit in our telic structure?

We can represent by means of a unit line segment the epistemic probability of a proposition <p> for a subject S and time t, and we can represent by means of a parallel and aligned unit line segment the confidence that S reposes in <p> at t.

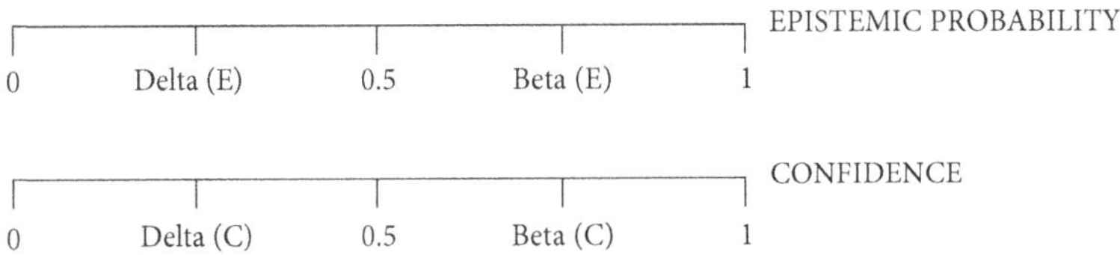

On any given question that you might take up, your positions on these two dimensions should ideally lie on a perpendicular to both unit segments. That is to say, you should proportion your confidence to your evidence as close as possible to that perpendicular relation.[4]

Confidence is itself an important part of telic structure and subject to telic normativity. Of course you can allow your confidence to be biased inappropriately in all sorts of ways. But you would then fail in the proper epistemic aim of confidence. The proper epistemic aim of confidence is to reflect your degree of evidence, positive or negative, on the question taken up.[5] Given this distinctive aim, we can assess your degree of

[4] I view the thinker pondering a "whether" question as follows (assuming for simplicity that nothing but the balance of one's evidence matters to whether and how one should answer the question): At that time t, the thinker S has a body of evidence bearing on <p?> either pro or con, a "total pertinent evidence set." S's epistemic probability on <p?> then aligns with the strength of the support lent by that body of evidence, on balance, either to <p> or to <not- p>. By Beta(E) I mean the balance of evidence such that a balance of that weight or above would rationally justify our thinker in adopting the policy to affirm that p in pursuit of apt affirmation. By Beta(C) I mean the degree of confidence such that confidence of that degree or above would suffice for the thinker to adopt the policy to affirm positively in pursuit of aptness on whether p.

[5] More strictly, it is to reflect how competently you would affirm in the endeavor to affirm aptly, since one can be properly extremely confident of something that is not based on evidence

confidence on any given question according to a straightforward AAA/SSS structure.[6]

Wherever your confidence might fall, even at the 0.5 point on the line segments above, it can be assessed in accordance with the AAA/SSS structure of telic normativity. It can be assessed as accurate, as adroit, and as apt. All that is required for such assessment is that there be an aim, and an attempt constituted by that aim. And, again, your confidence *can* and *should* have an aim: namely, the aim to reflect your degree of evidence, which may put you in a position to know. Epistemically, then, confidence can and should attempt to attain that aim. A thinker's confidence is *alethically rational* depending on how adroitly it attempts to attain its aim. Any instance of alethic confidence is thus assessable telically in AAA terms, and the competence exercised then has our triple-S structure: situation, shape, and skill.

True, the aim of confidence is then quite different from the aim of judgment. For any given question, confidence properly aims at reflecting degree of epistemic probability, whereas judgment aims to get it right aptly on that question, through alethic affirmation. These *are* different, yes, but they are tightly bound together in our account of the epistemology of judgment. Let us see how.

2. Gnoseological competence (the competence constitutive of knowledgeable judgment) is two-ply. It consists of competence to set degrees of *confidence*, a setting often based on epistemic probability, along with competence to *judge* adroitly based on one's degree of confidence. (This latter would involve discerning how confident one should be as a basis for making a judgment.) Let's consider these in order.

a. The gnoseologically proper aim of one's degree of confidence on a question <p?> is the aim to reflect one's degree of epistemic probability on that question. Given this aim, degrees of confidence fall

at all, not now, not ever. Here I have in mind, for example, the hinge- like components of folk commonsense, which we acquire through proper child development, with no reliance on any "evidence" properly so called (with no "ratiocination," as Wittgenstein puts it when he recognizes how for the child light dawns gradually on the whole). Alternatively, one might allow that null evidence can suffice in those and other cases.

6 AAA/SSS: AccurateAdroitApt/SituationShapeSkill.

under an AAA/SSS telic framework, with its distinctive telic normativity. In this respect, degrees of confidence join alethic affirmations, judgments, beliefs, propositional seemings, and propositional experiences.

b. On the present proposal, a thinker's proper management of their degrees of confidence is essential for their gnoseological competence to make judgments. Thus, S's proper judgment on a question requires their prior degree of confidence on that question, which yields two stages for AAA/SSS assessment. We can assess the degree of confidence, and we can assess the judgment.[7]

c. The adroitness of your *judgment* on whether p at a given time now requires the adroitness of your degree of *confidence* at that time on whether p. Moreover, the aptness of your judgment on whether p requires the aptness of your degree of confidence at that time on whether p.[8]

d. However, your judgment on whether p could possibly fail to be apt at t even when it was based adroitly on your apt degree of confidence at that time on whether p. This is because the truth of your judgment does not follow from the aptness of your degree of confidence. The aptness of your degree of confidence requires only

[7] Such "management" need not be subject to any arbitrary power to decide at will, and even less is "*proper* management" subject to any such power. The doings of the "manager" must of course be *deeds*, i.e., *attributable* doings of their own, and subject to motivation through reasons. A thinker can manage their degrees of confidence under rational motivation, however, even when the pertinent deeds come about for *reasons* but not through sheer acts of will, not through acts that the thinker could have omitted "at will," even arbitrarily.

[8] It might very reasonably be wondered why the degree of confidence must be apt in order for the judgment to be apt. Well, compare a case where one reasons from premises through lemmas to a conclusion that p, one that is then believed on the basis of that reasoning. If the reasoning is in essential parts inductive, then it could be adroit and yet false at one or more premises or lemmas. However, for the conclusion to be *apt* based on that reasoning, it must be that the thinker gets it *right* on that conclusion in a way that manifests sufficient competence and hence does not derive essentially from *luck*. Yet given the reasoning as described, this will be implausible. Through that stretch of reasoning, in the example, the thinker gets it right through essential reliance on knowledge-denying luck.

Given the essential role of confidence in the basis for epistemically evaluable judgment, the same intuition will presumably apply. It will seem implausible that the thinker's judgment is correct through competence and not luck, if the thinker's degree of competence reflects the epistemic support provided by their evidence on the question pondered, but does so essentially through luck and not competence. Once the rot of luck enters the basis that way, it will plausibly affect the outcome conclusion as well, so long as that conclusion depends for its status essentially on that basis.

that this degree of confidence aptly mirror your epistemic probability re <p?>. And you might base your judgment that p on that degree of confidence with excellent adroitness even when it was false that p. So, the fact that your judgment was so based does not entail the aptness of your judgment that p, since *this* aptness requires that it be true that p.

3. Again, your *alethic affirmation* of <p> is accurate iff it is correct (true); it is adroit (competent) iff *it* manifests sufficient confidence that is adroit; and it is apt iff its *success* (its attaining truth) manifests a competence constituted in essential part by apt sufficient confidence—above beta/C.[9]

Correspondingly, your *suspension*, on a question whether p, is accurate (succeeds) iff it succeeds in the aim of suspension: namely, the aim to affirm iff affirming would be apt, which requires that it align with apt confidence that lies within the interval from delta/C to beta/C. Your suspension is adroit (competent) only if it is based on such confidence. And your suspension is apt (successful because competent) only if the attainment of its aim manifests both your competence to align your degrees of confidence with your corresponding degrees of epistemic probability, and also your competence to judge or suspend within the respective proper bounds of confidence.[10]

But why should you suspend in the interval between 0.5 and beta/C instead of affirming alethically in that interval, and why should you suspend in the interval between delta/C and 0.5 instead of denying alethically in that interval? After all, you are still likely to get it right if

[9] It's an interesting question how well this account corresponds to Cartesian epistemology. Descartes's clarity and distinctness clearly comes in degrees. Also very clear and explicit in the *Meditations* is the principle that you properly judge that p only if it is sufficiently clear and distinct to you that p. And he also distinguishes between something *seeming* (very) clear and distinct to you and it really *being* that clear and distinct to you. It must be *actually* sufficiently clear and distinct to you that p if you are to judge properly that p. So, does Descartes's degree of clarity and distinctness correspond to our dimension of epistemic probability? Consider how clear and distinct a proposition seems to you. Does that constitute or correspond to your being confident of its truth to that degree? Finally, Descartes of course has crucial use for an agential faculty of judgment, exercised through our free will. So it is intriguing how closely Descartes's framework corresponds to the one sketched here.

[10] This is an initial account of the epistemic normativity of suspension (more exactly, of its gnoseological normativity). The discussion to follow will aim to go deeper.

you reverse those policies, by affirming and denying respectively in those intervals.

Yes, that *would* seem proper for a quiz show stab at an answer. But it would not be proper for an oncologist's diagnosis. The proper aim of the oncologist is not just getting it right but getting it right *aptly*, which requires getting it right adroitly. One must aim not just for *some* degree of adroitness but for adroitness period, adroitness *enough*. So, one must aim to affirm alethically (and positively) only with confidence above the pertinent threshold of "adroitness enough," namely beta/C.[11] (And similarly for the alethic affirmation.)

4. Notably, all of this assessment is relative to the location of the proposition in question for you (at the time t of assessment) on the epistemic probability dimension, on that unit interval. And no assessment of that has been entered above. That has just been taken as given. But is that appropriate? Is it fine that a given proposition lie wherever it may do so on the epistemic probability dimension EP, for any given proposition P, subject S, and time t?

What about negligence or recklessness? What if your total evidence on the question derives essentially from negligence or recklessness? And where would this assessment belong: In intellectual ethics or in theory of knowledge (gnoseology)? Well, if that judgment or belief rests on negligence or recklessness, does that reduce its standing on the dimension pertinent to whether it is a case of knowledge (on the gnoseological dimension)?

What of fabrication? A billionaire might set up a think tank tasked with tracking their changing political opinions so as to block contrary evidence and fabricate favorable evidence. Their degrees of confidence on important political issues can now easily align with the epistemic probability for them of the propositions that they believe. But how adroitly do they then proceed epistemically?

[11] The account here is again Cartesian. At an epistemic juncture, the Cartesian objective, one highlighted by telic virtue epistemology (TVE), is that of making an alethic attempt if and only if it would be apt. This is to be distinguished from the Jamesian objective of attaining truth and avoiding falsehood. There is a distinctively Cartesian objective (like one found also in Aristotle).The appendix to Chapter 3 provides textual evidence for these claims.

Suppose we say that such fabrication, negligence, and recklessness are matters of intellectual ethics with no constitutive bearing on whether the subject knows. If so, they do not touch the epistemic justification constitutive of knowledge. But that seems most implausible. Our focus here is moreover on a philosophical theory of knowledge, and so on *what is constitutive of knowledge*. For terminological convenience, again, we are using the term "gnoseological" to specify the sort of epistemic justification that can be constitutive of knowledge.

Consider, then, the AAA/SSS assessment both of degrees of *confidence* re a question and also of *alethic affirmation* on that question. If determined just by how closely the confidence is proportioned to the subject's evidence, such assessment is independent of any assessment of the question's location on the epistemic probability dimension for that thinker at that time. But we have seen why *epistemic* assessment of that location is appropriate and relevant, and also why that assessment is not only epistemic but also *gnoseological*.[12]

Inquiry takes means towards certain intellectual or cognitive ends. Let us next look into what is generally involved in such activity.

C. Means–End Reasoning and Means–End Action

1. Two forms of means–end reasoning and means–end action may be distinguished: content-focused vs. non-content-focused.

First example: you give Mary a gift in an attempt to please her by giving her possession of something she wanted to have, but you may also

[12] It is an assessment of a sort of intellectual, cognitive status of a belief that is potentially constitutive of knowledge, when that belief does amount to knowledge. This is a status both (a) logically independent of the mere truth of that belief, and (b) *constitutively* by virtue of having which a belief might amount to knowledge. (Any practical advantages provided to the thinker by hosting their belief would then be irrelevant to the *gnoseological* assessment of that belief, *including* intellectually "practical" advantages as to whether and how that belief might aid the success of future inquiry. The latter would seem relevant to a certain *epistemic* assessment of that belief, but not to its *gnoseological* assessment. You don't get to know that an issue of the *National Inquirer* is a reliable source simply because that issue happens by accident to contain only truths, and a trove of them. This latter fact is quite irrelevant to how *gnoseologically* competent is your belief of that fact. You are not relevantly, gnoseologically justified in believing that fact about that issue of the *National Inquirer* simply because your belief would happen to have such downstream epistemic benefit.

aim to please her by the act of giving her the gift. In this second attempt "it's the thought that counts."

Here's one more jolly holiday season, and you must buy some gift for someone who has everything. You may of course lose hope of giving them anything they will use or even want to have. Yet you must buy and give some gift anyhow. Here one might aim to give something the recipient will appreciate, but even if there's no hope of that, one still gives the gift, as the sheer giving of it may still please them well enough. In this case the success of one's attempt to provide something to the liking of the recipient is a kind of spandrel success, a sort of indirect side effect. Here it's the aiming that has the desired effect of pleasing through the receipt of their gift, and not through one's ostensible means to that end, which is giving possession of the gift. (Since in our example one makes a double attempt, both to give something pleasing and also to please through the making of that first attempt, therefore that *first* attempt might yield success for the second attempt in two ways: in our spandrel sort of way, as well as in the normal instrumental means–end sort of way.)

In our example of a chess game with a young opponent, one's deeper aim is to lose and help strengthen the child's love of the game. Wanting him to *really* win, one aims to further that by playing seriously, once convinced that he is by then the better player. This example is unlike the gift-giving example. In the chess example it would be absurd to try to attain one's deeper objective through the *content* of one's attempt. That would be to attempt to lose by winning. But the correct analysis is that one tries to *really* lose by seriously playing to win. This is why one's means–end action is non-content-focused. One is not trying to lose by attaining the success of one's action taken as means. That *would* be absurd. Nevertheless, one does try to really, honestly lose, although one also seriously *tries* to win, where this trying is a means to one's dominant objective of *really* losing. By layering the attempts, the agent avoids incoherence.

2. Consider now your objective when you deliberatively suspend. You endeavor to attain a knowledgeable answer to your question. That's what you want, and what you aim for through your inquiry. So, if your suspending on that occasion is deliberative, then you suspend while still

engaged in a proper resolution of your question whether p. Since you are aiming to resolve your question not by guessing but by judging, and since you want both to succeed and to avoid failure, what you aim for is to answer if and only if you would answer competently enough, indeed aptly. And this is then the basis that you need. You need to be well enough assured that if you answered alethically you would succeed aptly, and avoid failure. Only on this basis could you be properly assured that your *judgment* would succeed, as your *alethic affirmation* would be not only correct but also apt.

Given thus your proper aim in suspending, it seems absurd that you could attain your *dominant* aim by suspending, whether properly or not. The dominant aim of your inquiry is that of settling the question knowledgeably, through knowledgeably apt alethic affirmation (positive or negative). Obviously enough, suspending could not then function as a *constitutive* means to that aim.

But is that the only way suspending could function as a means to your aim? Not at all; we've seen an alternative way, that of spandrel means.

We next take this up more expansively.

D. Action and Forbearance in Epistemology: Judgment, Inquiry, and Suspension

1. We first take a step back to take note of how judgment is related to inquiry, and inquiry to suspension.

Telic virtue epistemology introduces *states* of judgmental dispositions (some of which are policies, really). We postulate both conscious judgments and also mental acts (or psychological episodes) that figure in implicit reasoning, and have a truth-directed teleology. Both of these are subject to our AAA/SSS account, on the model of conscious alethic affirmations and judgments. On top of that, we also recognize dispositions to issue such judgments or acts, among which would figure judgmental dispositions (or policies, when these dispositions are sustained agentially, as are for example our driving policies).

Given this background, how can we explain within TVE when it is that suspension is epistemically appropriate or required? When, more specifically, is it *gnoseologically* appropriate or required? As a preliminary, we first consider what it is to engage in consciously deliberative inquiry as one ponders a question.

2. Our conscious aim as we ponder a question is normally a knowledgeable answer. We'd like to affirm alethically in answer to that question, successfully getting it right. But our aim then goes beyond the sort of aim adopted by the quiz show contestant, who is satisfied with just getting it right. He affirms alethically, aiming at truth, and that can be the full extent of his epistemic aim as he tries to win the prize. Normally our aims go beyond that of the contestant, however, as we try to answer our questions not just correctly but knowledgeably. We aim to get it right through competence, not just through a lucky guess.

3. Such inquiry is thus a special case of consciously intentional goal-directed action, a means–end attempt, aimed at attaining the end by consciously bringing about the means. Such an attempt is made by conscious use of some deed (some doing attributable to the agent as their own doing).

4. And how is such inquiry related to judgment? Initially at least, these seem incompatible. You cannot both inquire and judge, we may think, as that just seems incoherent.

Our aim as we inquire, however, is to affirm alethically and aptly the right answer to our question whether p. Suppose in a particular case the right answer to our question whether p is that p. We may then affirm alethically that p, while aiming to affirm not only alethically but aptly. This is then a judgment on our part on the question whether p. Why then are we not inquiring? Supposedly, inquiry is consciously intentional goal-directed action aimed at truth or knowledge. Is that not precisely what judgment is?

Still, is our aim when we judge *of the right sort* to constitute inquiry? Well, our aim when we judge is to get it right by aptly affirming alethically. We thus aim for a kind of knowledge, namely apt alethic affirmation (animal knowledge). And that is supposedly a primary aim of inquiry, namely knowledge, in the sense of competently and aptly attaining truth. So, why is this not inquiry?

5. Have we not arrived at the conclusion that all judgment is inquiry? No, surely the more plausible view is that inquiry is a preliminary to judgment. When you are already judging, this means that inquiry has concluded. Inquiry is often aimed at determining whether and how to judge. When you now go ahead and judge, this no longer aims at determining *whether* to judge, and if so how. When you consciously inquire on whether p, you consciously take up your question with a view to alethic affirmation at a minimum, or to the more ambitious aim: to *judge* (to affirm on whether p, to affirm alethically, and not only correctly but aptly).

6. Let's consider consciously means–end intentional actions in general. In another example of that, you aim *to walk next morning all the way to the train station before 8 a.m.* Preliminary means may include setting your alarm clock the night before, and putting on your shoes that morning. Constitutive means would involve taking steps sequentially that morning until you get to the station by 8 a.m., and more specific plans may be set and may change as you get into it, so that you may speed up or slow down as you assess the time available. So, the constitutive means involved will include taking those steps sequentially. And the constitutive means to walking to the station may now qualify as preliminary means to the end of *entering the station by 8 a.m.* By taking those preliminary means one literally puts oneself in a position to take the constitutive means to thus entering the station once one is at its threshold early enough.

7. Turning to epistemology, let's consider whether inquiry must be *preparatory to* rather than *constitutive of* attaining one's dominant aim, that of answering one's question knowledgeably.

Inquiry then would encompass things that one does as one attempts to put oneself in position to answer one's question knowledgeably. For telic virtue epistemology, inquiry would then seek to secure a triple-S profile (SituationShapeSkill) constitutive of complete competence to answer that question. That way, when one did answer one's question correctly through the exercise of such competence, one's answer would be alethically apt. And this is the aim constitutive of judgment.

8. If that is the relation of inquiry to judgment, how then is inquiring related to suspending? This depends on the kind of suspending. Deliberative suspending requires inquiring, since to suspend deliberatively is to suspend in the endeavor to judge successfully on the question (through an apt alethic affirmation).

By contrast, anti-deliberative suspending goes to the opposite extreme: it requires *not*-inquiring. In both cases you intentionally omit judgment altogether, whether positive or negative. In one case you do so while still engaged in attaining an apt alethic affirmation, but in the other you have no such ulterior aim.

In either case, when by suspending you endeavor to attain an apt alethic affirmation on the question under inquiry, your endeavor cannot possibly have the form of taking *constitutive* means towards your objective of a successful judgment on that question. How then are you still aiming for a knowledgeable answer to your question? Perhaps your endeavor must rather take *preliminary* means to a successful judgment? We next consider this.

5

When and How Is Suspension Apt?

A. What Makes Suspending Epistemically Appropriate?

1. How should we assess suspending? More specifically, how should we assess it gnoseologically, with respect to our normal epistemic aim when we take up a question? Our aim here is to answer that question knowledgeably.

We had concluded that the epistemically pertinent suspending is not that of simply dropping the question. Such abandonment is a non-deliberative suspension that is of course subject to all sorts of assessment, including prudential and moral assessment. One might assess it in intellectual ethics, in accordance with theory of inquiry more specifically. It may be a big mistake to abandon that question, for example, given important aims of inquiry that one either has or should have at that time, for the intellectual benefit of oneself or one's community.

2. None of that would be immediately and directly relevant to whether one proceeds with gnoseological propriety in thus suspending. Such proper procedure—procedure that might help constitute knowledge if successful in its *dominant* objective—is determined by what one should do *in the endeavor to answer one's question knowledgeably*. Within TVE (telic virtue epistemology), the pertinent gnoseological aim is that of *aptly* answering that question alethically, through apt alethic affirmation that gets it right on the question not just by guessing but through competence.[1] Of course, one's attempt to do this—to answer one's question

[1] There is thus a fascinating reversal in the skeptical philosophy of Pyrrhonism, as they explicitly take *suspension* as their dominant aim. They thus become purposeful inveterate contrarians, always seeking to counterbalance whatever positive case may be abroad in favor of given answers to given questions. They remain skeptics ("inquirers") by persisting in the pursuit of data and arguments that may bear with epistemic and even gnoseological propriety on

Epistemic Explanations: A Theory of Telic Normativity, and What it Explains. Ernest Sosa, Oxford University Press (2021). © Ernest Sosa. DOI: 10.1093/oso/9780198856467.003.0005

aptly—can itself succeed more or less aptly. This is to say that one's *judgment* on that question can be assessed for success, and also for competence, and for aptness.

3. That being so, how then does one suspend properly on a given question? The assessment of a thinker's performance in respect of *gnoseological* competence requires the thinker's retention of the objective constitutive of inquiry into that question. Abandoning the judgmental question (and thus the judgmental inquiry) is then out of the question. Gnoseological assessment of any case of suspending requires that it be *deliberative* suspending. Only such suspending is assessable with respect to the thinker's endeavor to attain a knowledgeable answer to the given question, which would be an apt answer, not just a true answer.

When suspending is gnoseologically rational and justified, therefore, it must be by relation to that objective. Obviously, though, suspending cannot be a proper *constitutive* means to that objective. Perhaps then suspending would be gnoseologically appropriate by being a proper *preliminary* means to that objective?

Yes, suspending may often have that sort of spandrel status as one inquires into a question. In inquiring, the thinker must aim to judge if and only if judging would succeed. That is required for proper performance on the given occasion. However, proceeding that way may have a spandrel effect, if it turns out that one must suspend rather than judge. In that case, proper procedure has the consequence that one must *omit* judgment. (Compare how my attempt to *really* lose to my young chess opponent requires that I play to win, and how this might have a spandrel outcome contrary to what I aimed for by proceeding that way.) So, my

the questions of interest to them. But their persistent dominant objective is suspension, not knowledge, at least on matters of objective value. They wish to protect themselves from any belief in any objective value, as in their view this is liable to lead them astray, as they will then fear that they are falling short or worse in respect of the objective value that they might or even ought to attain in or through their actions. Of course, it seems conceivable that they may fail in their attempt to attain suspension, as despite their best efforts the case they build through inquiry into a given question of objective value may remain conclusive for affirmation, either positive or negative, so that they are blocked from proper equipollence and attendant suspension. This would then be a spandrel outcome analogous to the spandrel win in my earlier example in which I play against a grandson in a chess match that I aim to lose (to really, seriously lose).

proper procedure *toward the objective of now knowledgeably answering my question* may result in my *properly* suspending, with gnoseological propriety as I aim for knowledge of the answer. And we can see how I *properly* suspend that way, in that endeavor, even if my suspending ensures that I do *not* answer my question knowledgeably, since it turns out that I must not so much as judge.

In addition, suspending now may be a means to an apt answer to that question in due course, and a thinker may suspend as a spandrel outcome of properly pursuing that objective, and also as a means to eventually attaining it.

What is not at all clear is whether suspending can be epistemically appropriate *only if* it is done that way, as a means to *eventually* answering one's question knowledgeably.

4. Why must we commit that way when we properly suspend? Why must we commit to our suspending's somehow *leading* as a means to a knowledgeable answer? That seems unclear and uncertain. It seems rather that our stance in suspending could be twofold: it will of course be obvious to us that suspending will not provide constitutive means to our objective of answering our question aptly on that occasion. However, we might still remain quite unsure, indeed perfectly neutral, on whether by means of suspending we might *later* attain an apt answer to our question.

Might we not suspend at a given time with no decision whatsoever as to whether we will continue to pursue inquiry *even in the very nearly immediate future*? All that is required for the suspension to be gnoseologically based and appropriate is that the intentional omission of judgment be motivated, not *exclusively* by boredom, or the pressure of other business, or by any other practical concern, but that it be sufficiently motivated on the basis of insufficient apt confidence: that is, on the basis of a confidence level *neither* high enough for positive affirmation *nor* low enough for denial. All that is required is that the intentional omission be motivated this way by such middling confidence, and aptly so.

It is not even ruled out that one's omission, and even one's intentional omission, be overdetermined. All that is required for gnoseologically appropriate suspension is that the intentional omission be sufficiently motivated by an intermediate level of confidence, between delta/C and beta/C. One suspends when one's intentional omission of affirmation is based on one's confidence being insufficiently high to affirm positively (below beta/C) and also insufficiently low to deny, to affirm negatively (above delta/C). And one's suspension is deliberatively gnoseological when it is thus based on confidence that is itself gnoseological in aiming at properly mirroring one's epistemic probability on the question under inquiry.

The gnoseological appropriateness of one's suspension then requires that one's confidence level lie above delta/C and below beta/C, *appropriately* so. For this to be so, one's confidence level must be appropriate, which in turn requires that one's epistemic probability be appropriate: not tainted by fabrication, or negligence, or recklessness.

5. How to assess suspending gnoseologically, initial take:

> When you inquire into a question (aiming to answer it knowledgeably), you suspend properly (gnoseologically properly) on that question *if and only if* you do so based sufficiently on being out of position to judge with success, where to judge with success is to answer aptly.[2]

Within TVE, that amounts to the following:

> You suspend properly on a question when you inquire into that question (aiming to answer it knowledgeably) iff you suspend based sufficiently on your lack of the complete (SSS) competence required in order to answer that question aptly.[3]

[2] So, on some level the thinker must be responsive, at least functionally and implicitly, to being thus ill-positioned.

[3] Equivalently: You suspend properly on a question (when you inquire into that question) iff you do so based sufficiently on your being out of position to answer it, to answer it by combining the following two things: (a) affirming alethically while (b) the correctness of your affirmation would manifest your pertinent epistemic competence. (Based "sufficiently," meaning that, even if other motives may have overdetermined your then suspending, *this* motive of yours would have sufficed psychologically on its own.)

And this aligns with a considerable objective of proper suspension: that one's suspending should reflect one's sensitivity to whether one is in a position to know, in a position to judge with success (in a position to attain knowledge, at least on the first, animal order).

6. Earlier we considered an initial TVE account of the normativity of suspension, an earlier version of the following:

> Your *suspension* on a question is your intentional omission of affirmation (positive or negative), motivated by the following aim, on that question: the aim to affirm alethically iff your alethic affirmation would be apt (and thus aligned with your apt confidence within the interval from delta/C to beta/C). In other words, to suspend thus is to intentionally omit the following: *constitutively attempting to attain an apt answer to that question, by affirming, whether positively or negatively.*

Such suspension is deliberative and gnoseological in virtue of a distinctive aim: that of *judging if and only if one's judgment would succeed.* Your suspension thus understood is *accurate* iff it succeeds in its aim. Your suspension is *adroit* only if it is based on such confidence. And your suspension is *apt* iff its attainment of its aim manifests both your competence *to align your degrees of confidence* with your corresponding degrees of epistemic probability, and also your competence *to judge or suspend within the proper bounds of confidence.*

7. Again, to suspend deliberatively and gnoseologically is to intentionally omit judgment, positive or negative, in the endeavor to attain the following aim:

> so judging if and only if the judgment would succeed.

That is to say, it is to affirm alethically in the endeavor *to so affirm if and only if that alethic affirmation would be apt.*

If you so suspend gnoseologically you do not *just* abandon the question in boredom or disgust. That would be a non-deliberative suspension devoid of gnoseological standing. Rather you must suspend in *proper* pursuit of your dominant objective on the question under inquiry. Hence you must not *inappropriately* fail to gather pertinent available evidence.

Such deliberative suspending is thus gnoseologically successful if and only if you suspend while satisfying all of those conditions.

According to TVE, that involves your being out of position to judge successfully, lacking the required competence that would put you in such a position, the competence in virtue of which if you judged you would do so with success, as you would alethically affirm with aptness. And it involves also your continued pursuit of your gnoseologically dominant objective, which is a knowledgeable answer to your question under inquiry.[4]

Your suspending on that question is then adroit if and only if it manifests the pertinent gnoseological competence, which includes the competence to omit further gathering of evidence when this is appropriate.

More is required for the *aptness* of your suspending. This requires not only that your suspending manifest such competence but also that the *success* of your suspending also manifest such competence. Consider your competence to attain the following on a given occasion:

> to judge iff your judgment would succeed.

Such competence must be manifest in your then suspending, in your then *intentionally omitting* judgment. It is a competence that must be thus manifest if your suspension is to be apt. So, it must be that you are guided to omit judgment by your competence to accomplish the following: to judge if *and only if* your judgment would succeed.

[4] It is their scorning this as a dominant objective that makes Pyrrhonian skepticism anti-gnoseological. Their dominant objective is rather suspending than knowing on whatever question may be pondered, or, more modestly, at least when the question is one of objective value. However, Pyrrhonism thus conceived seems doomed to incoherence, doomed to forfeit the calm ataraxia that seems fundamental to the preferred way to eudaemonia. Why so? Because one falls short of their desired ataraxia not just *when one pursues objective value* but *when one pursues whatever*. Worry would seem to attend pursuit itself, not just pursuit of value considered objective. But Pyrrhonists do not forswear pursuit. They still pursue ataraxia and thereby eudaemonia. Either they consider these objectives matters of objective value or they do not. But it really does not matter. Either way the worry of failing will dog their pursuit and deny them ataraxia and thereby (in their own view) eudaemonia.

Accordingly, in order to be adroit (competent), your suspension must then manifest your more specific competence to tell that your judgment would *not* succeed, which is why you omit judgment. And, in order to be apt, the *success* of your suspending—your attaining the objective of judging iff your judgment would succeed—must itself manifest the pertinent adroitness (competence) with which you suspend.

Aptness is what would make your suspending epistemically creditable to you, and not just an epistemic success by mere luck. The success of your suspending must be creditable to your epistemic competence. This means that your suspending must attain its objective, which is to judge iff your judgment would succeed. In addition, its attaining of that objective must not be just by luck. It must rather be creditable to your relevant competence. It must reflect your ability to guide your epistemic performance so that *through pertinent competence* you attain that outcome.

B. The Importance of Proper Inquiry and Omission of Further Inquiry

1. We earlier noted how apt cognitive performance must be based on a total evidential set that is *properly* taken by the thinker as a basis (which must avoid relevant negligence, recklessness, and fabrication). Thus, the sheer experiences that (partly or wholly) constitute such evidence, and the seemings in line with such experiences, must themselves be apt. (Propositional experiences fall under AAA/SSS normativity in the functional mode, since they have an alethic aim, to represent the environment correctly.) And one must also take *proper* account of the relevant evidence in one's possession, while *properly* omitting any further inquiry, any further gathering of relevant evidence.[5]

[5] This TVE version of evidentialism is distinctive in allowing that a thinker's pertinent evidential set with respect to a given question <p?> can be the null set. Intuitive knowledge for example can derive from sheer understanding of that question <p?>, so that, given just that understanding, the thinker is well placed to judge competently. No extraneous data or other evidence is required. The set of such data or evidence is hence null. Yet the SSS profile of that thinker at that time on that question suffices to give them the competence needed for

2. The propriety of one's judgment seemed then to depend ultimately *not only* on the propriety of the positive stances that one takes and the degree of competence that is manifest by those stances, and on how such competence is then manifest ultimately in one's getting it right with one's judgment. That is necessary but not sufficient. It emerges that we *also* need an epistemic assessment of things that one does *not* do, of the propriety of certain omissions. These omissions—omissions of inquiry, for example—must also be appropriate enough.

That introduces an epistemic propriety of *omissions*, one that now seems required. We must be able to rely epistemically on omissions as well as on commissions. What matters to the reliability of commissions is how likely we would be to get it right given how the commission is guided, for example through its basis.

What makes it *proper to rely on given omissions*? This is different. Here what matters is that one should be able to believe despite the omission, which is properly taken (at least implicitly, functionally) not to damage unduly that belief's pertinent quality.

3. An important connection now emerges between the reliability of commissions concerning a question under inquiry, and the "reliability" of omissions pertinent to that question. And this reveals a main reason why an omission of inquiry is negatively assessable. Such omission is negatively assessable when *because of that omission* one is denied reliable enough competence to judge successfully on the question under inquiry.

Consider judgment based on a truncated evidence set, a set that might be importantly augmented with the additional inquiry. It may well be that additional inquiry is required for a reliable enough answer to the question under inquiry.

As initial returns come in on election night, for example, one may gather *some* evidence as to the identity of the winner. But, even supposing that the electorate is known to be highly homogeneous, such evidence may still fall far short of yielding a reliable enough prediction. Accordingly, if one omits the inquiry essential for gathering such

competently enough getting it right, so that the success of their alethic affirmation is due not to accidental luck but to sufficient competence.

required additional evidence, this may result in one's lack of enough competence to judge on that question.[6]

4. Omissions and their propriety bear thus on the epistemic standing of one's total evidence set pertinent to a question whether p. And such epistemic standing then bears in turn on the competence exercised when one affirms, positively or negatively, rather than suspending. And this competence then matters to whether one's judgment, whether positive or negative, is itself apt.

5. What if one opts to suspend rather than judge on that question? How should we assess such suspension?

We are supposing the suspension in question to be still gnoseological and deliberative. The suspension of interest is hence not that of abandoning the question through loss of interest. Rather, while still pondering the question, one suspends by intentionally omitting judgment both positive and negative.

And now for a surprising question: Is there not a radical disparity between the requirements for suspension and the requirements for judgment?

Take again your question whether p. In order to judge on that question, either positively or negatively, you must properly acquire relevant evidence that provides a sufficient balance of support for the judgment that you make, and you must render your judgment at that moment while then *omitting* further inquiry *properly*.[7]

So, judgment requires of the subject/agent an evidence set that meets those requirements. By contrast, suspension requires nothing of the sort, or so it appears at first blush.

[6] And here one may incur low assessment and even blame, whereas if some glitch occurs and the election is declared invalid, everyone may suspend sans fault or blame, and with no hope of ever knowing.

[7] However, the omission need only be proper in that one is then already in a position to judge appropriately on the question pondered, without pursuing or even awaiting any further evidence; which does not rule out the need or desirability to continue inquiry for other intellectual objectives. Thus, while in a position to judge, one might still properly aim to make *more sure* on that question, which would justify yet more inquiry. One can surely properly "inquire" when one continues to seek relevant evidence, with a view to making (more) sure.

6. What seems quite proper—indeed required—of the subject/agent who suspends is that they intentionally omit judgment provided *just* that their body of pertinent evidence falls short, and would be inadequate as a basis for judgment, especially when they know this full well.

The requirements for apt suspension thus seem easier to meet than the requirements for apt judgment. Skeptics seem thereby to enjoy an important advantage over dogmatists, an advantage aligned with our distinctive perspective on gnoseological normativity. The ostensible advantage derives *not* from the hard work of a skeptic who adduces considerations that counterbalance any basis that a dogmatist may have for judging as they do. The advantage we now ostensibly uncover derives *rather* from the proper wariness of a skeptic who has been too often awakened from dogmatic slumbers. Such a skeptic might well refuse to render a judgment on question after question, based on such conservative caution, on the suspicion that further evidence might make a serious difference.[8]

But is such suspension appropriate *gnoseologically*? What gnoseological assessment assesses is always the performance of a thinker who aims for a knowledgeable answer to a preset question. Consider then the relevant suspension at a given moment when the question is still pondered by the thinker. This suspension must be deliberative by still falling under the dominant aim to attain a proper answer to the question under inquiry. The proper objective is *to judge on that question if and only if such judgment would succeed.*

What we then assess is the performance of a thinker at an instant when they (continue to) ponder that way. What the thinker may or may not intend at any later time is not under assessment just then. What the future holds is as may be, and has no evident bearing on what the thinker properly does at that very moment, no evident bearing vis-a-vis their dominant objective to judge at that moment if and only if their judgment would *then* succeed. So, the proper comparison in assessing whether the skeptic has it gnoseologically easier than the dogmatist concerns the requirements for proper judgment versus the requirements

[8] Recall Descartes's early procedure in the *Meditations*, as he reviews how often his comfortable opinions have turned out false: that is to say, how often later evidence has overturned those opinions, and his resolution no longer to trust such standing beliefs implicitly, at least for the duration of his special, philosophical inquiry.

for proper suspension at that moment, when the dominant aim is answering the question knowledgeably, with a successful judgment (that is, with a fully apt alethic affirmation).

7. We return to our question: *Are* the requirements for proper suspension really less stringent than the requirements for proper judgment? The reason why the skeptic is thought to have it easier is that they supposedly need not worry about having neglected to gather more evidence. They can properly suspend with assurance regardless of what they may have done by way of inquiry, even if they have conducted woefully inadequate and incomplete inquiry. Obviously, this is not true for judgment. One could hardly judge with proper assurance based on such flawed inquiry.

That reasoning is not wholly convincing, however, once we focus on what is under assessment in the cognitive performance of our thinker at a given moment. What is then under assessment is whether they proceed appropriately at that moment. And this is the assessment of whether their performance is appropriate *gnoseologically*: that is, whether what they do is appropriate with a view to their dominant aim, which is to answer their question (whether p) knowledgeably. It does seem crystal clear that they would not proceed appropriately if they judged on that question when their inquiry was flawed through inadequate gathering of required evidence. The question now is whether the quality of their inquiry is irrelevant (gnoseologically) to the appropriateness of their suspension. And this seems unobvious. We need a closer look.

8. Suppose one had taken up a question and had omitted even minimally adequate gathering of relevant data (where such data must be sought, and would not just come unbidden). Surely, one must omit judgment at that time. This seems the only appropriate option (gnoseologically). Wherever the fault may lie for one's inadequate position on the question, one must now omit judgment. But if this is clearly what one is epistemically required to do with respect to one's objective *to judge if and only if one's judgment would succeed*, how then could one possibly go wrong in thus intentionally omitting judgment, which would be to suspend? Isn't this conclusive? What more is there to say?

9. That one *could* perhaps go wrong emerges with an alternative response to our conundrum. Our thinker would now be seen to occupy a tragic position where they cannot possibly succeed, no matter what they do, not gnoseologically, not while retaining their objective to answer their question knowledgeably, with an apt alethic affirmation. Obviously, they are unable to do the right thing by judging, since their evidence set is so poor (and, let's say, even evidently so). Must we not say that it is only right and proper for them to suspend?

No, not clearly. Why not rather say that if they intentionally omit judgment, then again they fall short, with a view to attaining a knowledgeable judgment on that question? Might they not be in a position where, no matter what they do intentionally, they will be acting inadequately. For whatever reason, whoever may be at fault, they are out of position to act with gnoseological adequacy on the question cognitively before them. They are in a position neither to judge nor to suspend deliberatively on that question.

Yet that seems outrageous. How can that be so? Here an analogy may be helpful.

10. Suppose your objective is to get home by midnight. You are far away and must choose at a fork in a network of roads that you must use in order to get to your destination on time. You take the left fork and travel far along that road, which turns out to be unfortunate as you are now in a position at a new fork where no choice will lead to success. Whether you take either side of the new fork, or whether you take neither side, as you stay put or go back, there is now no way for you to get home by midnight. So, at the new fork there is no telically appropriate thing that you can do, with respect to the given objective. No matter what you do, it will be inadequate with a view to your dominant aim on that occasion, which is getting home by midnight. Please note well the content of the claim. The claim is not just that whatever you do will fall short of success. The claim is *rather* that whatever you do will be telically *inadequate* (in any case, but perhaps even culpably so).

11. That provides a model for our gnoseological assessment of the inadequate inquirer. Consider the traveler aiming to reach home by midnight and the inquirer aiming to answer their question knowledgeably at t. Both of these reach a fork where they cannot possibly act adroitly no matter what they do. Telically they are in that tragic position. There is now no way for them to attain their objective, and no way for them to proceed in a way that will even further that objective. Telically, they are hence negatively assessable whatever they may do. And the reason why they are negatively assessable is that, gnoseologically, they are inappropriately related to the question.

That might be a matter of epistemic bad luck, the sort of bad luck that might have attended their lack of competence for successful judgment. A thinker may thus lack the ability to judge with success on a certain question, and this may crucially affect the assessment of their performance vis-a-vis the question that they take up. Here again, through lack of ability, they may be out of luck with regard to epistemically appropriate procedure. Now the bad luck is constituted not by lack of evidence but by lack of ability, more generally, including lack of skill. Again, there may be *nothing* the thinker can do that will be epistemically adequate (gnoseologically, with respect to the given question under inquiry).

Note well, though, that the lack of ability posed here is not just the inability to judge with success, to alethically affirm aptly. It is rather the inability to either aptly alethically affirm (to judge with success) or to aptly omit alethic affirmation, aptly suspend. The subject may be condemned to deep inadequacy of performance simply through such lack of competence.

A further distinction is important for the telic normativity of suspension. Mere deficiency through bad luck or through just the happenstance of your lacking skill, shape, or situation is one thing. That would not sustain any negative gnoseological assessment of the thinker or of their doxastic performance. Negligence goes beyond deficiency, however, in assigning fault to the agent for their deficiency. The need to suspend might derive from a fault assignable to the thinker. This is when the subject's need to suspend is to the thinker's discredit.

12. Suppose while pondering a given question one negligently omits the inquiry that would uncover the plentiful available evidence. Might one fail to suspend with propriety simply because one is *not* in the position in which one *should be*, a position in which one *would have been* had one proceeded appropriately? If that is the right view, then through *inappropriate* inquiry one might end up where, no matter what one does, one will fall short epistemically. More specifically, one will then fall short *gnoseologically* no matter what one does. One's intellectual action will be inapt and maladroit, whether one judges or suspends.

Although seemingly incredible, at least initially, that conclusion deserves consideration.

13. Would one then attain aptly the objective proper to deciding on the question pondered? Of course, one could not then *judge* aptly.

What if one deliberatively suspends? One then still has the objective of judging if and only if one would judge with success. And one does attain this objective. *Since* one could not then judge with success, *since* one could not affirm alethically with aptness, *therefore* in intentionally omitting judgment one does attain that biconditional objective: judging iff one would judge with success. *Still the question remains*: Does one attain this objective *aptly*? Is the attainment creditable to one's pertinent competence or is it just by luck?

In order to attain that objective aptly, one must attain it competently and because of one's exercise of competence. And what is the pertinent competence? The competence that matters here is one aimed at proceeding appropriately with regard to the question under inquiry when the dominant objective is answering that question aptly (knowledgeably, with at least animal knowledge).

14. Let's consider how you might be out of position to answer the question with successful *judgment*, i.e., with apt alethic affirmation.

Suppose you believe incompetently and falsely some premise of the reasoning that now leads you to the conclusion that p. Nevertheless you may be rationally justified to activate that belief lodged in your long-term memory, as there is now no salient reason for you to doubt its truth. And consider the reasoning, based on that justified premise alongside others, the reasoning that provides essential support to you for concluding that p, support whose removal would render groundless your belief that p. Say that everything in your reasoning is perfect, going forward all the way to the conclusion that p. At the time when you reach your conclusion, you have in view several beliefs derived, in that whole stretch of pondering, from earlier stretches of reasoning, whose earlier conclusions are now just retained in memory. These are the reasons now within your purview, now readily available to you in this whole present stretch of pondering. Despite the fact that, as of your present purview, the thing for you to do is to judge that p (given the deductively competent reasoning that goes from those present premises to the conclusion), still we judge your conclusion to be *gnoseologically inapt*, because of its reliance on those premises with the defective rational aetiology (even if that earlier aetiology is now irretrievably in your past).

15. Compare now the gnoseological standing of your *suspension* when it derives from inappropriate inquiry that neglects available evidence required for competent enough deliberation. Suppose what might then render evidence available or unavailable is mere physical or psychological possibility, independently of any moral or other evaluative concerns.[9] And suppose one opts to suspend, based on the fact that one is then obviously out of position to judge with success on that question. Does this suffice to make one's suspension apt? Does one *aptly* attain the objective of that suspension? The objective is to judge if and only if one would judge successfully: i.e., if and only if one's alethic affirmation would be apt. Well, *is* the aetiology of that outcome performance good enough? Is it good enough if it involves a bad enough omission of inquiry?

Very plausibly, granted, the quality of that aetiology does *not* now matter. It does not matter that one negligently failed to gather available evidence essential for answering the question competently. With awareness that one is out of position to judge with success, one has no choice but to suspend, and hence one suspends appropriately, since one just has no better option.

Recall, however, what the dominant objective is: namely, to answer the question knowledgeably, with apt alethic affirmation. Under the

[9] Here again, as at other crucial junctures, is it social or biological norms that determine whether evidence is sufficiently available? That is, must it be taken into account if your procedure on the question is to qualify as gnoseologically competent? If not, what is a better alternative?

heading of that objective, one has not proceeded appropriately if one has negligently missed available evidence essential for a proper answer to one's question.

If one suspends now, consider the failure to judge aptly, through failure to judge at all. This failure derives from the flawed inquiry that brings you to your present quandary. If you decide in favor of judging, that is obviously flawed. But even if you decide against judging, in favor of suspending, even then, arguably, your performance is still flawed, given your dominant objective.

Given your position relative to the question under inquiry, your suspending on that question still falls short gnoseologically. You should have conducted better inquiry, should have gathered the available evidence. And this bears on our assessment of your present performance, *whether* it is the action of judging on that question *or* the action of intentionally *omitting* judgment. In a way it is too bad that you must omit judgment, that you have left yourself no choice but to omit judgment. Perhaps you *should* now be in a position to judge. Only your negligence to gather evidence denies you that position now.

Crucially, that is not to say that you are better placed to *judge* now, positively or negatively. That is even worse than suspending. So, you are now at a tragic juncture wherein, no matter what you do, you will fall short seriously. You are like the driver who, having taken a wrong turn, is now out of position to do *anything* that will be telically commendable, from the point of view of their dominant aim to arrive home before midnight. Like that driver, you now have no available option that would be relevantly adroit or competent overall, all relevant things considered.

16. Note also, again, the similarity with our negative assessment of a thinker's conclusion based on brilliant inference from premises activated from memory, where those recalled beliefs are quite unjustified by their initial sources, now gone irretrievably from memory. Granted, the thinker is commendable for their reasoning from the premises they presently have to go on. And those activated premises even enjoy a kind of justification, that which normally attends beliefs in long-term storage when there is now no reason at all to suspect their standing. (And this is perhaps a good reliabilist *synchronic* competence, even if, once we take into account the fuller *diachronic* disposition involved, the deliverances of this synchronic competence are found to be seriously wanting.) Given what our thinker has to go on, they proceed admirably by reasoning as they do to that conclusion.[10] And yet the *overall* gnoseological assessment of their performance is negative nonetheless, because of the epistemic poverty of the indispensable premises.

Similarly, in a limited way we may assess our suspending thinker positively for omitting judgment, when it is so clear that their judgment would be unsuccessful. Compatibly, nonetheless, our fuller *overall* assessment may be properly negative, as our thinker is so ill-positioned from an epistemic point of view, because of highly flawed inquiry. They have traveled to a fork where no choice (whether left, right, going back, or standing pat) is now even minimally adequate. No matter what they do now, their performance will lack the sort of intellectual aetiology required for positive gnoseological attainment.

17. In order to understand why that is so, we must focus on what is under assessment. We are not assessing how well suspension may serve the thinker as a means to later inquiry that may yield a successful judgment after all. True, the suspension may be positively assessable *in that respect*, but that is not overall determinative of the gnoseological competence of the thinker's performance at the present moment.

Similarly, if the thinker had been in a position to judge successfully and had done so, then again that judgment might have put them in a position to later judge successfully. But that instrumental respect is not what makes the judgment positively assessable at the moment when it is made, in the respect of interest to us. What is of interest to us is the standing of the judgment at its very moment, and independently of how it might or might not contribute to any future judgment.

When we consider the standing of suspension at a given time, therefore, we are again focused on the thinker's performance *at that time*. The

[10] This is like the performance of a small-plane pilot who neglects to check the plane's fuel before takeoff and pilots brilliantly through a bad storm so as to land safely. Their safe arrival in their destination does manifest outstanding piloting competence, but the awful negligence denies it status as apt, much less fully apt. Nor is it so much as adroit (adroit outright, adroit enough, overall).

thinker's proper objective is to judge if and only if so judging would then succeed, and otherwise suspend (i.e., otherwise intentionally omit judgment). The focus is all on that instant, all in disregard of any practical objectives, in disregard even of any theoretical, intellectual objectives for the future. The focus is simply on how well that performance would do—vis-a-vis judging or suspending with gnoseological success—*on that occasion*: "How well does that performance do with a view to that sole objective?"

18. Taking the past into account has obvious relevance in assessing the judgment that the thinker might make on that occasion. Now their performance necessarily involves a *choice*: the choice, on the question under inquiry, whether to judge or to suspend.[11] And we have seen how the thinker's performance in the forgotten past can bear crucially on the assessment of their present judgment. Similarly, then, their performance in the forgotten past might also bear on the assessment of their present suspension. Past failures of our thinker might bear on whether they are now in a position to make a proper choice vis-a-vis the dominant gnoseological objective: namely, attaining a knowledgeable answer to the question under inquiry.

Compare your *judgment* based on premises believed with high justification as of the present moment, lodged as they are in your long-term memory. Such beliefs can be activated with default justification, absent any specific reason to question them. So there is a way in which our thinker might be brilliantly justified in believing a conclusion that they derive from such premises through insightful reasoning. Compatibly with that, however, that conclusion may be epistemically (gnoseologically) unjustified and no candidate for knowledge, given the disqualifying sources of its entailing premises, even if they *now* enjoy the standing of stored beliefs free of any specific doubt.

[11] But please do not assume that such a "choice" must be arbitrary. No, it might rather be rational, motivated by compelling reasons. Judgment and belief can be free and involve decision or choice that is rationally motivated while not arbitrary. Too often belief is said not to be agential because not "voluntary," while a "voluntary" decision is supposed to be one that you could have reversed arbitrarily. Judgment and belief might not be owed to arbitrary volitional agency while still rationally agential, as is a vast amount of our ordinary agency.

So, *all* gnoseological things considered, it may be that our thinker really ought to suspend, and not to judge. *All such things considered*, they are terribly positioned to judge. And that is so even if in a clear sense they are highly justified in judging (*relatively* so), since that is what they do based on brilliant reasoning from premises *now* justifiably available through activation of beliefs in long-term memory.

19. Some further comparisons may be helpful.

In a first case, your objective is to compete in a rifle shooting competition and to hit your target as close to the bullseye as possible when it is your turn to shoot. However, you fail to prepare properly. Through negligence or recklessness, the rifle you have brought to the competition has a short range, whereas what you need is a long-range rifle. So you don't even take a shot. You intentionally refrain from shooting, knowing that you'd have no chance of success. And from one point of view that is what you must do. It is only wise for you to forbear that way. Yet, your forbearing is most deplorable telically, given your dominant objective, which is to shoot aptly at that target. And you are to blame for *having* to forbear thus. This is now due to your culpable negligence. So, despite its being the only thing for you to do in the circumstances, you are also tragically in a position where there is nothing telically appropriate (adequate) for you to do. Your forbearing—your *having* to forbear—is not commendable, relative to your dominant objective. Shooting would be even worse, yes, but even forbearing is still inapt and maladroit, because of your culpable negligence.[12]

[12] Can we resist this conclusion by distinguishing "having to forbear," in general, and "having to suspend" specifically, from actually forbearing? But how is this different from distinguishing "having to fail" (through culpable negligence) from actually failing. Take the small-plane pilot who runs out of fuel and crashes short of their destination. Can we say that they are blameworthy for having to fail, and even for having to crash (given how short they were of fuel because of their negligence), but not for the failure itself, not for the failure to arrive safely at their destination?

Compare the thinker who has to suspend through culpable negligence to inquire properly, and who does suspend, thereby failing to attain the knowledge that they would have attained otherwise. Should we say that they are assessable negatively for having to suspend, for having to fail that way to attain their dominant objective, the objective of answering their question with a knowledgeable judgment? And should we add that the failure itself is not to be assessed negatively, nor is the suspension?

20. For variety, take next an ostensible Major League Baseball game.

It's just a movie, though, a comedy of errors. Some hapless Joe is suited up half-drunk in the locker room and pushed to the plate against an ace opposing pitcher. He is aware enough to realize he should not make a move, and stands there until (as it happens) he gets the walk. Does he deserve credit for his intentional omission of swings? He does realize that this is what he needs to do, as he can hardly see the blazing pitches. But his performance is nothing like that of the champion hitters who can discriminate with high reliability when to swing and when not to swing, so as to earn credit not only for the swings but also for the omissions. Our hapless Joe is the butt of a comedy of errors and would not earn much credit either way, neither for swinging nor for forbearing. This despite the fact that, given their level of skill, and their chances of success with a swing, they must indeed forbear swinging. So, relative to their nearly zero skill, they must forbear, yes. But, first, their low skill deprives them of nearly any chance to creditably swing and succeed thereby. And, second, it deprives them also of much chance to creditably omit a swing. We might plausibly suppose them to be somewhat better off just holding on to their bat motionless, which makes it preferable for them to omit swinging. But the credit would be minimal and laughable.

21. These ideas about the normativity of suspension will make no sense unless we recall that the assessment here is gnoseological, having to do with the status of judgment that is pertinent to knowledge, the status, beyond mere truth, by virtue of which a judgment is constituted as a case of knowledge. So, the criteria pertinent to assessment of that status will be criteria pertinent to the attainment of knowledge.

A judgment might have a kind of rationality by being properly based on stored beliefs now activated for use in answering the pertinent question (the question answerable through that judgment). But this sort of rationality is neither necessary nor sufficient for a judgment to be knowledgeable. Not necessary, because many judgments can be knowledgeable just through activation of a knowledgeable belief, sans any reasoning at all. Not sufficient, because a judgment that is rational that way can fall way short of knowledge if the activated beliefs are sufficiently defective in their sources, which may now lie irretrievably in the thinker's past. There is of course still a kind of rationality that pertains to such judgments, even if it is not necessarily gnoseological. It is a kind of rationality that is relative to the position that the thinker happens to occupy, which we have seen to be possibly quite defective gnoseologically in various ways.

22. In conclusion, we see a similar upshot in the case of suspension. Suspension may be highly rated *relative to the thinker's position, even if this position is gnoseologically defective.* In this case it might well enjoy a high degree of rationality even if it is quite incompetent and inapt. *As of the present moment*, our thinker might suspend under conditions that are gnoseologically spoiled because of their defective derivation. The spoilage may now derive from negligent omission of inquiry. Suppose you obviously should have conducted further inquiry in pursuit of a knowledgeable answer to your question. Because of that, your present suspension may now be gnoseologically subpar. Concerning your decision *whether to now judge or suspend*, you are ill placed. In your position you will fall seriously short no matter what you do. And this is compatible with your doing very well *relative to that (inadequate) position.* Relative to that position, you are doing perfectly well by suspending. As with the rifle competition, there may be nothing better you could do, *given your position.* Indeed, all the other alternatives may be clearly worse. Compatibly, though, your suspension may still be terribly subpar, *all gnoseological things considered*, because of the low quality of your position, for which you are to blame. And so your suspending, your *having* to suspend, is still gnoseologically blameworthy and to your discredit. (Your suspending is as deplorable, and as discreditable, as is the rifleman's forbearing from taking a shot, or the hapless batter's forbearing from taking a swing.)

The skeptic has no special advantage. Their suspending may be quite discreditable epistemically. This is so if their position on the question is lacking through negligent inquiry, for example. And that is presumably a way in which the Pyrrhonian skeptics could have properly insisted that they remain inquirers ("skeptics"). Still standing is then of course the question of whether their inquiry is flawed or competent. It would remain to be seen what is required for proper pondering and resolution. What more specifically is *gnoseologically* proper? These are questions addressed in earlier chapters.

6

More on Suspension

Its Varieties and How It Relates to Being in a Position to Know

1. A broader view of suspension.
We have focused above mainly on occurrent judgmental suspending, a particular sort of suspending.

Suspending comes in many varieties, however, some of which are determined by two divides: one between occurrent and dispositional suspending; and another between judgmental and functional suspending.

To suspend judgmentally is to consciously and intentionally forbear from judgment (either positive or negative) on a given question. Functional suspension, by contrast, is constituted rather by the agent's *sub*consciously forbearing from teleologically functional (aimed) belief and disbelief.

Earlier we focused on one of those forms of suspension: the consciously intentional omission of judgment, whether positive or negative, on a question taken up. What follows takes up suspension more generally, to include the teleologically functional and not just the judgmental, both in occurrent and in dispositional forms, and both the instantaneous and the deliberately stable and longstanding; and more.

On the first order, suspending is comprised of *absences*: the absence of affirming/believing and the absence of denying/disbelieving. Suppose you are confident of the truth of a certain proposition to a degree that lies within a span from some threshold below 0.5 to some threshold above 0.5. No degree of confidence would seem apt to yield inherently and necessarily either a disposition to affirm or a disposition to deny on your part. And it is *these* dispositions that determine whether you relevantly "believe" or "disbelieve," on our conception of these states: i.e.,

Epistemic Explanations: A Theory of Telic Normativity, and What it Explains. Ernest Sosa, Oxford University Press (2021). © Ernest Sosa. DOI: 10.1093/oso/9780198856467.003.0006

whether you alethically affirm or deny, or whether you would so affirm or so deny, simply in the endeavor to do so aptly. So, it remains that on the first order there is not much, if anything at all, that constitutes the suspending. Of main relevance on the first order are simply *absences*—the absence of believing and the absence of disbelieving—that is to say, the absence of a relevant disposition to affirm and the absence of a relevant disposition to deny.

However, is there *never* anything that positively constitutes suspending? Might it not be simply a credence (or a degree of confidence) within certain thresholds of belief and disbelief? This would be a credence that lies between the disbelief threshold delta (a threshold below 0.5) and the belief threshold beta (a threshold above 0.5).

Agency is still involved here, however, whether in the form of *intentional* deeds, of *acts* involving decision or choice; or in the form of non-intentional deeds (attributable doings); or in the form of *sustained* intentions that may involve such deeds (either by deriving from them, or by being intentions—or, better, policies—to perform them in certain conditions; or both); or in the form of agential dispositions to perform such deeds (even if these deeds and the dispositions to perform them are both of them subconscious).

Why so? Why is agency still involved? Because it is one thing to host a credence of a certain degree (with that degree of confidence), and quite another to host a credence of such intensity *while that degree lies within the relevant interval, above the disbelief threshold and below the belief threshold.* This latter requires the enclosure of that degree of confidence within those thresholds. But its being so enclosed depends on the locations of the thresholds.

So, what determines those locations? Well, suppose first that the belief threshold is *defined* as the threshold at or above which one affirms or is disposed to affirm if one then endeavors to affirm aptly. Suppose, second, that the belief is *judgmental*, and that the disposition to so judge takes the form of a *policy*. If this policy is sustained freely, as policies are generally sustained, then the being enclosed of that degree of confidence within those thresholds is determined freely, through the free determination of where one begins to affirm and of where one stops denying.

But if one freely determines where one starts affirming (or becomes willing to do so, or by policy would do so), then plausibly one freely determines when one does *not quite yet* affirm (or become willing to do so, or by policy would not yet do so). And if the free determination of where one starts affirming is constituted by an intention to do so, then plausibly the free determination of where one does *not* yet affirm is *also* constituted by an intention, the intention *not* yet to do so. When one properly *deliberates* on an option and one has not yet decided, this lack of decision is no doubt intentional, and plausibly implements an ongoing intention not yet to opt, either affirmatively or negatively, and not to do so until the balance of reasons adequately supports one's opting as one does.[1]

Objection: "When one deliberates without yet having opted among affirming, denying, *or suspending*, one *already* intentionally omits affirming and omits denying. So, this intentional double omission cannot be what amounts to suspending."

Reply: Good point, though a point about *one* variety of suspension, *settled* suspension. What this reemphasizes is that suspension has significant varieties. We here have reason to distinguish between *provisional suspension*, or *time-slice suspension*, which might occur when one is still deliberating, and *conclusive, or settled, suspension*, whereby one suspends not just gnoseologically, while still endeavoring to attain successful judgment, apt alethic affirmation. When your suspension is conclusive on a question, this betokens a loss of epistemic hope and drive on that question, perhaps for excellent reasons, and comes with *abandonment* of the question, as one gives up inquiry.

One might of course end inquiry temporarily without opting for any such settling attitude and settled outcome. (Perhaps one needs to eat or drink or take a nap.) In this case one *defers*. One might even defer indefinitely, as one reaches a point where one sees no good way to continue

[1] Our reasoning develops the view that agency is involved for the special case of *judgmental* belief, whose metaphysical core consists of consciously intentional attempts. The broader view involves not only such consciously intentional agency but also the functional agency of attributable deeds, which need not be consciously intentional. Compare the discussion in Chapter 10 of the deeds that our BIV might perform, deeds that the BIV thinker cannot bring to consciousness (for lack of required concepts) while they are performed nonetheless, attributably to the thinker who performs them systematically in the exercise of their cognitive competence.

inquiry. One might then end inquiry without *conclusively* affirming, denying, *or* suspending. One reaches *no settled attitude* whatsoever, and simply redirects one's attention, and eventually the whole question may just drop out of mind, without your having done anything intentionally to bring that about.[2]

2. What constitutes intentional omission?

Settled, conclusive suspension is hence a kind of attributable double omission. This might even be intentional. Say one faces an option whether to wiggle a certain finger. One might decide to do so, whereby an intention is born, one soon implemented. Alternatively, one might decide *not* to do so. However, might one simply intentionally *not* wiggle that finger, with no benefit of corresponding intention? Not plausibly: after all, what makes an omission intentional if not the intention to omit?[3]

Of course, an intention need not be at the surface and focus of one's consciousness in order to so much as exist. An intention can be subconscious, as when one tries to put on the brakes in response to the sight of a red light, while engrossed in conversation. Even if the brakes are stuck, one tries to put them on. What gives positive substance to such trying? One possibility is that it is a present-directed intention, even if it is *sub*-conscious. But a second possibility is that it is simply a deed of the driver, an attributable doing, one that is brought about appropriately at just that juncture in the exercise of that driver's driving competence. (It might be denied that in such a case one does really try, but how plausibly?)

The foregoing suggests that omissions (and actions more generally) can be attributable in any of three ways at least. One way is for the omission to correspond to a present-directed intention, whether conscious or subconscious, an intention to persist in omitting. A second way is for the omission to derive from a past decision to omit indefinitely, even if the continuing omission is no longer accompanied by a present-directed intention to keep on omitting. The continuing omission cannot remain

[2] The place of suspension and related epistemic matters is insightfully discussed in Matt McGrath's "Being Neutral: Agnosticism, Inquiry and the Suspension of Judgment," forthcoming in *Nous*.

[3] Alternatively one might just take 'intentionally' to be short for 'intentionally, *by design*.'

intentional, however, absent any continuing intention to omit, *unless* it continues to be mnemonically owed to the earlier decision to omit.

Suppose the relevant mnemonic efficacy lapses, so that now the omission continues only because the whole matter is forgotten, and one simply fails to concern oneself with the relevant options at all. At this point one simply omits, without this being plausibly intentional. And at this point one *may* still omit attributably to oneself. But if none of those three possibilities is any longer in place, then one *also* stops suspending. One then simply *fails* to act, without *forbearing* action (without *suspending*, in the epistemic case).

So we have recognized four distinctions among ways to forbear action (applicable to the special epistemic case of suspending judgment):

- first, between consciously intentional versus subconscious forbearing;
- second, between subconscious forbearing that is still intentional, versus subconscious forbearing that is still attributable to the agent without being intentional;
- third, between provisional versus conclusive forbearing (including suspending judgment as a special case);
- fourth, between suspending made intentional and constituted by a present intention to suspend versus suspending made intentional and constituted by deriving mnemonically from an earlier intention to conclusively suspend (even without a continuing present-directed conscious intention to suspend).

3. Being in a position to know.
We need to distinguish a *weak* position to know, from a *strong* position. The weak position goes with *could*, but the strong position goes with *would*, in a way that should be clarified as follows.

Take an archer who has the skill and the situation to hit the target (has the bow and arrows and is well situated with respect to the target), but whose shape is questionable. He has had just enough to drink that it is indeterminate (or nearly so) whether he would then shoot in proper shape. As the drink wears off, he may be in a range of seconds where a split second might make the difference between being in proper shape and not being in proper shape. So it is just not clear whether if he shot "now" he would shoot with compete SSS competence. (For simplicity, I assume that a sharp line divides being in proper shape from not being in proper shape.)

In that case it may be hard to tell whether as such an archer you'd be in a position to succeed aptly at t. This is because it is so iffy whether you'd be in the required shape at that time, a shape that would give you the SSS profile whereby if you tried to hit the target you would be likely enough to do so aptly, through competence.

Plausibly, whether you are then in a position to succeed aptly depends on whether you have such an SSS profile. But there's a case that insinuates doubt. In that case you may have the triple-S profile to succeed reliably enough when you try to answer a given question, but although you have that threefold competence you would not exercise it; rather you would affirm through wishful thinking and not through sober competence.

Suppose you are a pistol shooter who is terrible with the left hand but nearly infallible with the right hand. You may then have a superb ability to hit the target before you while sorely lacking the competence. How so? Well, suppose you incorrectly assess your own skills, reversing the correct assessment. You think you're great with the left hand and terrible with the right hand. So, at t, you would shoot with the left hand and would perform terribly, while neglecting your superb right-hand skill. You have the *ability* since you could easily use the right hand, but you lack the competence since you so often would use the left hand instead.

As such a pistol shooter, are you in a position to succeed aptly at t? In a weak way yes. You have a triple-S profile such that, if you exercised it, you would be extremely likely to succeed, and your success would manifest that competence. But you are not in a strong position to succeed aptly at t. This is because you in fact would not exercise that marvelous triple-S profile. Rather, you would exercise the sorely lacking left-hand profile.

On a particular occasion, you might normally assess your skills well, and would normally use your right-hand triple-S profile. Consider then whether at that particular instant you are in a position to succeed aptly, and suppose that although *normally* you would use your right hand, *on that particular occasion*, for whatever reason, you would favor your left hand. You do then enjoy a superb competence to pistol-shoot with success, since you would nearly always use the right hand. And even when you would choose the wrong hand you do retain both the general competence and ability to shoot with success (by using your right hand, which you nearly always would do).

Yet at that time t, when for whatever reason you *would* pick the wrong hand, you are no longer in a strong position to succeed aptly (even if you are in a weak position to succeed aptly).

4. We now have a choice between a weak position and a strong position. So, which of these is more helpful for understanding the normativity of suspension? What *should* you be sensitive to in determining whether to suspend? Is it enough to be sensitive to whether you are in a weak position to succeed aptly, or must you rather *also* be sensitive to whether you are in a strong position?

Surely you should suspend whenever you fall short of a strong position to succeed aptly. You may be either in a weak position or in no position. Either way you should suspend. What you need in order to succeed aptly is the complete SSS competence that you would exercise if you tried, and by exercising which you *would* attain aptness. If you lack any of the three S factors, or you lack the pertinent disposition to use the SSS (right hand) competence that you *could* use, you should then suspend, since you would thereby fall short of aptness. However, on the assumption that the whole array of options is under your control, and available for your choice, what you should do all things considered is to exercise your competence, one that by hypothesis you do have and can exercise.

5. Consider the timing pertinent to gnoseological assessment. We are focused on assessment of cognitive performance on a given question at a given moment, where the choice is between judgment (positive or negative) and suspension. The proposal before us is that suspension (deliberative intentional omission of judgment) must be based on the thinker's sensitivity to whether they are "in a position to know" at that specific time. For this to work plausibly I assume that it must be tantamount to

the following: that suspension must be based on the thinker's sensitivity to whether if they were to judge at that very moment, then they would (likely enough) judge with success. (This is why our "position to know" involves *would* and not just *could*, and it is also why its focus is strictly on a given instant.)[4]

[4] Arguably an alternative notion of being "in a position to know" has its own important uses, as is argued in Christopher Willard-Kyle's insightful discussion, "Being in a Position to Know Is the Norm of Assertion," forthcoming in *Pacific Philosophical Quarterly*.

However, I cannot see how that alternative notion bears on the normativity of suspending. This is not just because of an emphasis on *could* rather than *would* in how we understand being in a position to X. It's also because the scope of performance envisaged may be allowed indefinitely long temporal extension. So, one's "being in a position to know" might thus leave it open that it may take some years before one does come to know and shows thereby that one was in a position to know. It might take years to prove that theorem, as with Fermat's Last Theorem. Nevertheless, despite having been thus in a position to know after years of reasoning, you may have been right to suspend during all that intervening time. So, what made all that suspending gnoseologically appropriate can't have been your failure to be in a position to know in that alternative sense, since in that sense you were all along in a position to know (after years of proper reasoning).

In our preferred sense here, by contrast, you (the mathematician) were not in a position to know until the very end. At the intervening stages during all that stretch of reasoning, you were never in a position to know. This is because at no time t in that stretch (prior to the very end) were you in possession of a basis that would have been your basis for judging on the pertinent question, whereby you would have known. This is what made it gnoseologically appropriate, indeed imperative, for you to suspend at every such instant t.

PART III

THE TELIC NATURE OF KNOWLEDGE, AND SOME MAIN VARIETIES

7
Knowledge, Default, and Skepticism

Virtue epistemology takes its own approach to the questions of traditional epistemology. What follows will focus on a distinctive notion of default assumptions, which enables a fresh treatment of philosophical skepticism. The response to the skeptics will be that they've mistaken what's required for the epistemic quality of ordinary judgments and beliefs. This treatment of skepticism is enabled by an analogy between epistemic and athletic performance, and between episteme and praxis more generally.[1]

Our virtue epistemological approach relies on a category of default assumptions that is different from any "default justification" or "entitlement" already in the literature, if only because ours is embedded in virtue theory and is to be understood thereby.[2] Wittgenstein comes closest in *On Certainty*, though his own ideas are also unhinged from any broader virtue epistemology.[3]

[1] And this is really more than an analogy: telic virtue epistemology takes judgment and judgmental belief to *be* forms of praxis, of intellectual praxis.

[2] Two comments about this sentence: First, a stylistic observation about the occasional use of the first-person plural and its grammatical variations, in this sentence and elsewhere in "our" main text. My use of that device is meant to encompass my auditors or readers, so that for example 'our virtue epistemological response' denotes the virtue-epistemological response that will be of interest to "us," meaning to those who do or will consider it. Second, in writing that sentence I have had in mind mainly the work of Tyler Burge, Fred Dretske, Peter Graham, Christopher Peacocke, and Crispin Wright, whose respective ideas of "entitlement" or "default justification" bear surface similarities to the one developed in our main text (as in their work cited in our bibliography). Despite those surface similarities, the proposal here is quite different, as it is deeply embedded in virtue theory, which bears on the assessment of epistemic performance (such as judgment and belief) only as a special case. In our virtue theory such default assumptions are in place across domains of human performance generally.

[3] A take on Wittgenstein's hinge epistemology is offered in Chapter 11.

Epistemic Explanations: A Theory of Telic Normativity, and What it Explains. Ernest Sosa, Oxford University Press (2021). © Ernest Sosa. DOI: 10.1093/oso/9780198856467.003.0007

A. What Lies Ahead

The epistemology here is focused on knowledge itself, not primarily the word, nor the concept. It is knowledge friendly in that it takes the phenomena of epistemology to be best delineated through our concept of knowledge.[4] Truth is important, but it will not do the job on its own. We would of course like to understand the ways in which human beings harvest truth so as to flourish. But that project is distinct from the project of understanding the nature, limits, and value of human knowledge, the project of epistemology that goes back to Plato's *Theaetetus* and *Meno*. Our inquiry is in this latter line.

We begin with a question.

B. What Is a Background Condition?

Athletic attempts have a likelihood of success normally determined by the athlete's skill, shape, and situation, or "triple-S profile." The success of an attempt is creditable only if sufficiently owed to the agent's pertinent triple-S competence. In managing their performances, athletes must heed their level of skill, along with how tired they are, how far from the target, and so on, for the various skill, shape, and situation factors that are known to affect performance. Still, *many* factors they can properly ignore, as they stay in the "background." In a night game, for example, they can ignore the lighting system, even when the lights are *in fact* poised to fail without warning. As an athlete, one is not negligent for ignoring such factors, with a default assumption that they are of no concern, absent indication to the contrary. What would be negligent is to reduce one's attention to the ball and the field so as to ponder such imponderables. As for the relevant "background conditions," one need only assume that they are in place, which one can do if no defeater intervenes, such as flickering lights, or an alert on the PA system.

[4] The discussion to follow will continue to focus on one main side of epistemology: its judgmental, reflective side. But the teleological orientation of our account and its telic normativity can be extended to the epistemology of functional, animal knowledge. The guiding concepts here are the telic concepts of attempt, success, competence, aptness, and achievement, all of which span the distinction between attempts that are consciously intentional and those that are functionally teleological.

Background conditions come in three sorts, corresponding to the triple-S structure of competence. They can concern either the skill, or the shape, or the situation of the performer, each of which would normally bear on a given attempt's likelihood of success. But each has its own distinctive bearing. When drunk or in the dark, for example, archers might fail miserably even while retaining their skill.

A background condition is one that must hold if the relevant S factor is to be in place at the time of performance. The presence of the pertinent skill, shape, or situation will thus entail respective background conditions. What puts such conditions in the *background* is that, although they must hold, you can perform fully aptly without *knowing* that they hold. Nor need they hold *safely* if your performance is to be apt.

Background conditions thus pertain to competences generally. When an agent performs, in whatever domain of performance, relevant background conditions might easily have been missing, even when they are present in fact. They might thus be present just *by luck and unbeknownst to the agent*, with no detriment to the quality of that performance, nor to the credit earned by the agent for its success.

In this section, I have introduced the idea of background conditions by pointing to examples and by suggesting some salient features. For a given agent, time, and performance, a "background condition" is, for one thing, a condition whose holding is necessary for a given SSS competence to be possessed by that agent at that time. If baseball players are to retain their various SSS competences, for example, as they perform in a night game, the lights must stay on.

Darkness would deprive fielders of the ability to track fly balls through their vision and their hand–foot–eye coordination, so as to reliably make their catches. Why then is the continuing presence of the lights only a *background* condition for baseball fielders? That is because, as they run aiming for the catch, while keeping the fly ball in view, they need not *know* that the lights *will* stay on, nor need that be at all a *safe* condition. Background conditions need only be true, even if unsafe and unknown.

So, I simply take note of the fact that such background conditions are pervasive in human performance domains, that this seems so hard to deny. It would be nice to have a general theory, for arbitrary agent, time, and attempt, of what makes a condition a *background condition* for that agent's possession of a competence to succeed. Fortunately, though, we need not await such a general theory in order to use the notion so as to illuminate issues of epistemology, in the way to be essayed below. That, anyhow—epistemic explanation—is what we will aim for in the next section, while wielding our "background conditions."

C. Radical Skepticism and Relevant Alternatives

Our account enables a response to the skeptic independent of the modal remoteness shared by many radical skeptical scenarios.

Consider again the quality of an athlete's performance and the credit earned for its success. As noted, imminent background danger might have zero bearing on either quality of performance or credit for success. Nor need the agent rule out all such danger, some of which may be "irrelevant."

Analogously, *epistemic* agents may not be required to rule out irrelevant skeptical alternatives, apart from assuming that no such danger will be realized in fact.

Take for example the "brain in a vat" scenario. On the standard conception of that scenario, its *actuality* would of course affect one's epistemic performances, just as the lights' going out would affect the performance of players in a night game. However, the merely modal fact that the scenario *might easily* occur may be harmless to the quality of epistemic performance, just as the merely modal fact that the lights might easily fail is harmless to the quality of athletic performance. Nor need one *knowledgeably* rule out that skeptical scenario if one's performance is to be *fully* apt, any more than nighttime athletes need knowledgeably rule out the malfunction of the lights, on pain of forsaking full aptness.

An initial response to our skeptics is that they've mistaken what's required for the epistemic quality of our ordinary judgments and beliefs. *Their mistake is like disparaging a superb baseball catch as due to discrediting luck because, unbeknownst to the fielder, the lights could so easily have failed.*[5]

[5] And that's also how one might go astray in denying that Barney can know they see a barn, when in fake barn country.

A distinctive response to radical skeptics is thus enabled by that analogy between epistemic and athletic performance, and between *episteme* and *praxis* more generally.

Our approach also suggests a way to understand the appeal to "relevant alternatives" in responses to skepticism of years ago. At that time, the notion of relevance remained obscure, where the present approach might now shine its light. In our framework, an alternative is relevant if and only if it is one that the subject needs to rule out specifically (either through explicit judgment or through implicit belief), as its absence cannot be taken for granted by default. That notion applies pervasively in human life, and to epistemic performance as a special case.[6]

D. Adversity Ahead

Our analogy encounters an objection.

Consider the fielder's belief that he will make the catch if he tries. Suppose this belief to be no less apt than is the catch itself, despite the grave danger posed in each case by the fragility of the lights. If knowledge is apt belief, that stadium belief then amounts to knowledge. But this seems absurd, given how probable it is (nearly certain, by hypothesis) that the lights will fail.

We thus face a *reductio* of the virtue-theoretical thesis that apt belief is knowledge. Consider the analogy between the fielder's attempted catch and his belief that he will succeed if he tries. Suppose the catch is apt despite how lucky it is that its background conditions hold. Suppose the

[6] Moreover, when restricted to human *epistemic* performance, our background conditions are also akin to Wittgenstein's *hinges*. For a discussion of the relevant alternatives approach to skepticism and to the analysis of knowledge, see section 5.3 of the article on the analysis of knowledge in the *Stanford Encyclopedia*, by Matthias Steup and Jonathan Ichikawa. (References are found there to the relevant work of Stine, Goldman, and Dretske.) Our present approach also entails a crucial distinction between safety and relevance, but there is no real rapprochement between the two approaches. In my view, safety is not required for knowledge nor for apt performance generally. A performance of a nighttime athlete can be apt even if extremely unsafe (because of how unsafe is the lighting system). And a similar conclusion may be drawn about epistemic performances, where again grave danger, great risk of failure, seems compatible with success that is apt. Only the danger involving "*relevant*" alternatives can deny us knowledge. The foregoing is a first approximation, however, to be supplemented with the appeal to *security* in Chapter 9.

fielder's belief that he will succeed if he tries is similarly apt, despite the parallel luck in the holding of *its* background conditions. Since that belief is then an apt belief, our virtue theory declares it a case of knowledge. But, again, that verdict is very hard to sustain.

We need a step back to reassess.

E. The Place of Default Reconsidered

Suppose we awaken some morning with our body of stored knowledge containing its multitude of stored beliefs that we would severally endorse. That would be as normal as daybreak. But what if an alien force could have recently spoiled or thwarted our epistemic faculties? Suppose it came to a coin flip whether we would all be placed in a Matrix setting.

We're supposing that we were actually in close danger of that Matrix disaster, but that the coin flip turned out favorably for us, and the alien force moved away harmlessly. Once we knew all this, how would we properly react? Would we say: "right now we no longer know nearly anything"? After all, even if post-Matrixing beliefs matched earlier beliefs, this could only be by sheer coincidence, *not* through retentive memory, as (by hypothesis) the later contents would then come from the Matrix.

Here let us assume a radical Matrix scenario wherein victims' brains are envatted *and* massively manipulated, with all their beliefs removed and new ones inserted arbitrarily, in one fell swoop.[7] The point is that the post-insertion beliefs are related to the pre-insertion beliefs through nothing like retentive memory. Instead of retentive memory, what is operative is just the random procedure implemented by the Matrixers.

Does the *mere danger* of that epistemic disaster remove our ability to know as we normally do? Note well: in hosting our later beliefs we run

[7] Such massive manipulation is supposed for simplicity and effect. But even highly local manipulation will still give us a radical enough skeptical threat. And such local manipulation will not be blocked by externalist assumptions concerning theory of content or other plausible enough views concerning language or mind. It does not really matter for Descartes's skeptical doubt whether the Evil Demon acts across one's whole body of beliefs and for the full length of one's life. Skepticism about knowledge on that particular occasion is equally threatening, as he sits before a fire, if we consider that the Demon may be targeting just that particular agent at just that particular time.

the great risk of having been thus Matrixed. But this mere risk could hardly entail that massive loss of knowledge. Rather, even in full awareness of the danger we had lived through, we would still have attributed to ourselves the knowledge that we attribute in a normal morning unaffected by such danger. What is more, we would still have attributed to ourselves our body of background knowledge and I say we would have done so properly *and correctly*.

We could even suppose that, rather than a coin flip, the aliens ran a lottery, only by winning which would we have been allowed to retain our body of standing beliefs. Otherwise they would have thoroughly fooled us by Matrixing. Suppose we are informed by NASA, which provides powerful evidence that we had been besieged by those aliens and had luckily won their lottery. Should we conclude that our body of standing beliefs no longer constitutes knowledge? Given the picture that we would then have from NASA, if our body of standing beliefs is indeed largely true, this is a massive bit of luck. Only by luck are those beliefs largely true, as it was far more likely that our body of standing beliefs would have been massively false.

Only by luck were we not radically Matrixed. That is what we then believe, if we are convinced by NASA, as we are by hypothesis. Imagine yourself in that situation. Is it really an option to abandon the whole world view that we live by, through which we place ourselves in a surrounding jointly shared world, and based on which we act at every turn? Surely that is not an option. Must we then say that, despite our lack of any feasible alternative, continuing faith in our world view is wrong or inappropriate? Are we doomed to such incoherence? Not if we can find an alternative account of appropriateness, such as the account based on our default assumptions. On that account, the quality of our epistemic performances is unaffected by the NASA-recognized danger, in just the way nighttime athletic performance is unaffected by grave danger that the lights will fail.[8]

[8] It might be argued that the very knowledge provided by NASA acts as a sort of defeater-defeater that restores our background knowledge despite our knowing that we ran such high epistemic risk. However, this involves complexities that would need to be pondered. (For example, how can we take seriously the testimony of NASA, if it undermines itself, given that if there was indeed such massive luck in the workings of our retentive memory, including the

Full aptness is important on *both* sides of the episteme/praxis divide. Skilled athletes need to assess how likely they are to succeed, and must be guided thereby. In properly making that assessment, moreover, subjects are allowed to rely by default on the relevant background conditions, absent specific reasons for doubt. Why would that not be so on *both* sides of the episteme/praxis divide?[9] How could it not be so if the episteme side is just a special case of a broader praxis side?

F. Knowledge and Default

In a performance domain, agents aim at certain outcomes with their movements, representations, and affirmations (a baseball catch, say, a soccer goal, a medical diagnosis, or a legal conviction), based on proper default assumptions.

Our ordinary knowledge is also based on a proper assumption: *that no abnormal spoilers will intervene*. This implicit assumption helps guide our navigation in epistemic domains of expertise or common sense. Suppose our assumption is put in question, however, as we consciously question its truth. That is sometimes thought to import an epistemically consequential shift. We are warned that we can then no longer insist on ruling out spoilers by default assumption. In the new, more deeply reflective context, no such assumption is thought to be sustainable by default.

mnemonic faculties of the NASA personnel, how then can we even be sure that NASA is really to be trusted? Aren't we now left with suspension as the only epistemic option, as against our supposed knowledge?) Besides, the supposed remedy seems insufficient when we reflect that our whole body of standing background knowledge would still have been lost even if the interlopers had been undetected by NASA. Does this not *still* seem absurd? Note well: given the dependence of agential normativity *generally* on its basis in the knowledge of agents, all of life across the world would have lost its agential worth with any such massive loss of background knowledge.

[9] The kinship between some at least of Wittgenstein's hinges and our own background conditions comes again to the fore. Both are assumed by default to buttress our coherent commonsense perspective as well as the particular judgments that we make from that perspective. Hinges can thus enable our body of knowledge without our *knowing* them to be true, and without our reaching them as conclusions (through "ratiocination"). As with hinges, background conditions can be assumed to obtain, with assumptions that *stand fast* for us, and can properly do their enabling even when they are just assumed to be true, and even when that assumption is both unsafe and in ignorance. Chapter 11 will go into Wittgenstein's epistemological thoughts and how they relate to Moorean common sense.

The plausibility of such schizophrenia has been questioned by those who reject the doubts of radical skeptics as mere "paper doubts." And, I must say, if I consider how I would react to a NASA announcement about Matrixing extraterrestrials, I think I'd just proceed epistemically in pretty much the ways I would have proceeded absent the warning.

Would we really give up in such a case? Would we yield to universal suspension of judgment and belief?

I say we would do no such thing. Those of us who took the announcement seriously would just continue to try to place its warning in proper epistemic perspective, based on the best judgment we could muster, while those who dismissed the announcement would carry on with normal routines, which one could hardly do if entirely deprived of judgment.

And could we really be blamed, practically *or* epistemically? What other option would we have, really?

It is hard to see how life in general could possibly go on otherwise, given our pervasive dependence on knowledge of many and various forms. Even in the case of Robinson Crusoe, but especially in a complex social setting, we depend extensively on the judgmental knowledge that constantly fuels both our practical syllogisms and also the testimony that we need for coordinating action and sharing information.

Sure, but what we *would* do is one thing, along perhaps with what we *could not help* doing. Why think that we would *properly* continue to attribute our ordinary knowledge and justification to ourselves?

How can we avoid recklessness or at least negligence if we look away from the urgent NASA warnings? How is this case different from that of the surgeon who is warned about the fragility of the lights in her high-tech operating room? Why should we think of our situation when we receive the NASA warning as like the situation of the fielder and unlike that of the surgeon?

G. Default Assumptions Again

Our example of the Matrix-wielding alien force shows that our ordinary, common-sense domain contains *its own* default assumptions. Despite *knowing* that we had undergone such Matrix danger, we would have continued to attribute nearly all of the knowledge that we ordinarily self-attribute, which we surely would have done properly and *correctly*.

Could we have ruled out such Matrix intervention knowledgeably?

In what domain? When we face our varied quotidian questions, we act in line with our epistemic competence if we assume that no abnormal spoiler will intervene, including of course any Matrix intervention by extraterrestrials. Without a second thought, we standardly take it for granted that no such spoiler will intervene. When we turn out to be right on our quotidian questions, we thus manifest our competence, as we do also in making such default assumptions.

What if space scientists warn about a real threat of spoiler dangers? In addressing that question, are we beyond our normal everyday framework, so that default assumptions are no longer competent?[10] If we persist in making the default assumptions that are pertinent to judgment and belief, and we turn out by luck to be right, could the success attendant on our luck still be competent and even apt?

Within a virtue theoretic framework we *can* then still judge and believe with full aptness. The "fullness" of our aptness is constituted by two things in combination: (a) the aptness of our success, as this manifests not just luck but sufficient competence exercised by the agent, and (b) the aptness of that apt attainment, as *this* aptness is itself attained through the agent's competent assessment that they're then positioned to attain it. Their attempt may thus attain not only success, but also sufficient competence and aptness. Their attempt may thus be apt and "fully" apt, even while neglecting factors with negligible bearing.[11]

[10] This is again reminiscent of Wittgenstein's hinge propositions said to be like a riverbed for the flow of our beliefs over time. They might at first be lodged in the stable riverbed but later come loose and form part of the flow rather than the bed. We return to this antecedent in Chapter 11.

[11] A probabilistic account is of course an alternative that some will find plausible. So, my own proposal assumes that we are explaining performances and their competence and aptness through on/off judgments or beliefs and the practical syllogisms that they fuel. Our view of the role of on/off knowledge—and its place in creditable, successful attempts in general—is set within that context. It is beyond our purview to defend this framework against alternatives that dispense with on/off beliefs and with practical reasoning in terms of such beliefs and knowledge. To me it seems implausible that any satisfactory account of our agency and our cooperation can dispense with such judgments and beliefs and with the corresponding assertions that enable us to share information and coordinate action. In any case, our reasoning presupposes a framework of outright judgment, belief, and knowledge.

H. Deductive Closure

If we *can* rule out spoilers thus, if only by competent default assumption, can't we now *competently deduce* that no such spoiler *will* intervene? Can't we now thereby come to *know* after all that we need fear no such spoiler? Is this how we can agree with G. E. Moore that, within ordinary contexts, we do know the sorts of facts listed in his defense of common sense?

Let's return to the hovering Matrixers as their lottery determines our epistemic fate. If we lose, we will all be Matrixed. At that moment, all across the globe there will be an immense welter of human activity, all based on a corresponding wealth of knowledge how and knowledge that. Consider the fact of the lottery, its complex setting, and its monumental epistemic threat. Does such *danger* spoil that immense complex of activity in its entirety, since it all now seems epistemically baseless? I press my car starter, say, expecting this to start the car. And that is what happens, but only because miraculously we win the lottery and the spoiler force moves on harmlessly. Is that enough to take away my credit for starting the car? No? But how can I keep that credit if my knowledge is gone? True, I do attempt to start my car, and my car does consequently start. But is that success properly, fully *attributable* to me? Can a success through ignorance, through guessing or the like, still be fully creditable to the agent?

Suppose we do find it plausible that, in such circumstances, people worldwide would still properly credit themselves and each other for the success of their attempts. In line with that, suppose we do keep our full credit for the many things we do just as we win the momentous lottery. If we are to keep our credit, we must also keep our pertinent knowledge as the drama unfolds. I then know that by pressing its starter button I will start my car. And I could then *deduce* that I will not be Matrixed so as to preclude that anticipated outcome. So, could I thereby come to know after all that I will not be Matrixed, and also that we would not lose our fateful lottery?

Undeniably, I can thus deduce that we'll not be Matrixed, and later that we've not been Matrixed. But would that deduction give me knowledge of its conclusion, if I did not already know it to be true? How could I possibly know that no Matrix spoiler would intervene *even when a spoiler was nearly certain to intervene*? How could I know such a proposition to be true, based on the sheer assumption that it is true?

Our way with the skeptic thus requires the rejection of epistemic closure and transmission, its rejection at least when such closure is stated in full generality.

This route to denial of closure is compatible with rejection of every other route in the literature (Dretske's, for example, and Nozick's), all of which seem unacceptable (and different from ours in both scope and content). Ours comes trippingly with telic virtue theory in all of its domains. But the case must be stated with care.

Transmission is ruled out because it would be viciously circular in our example, with a distinctive twist. The vice would come from *assuming (by default)* that p and then arriving at the belief that p on that (circular) basis. So, the rejection of transmission in our case seems straightforward and unproblematic.

What of non-transmissive closure? Consider first this reasoning: *Must I not know that p if my basis for coming to know that q is essentially dependent on my thought that it is true that p?* This just begs the question viciously against our telic epistemology of default assumptions. After all, the appeal to default assumptions is predicated precisely on the idea that, no, we do *not* need to *know* the whole of the propositional basis on which we come to know that q by aptly so believing. The main idea behind the proposed use of default assumptions is precisely about some at least of the propositional basis for our conclusion that p. The main idea is that not all of that basis needs to be known, as some of it can just be assumed by default and without negligence or recklessness. And we have seen how this sort of default assumption figures in that sort of way across the immense variety of human performance domains. It is an important fixture of such domains that performers can make such assumptions with no negligence or recklessness, and can thus earn full credit for their performances and for their success. So, far from being a problem, this sort of denial of *such* non-transmissive closure is an important positive feature of the proposal.

Still, there is a serious problem of closure that we still need to face. Isn't it enormously plausible that if at a given time I know that p, and

I know that, necessarily, if p then q, then I can come to know that q through competent deduction, provided I did not already know it? (And I don't even need to know that *necessarily* if p then q; the knowledge that if p then q would suffice.) Yes, if I do know that p, and that if p then q, then it would seem that I can competently deduce that q, and *thereby acquire* knowledge that q, provided I did not know that q already.

Appearance here deceives, however, as that general principle has a discernible exception. If knowledge is subject to the telic normativity that makes room for default assumptions, then we can counter-reason as follows.

Suppose I do know that p, and know that if p then q, and competently deduce that q, and judge on that basis that q. Does it really follow that I thereby know that q? Well, the assumption that I *competently* deduce that q would seem to require that I not thereby incur any vicious circularity. But what if my knowledge that P is based, as it might well be, on a default assumption that q? If so, then the larger chain of reasoning based on which I arrive at the conclusion that q is clearly circular, and viciously so, containing as it does the conclusion as itself an essential premise.

So we see how once default assumptions are admitted as a proper fixture of the telic normativity of human attempts in general, and once we apply that to the special case of human epistemic (gnoseological) attempts, we must make an exception to the otherwise very plausible closure principle. In a case where your knowledge that p is based on an essential default assumption that q, then if you don't know that q, you cannot acquire knowledge that q based on your knowledge that p, not even if you competently deduce that q from your knowledge that p. This is because you may thereby incur vicious circularity in your broader reasoning on which rests your final conclusion that q.

Our ordinary knowledge is based on a proper assumption *that no abnormal spoilers will intervene*. That implicit assumption helps to guide our ordinary epistemic navigation. This all takes place within our ordinary epistemic domains, whether of expertise or of everyday common sense. Putting that assumption in question, however, seems an epistemically consequential shift. Can we then still insist on ruling out abnormal spoilers by default? In that new, more deeply reflective context, can any such assumption still be sustained so easily?

The reflective shift is said to take away our ordinary knowledge. In the ordinary domain itself we seem unable to knowledgeably rule out any such spoilers. Consciously reflective knowledge requires us to consider the possibility of spoilers, which would drive us *out* of the ordinary context and into a context of reflection where we can no longer just assume that we are free of spoilers.

Can we perhaps adopt a position like that of the athletes who carry on with their game even while knowing that the lights are about to fail (or nearly certain to fail). If they do carry on, they can plausibly earn full credit for performing full well athletically despite the fact that their default assumptions are made in the teeth of contrary *knowledge*, or at least in the absence of pertinent knowledgeable support. Can we take an analogous view of our judgments? It is surprising how tempting it is to answer here in the affirmative. I do myself yield to that temptation. To me the domain of epistemology is a special case of human endeavor with a telic normativity of the sort we have explored. And it is then a feature of that normativity to allow default assumptions that can properly support the performance of agents with no negligence or recklessness.

Epistemology is then similar to athletic domains in allowing default assumptions against abnormal spoilers, assumptions that fall far short of knowledge, and even of safety.

As we have seen, however, allowing default assumptions in our epistemology has an important epistemic implication. We must now reject familiar and general principles of deductive closure. Default hinges are assumptions that stand fast by being faultlessly assumed. By standing fast, such competent assumptions can buttress knowledge even if they are not themselves known to be true or even safe. But we can't possibly *come to know* that p by reasoning based essentially on the sheer prior *assumption* that p, not even if the assumption is true, nor even if it is true and competently assumed to be true. You cannot get to such knowledge through any deduction that relies essentially on a sheer assumption not itself already *known* to be true, not when the assumption has the very same content as the conclusion to be drawn.

I. Are We Not Confusing the Epistemic with the Practical?

Perhaps we would indeed properly continue to engage in quotidian judgment while disregarding the warning that *possibly* we are Matrixed by spatial interlopers, or indeed that this is *likely*. But might we proceed thus, on an assumption of normalcy, just because we have no *practical* choice? Even if we take the probability that we are Matrixed to be astronomically high, perhaps we must carry on based on the same continuing assumptions, so that we'd go through the day making the very same judgments that we would have made even had we not been privy to the NASA announcement. But why suppose this prudential decision to bear on the *epistemic* standing of the profusion of ordinary judgments that we'd still emit with abandon. Should we not then grant that any continuing justification we may have for rendering those ordinary judgments will be just pragmatic and not epistemic?

A powerful intuition, granted.[12]

Can it still be resisted? Can we resist it so as to save our proposed *epistemic* role for default assumptions? Here follows an argument for the affirmative.

Consider first an analogous example. I am about to play chess with an opponent at the public chess space in Washington Square Park. Night has fallen just prior to the match, as onlookers gather. Suddenly a stranger emerges from the darkness holding an iPhone, eyes me intently, points at me with cocked thumb and index finger, and just then I see this text on my iPhone: "I am looking at you. You must play. Play normally. If you do not play normally, we'll know and you'll be shot dead." Please fill out the context so that, as I then see it, I have an irresistible rationale to play normally. As far as my selection of chess moves goes, I then restrict myself to the reasoning that I would have used in normal chess.

Well, I do so to the extent possible, since normally I would not be motivated to play by the fear of being shot dead. Still, I make my specific

[12] My grateful thanks to Chris Kelp for pressing this concern.

chess moves based purely on chess considerations (except only for that overarching motive), and I do all this through my chess competence. So, the AAA/SSS structure would seem to apply in pure chess form, in which case I will earn chess-specific credit for any success that I may have.

We can imaginatively fill in details so that, given my fully convinced view of the situation, I have *no real option* but to keep on playing. On that hypothesis, I *must* play normally, I must stay in the game, and this for powerful practical reasons, given how I see the situation with full conviction.

Nevertheless, is it not obvious that these reasons have no bearing at all on the chess standing of any move that I may make in the course of that match?

That being so, here is the proposed analogy to the epistemic case.

Because we are essentially rational animals, we have *no real option* on how to proceed cognitively over the enormous span of the animal knowledge we rely on in any ordinary day. However, that applies equally to Mr. Magoo and to normal perceivers.[13] Any particular human, no matter how inept or adept, will be bound to proceed within some parameters of perceptual belief acquisition. But no one is likely to *entirely* avoid illusion and every other perceptual error. Even when we are informed that there is an even chance that we will soon be Matrixed, Magoo and I will each continue to exercise our animal competences, perceptual and otherwise. And our respective cognitive performances will not be thought to be on a par. Magoo will perform poorly, or at least much more poorly than I will. My success will be apt, through competence, so that I will attain a kind of knowledge, a first-order "animal" knowledge still denied to Magoo. And that remains so even if Magoo attains equally many *correct* beliefs entirely by luck, with nearly zero competence.

True, the question is trickier when we turn to reflective knowledge full well. Here, taking a leaf from the Pyrrhonists, we might forbear judgment. In our alethic affirmations, we might forbear aiming for aptness. We would then continue to perform on the first order—the

[13] The reference here is to the nearly deaf and blind cartoon character who regularly but miraculously escapes disaster at every turn, so that while he *does* regularly escape disaster, it's not true that he *would* escape. It's a *miracle*, after all.

level of animal knowledge—however poorly we might fare in doing so, since all our plentiful true affirmations would derive from luck and not from competence. Our continued first-order performance would be owed to an imperative of our animal nature.

However, the very rationality of that nature at its best might then move us to a general or even universal suspension of *judgment*, despite continuing to affirm *alethically* at every turn, as we are force-guided by our animal nature, by our perceptual competence.

So, with the Pyrrhonists we might continue to be guided by our appearances and their inevitable first-order functional belief outcomes, *but* with a crucial difference emphasized by those skeptics: While refusing to *endorse* those outcomes rationally, we would also refuse to make the corresponding *judgments*, so as to attain through such judgments the status of reflective knowledge or knowledge full well.

The inclusion of default assumptions in our virtue epistemology gives us an alternative to that dreary skeptical life. We can appeal instead to the analogy with the baseball fielder, by recognizing that there are things we can assume nonnegligently despite our not knowing them to be true and despite their lack of safety. That the lights will stay on is one such condition that the fielder can trust to be in place even without knowing this and even when it is highly unsafe.

The suggestion is further that when the space aliens are poised to Matrix us if we lose in their lottery, we can still trust that we are not and will not be Matrixed, and can proceed without negligence to exercise our normal animal competences.

Of course, that leaves much room for reflection requirements that still demand satisfaction—on pain of negligence or even recklessness—in the exercise of our cognitive competences. So, there will remain an important distinction between bare animal knowledge and reflective knowledge full well.

J. An Application: Barn-spotting

About the large wooden structure that he sees before him, does Barney know it to be a barn? Does he know this by trusting his visual appearances when he happens to see the one real barn in an area rife with mere façades? Opinions differ on this. Epistemologists are mostly reluctant to allow that Barney does "know." But many of the folk apparently disagree, and some epistemologists now take that side. How should we deal with this?

Let us first generalize beyond the particular example.

Suppose you judge that p on a certain basis of visual appearance, so that it visually appears to you that p—abbreviated here as A(p). Can you thereby know that p, through a default assumption that reality here fits appearance?

What if your assumption is not something you know to be true, nor is it even a safe assumption? What if it could very easily have been false, since in your modal vicinity A(p) comes mostly with ~p?

Our approach allows, however, that you can know that p even if you rely on an assumption that is neither safe nor known by you to be true. In particular, you can know that p even if you base your belief that p on your knowledge that A(p) and your assumption that if A(p) then p, and even if initially this assumption is just a hinge that stands fast for you and is neither safe nor known to be true.

What you do *not* know *with priority* in such a case is that your appearance is not misleading. In the familiar case of the fake barns, what you cannot rule out through *conscious reflection*, not knowledgeably, is the following: that you *seem* to see a barn without *really* seeing one. You cannot then know *with priority* that if you seem to see a barn, you do see a barn; in particular, you cannot know this so as to *thereby* obtain knowledge that you do see a barn, for you cannot know it *prior* to your knowing that you do see a real barn (nor can you even use it as a *non-posterior* basis for this latter knowledge).

It might be argued that we can rely on the known fact that the overwhelming majority of barn appearances across the face of the earth are veridical. Can't we then know that the one real barn in that vicinity is indeed a barn when it gives us the corresponding appearance?

Not plausibly. Compare a case where you enter a vast warehouse with millions of bags all of which contain only white marbles by the hundreds, with the possible exception of at most one bag. And you know that to be so. When you enter the room and pick up one of the bags at random you accordingly believe that the marble you draw from that bag is white, as you take it out of the bag, and you know that marbles picked at random from bags in that room tend strongly to be white. But what if that particular bag too has hundreds of marbles, all of them *red*, however, with the sole exception of the white marble that you happen to pick. Do you know that marble to be white as you take it out of its bag? Surely not.

So, at least for now we have reason to favor the approach through default assumptions of the form: if A(p) then p.

Your relevant default assumption is that *if you visually seem to see a barn, then you do see a barn*, which is a special case of our general default assumption, as we approach the world through our senses, that if A(p) then p, an ongoing assumption that *reality here tends to correspond to appearance (whether visual or of some other sense modality)*. This sustains the assumption made by epistemic agents, in their ordinary epistemic proceedings, on any given occasion, that they will likely enough succeed by believing in line with how things visually appear to them. And it is an *assumption* that according to our account of default assumptions, they can make *with priority*, and properly so.

The ordinary epistemic visual domain is thus a special case of *domains in which agents are allowed default assumptions*. The following assumption is one made generally by default in that domain: *that if here now one seems to see that p, then one does see that p.*[14]

K. Concluding Remarks

This chapter has introduced default assumptions and their normative roles. That makes room for a telic normativity that enables a better view

[14] This is a first approximation, however, since we must allow for the possibility of override or defeat. So, more strictly, the default assumption would take rather the form of one or another of the following: that if one seems to see that p, then probably one does see that p; that one's seeming to see that p tends to imply that one does see that p; or (instead or in addition) that cases of seeming to see that p are (generically) cases of seeing that p. These are contents the assumption of which will combine with one's seeming to see that p, so as to enable a rational basis for increasing confidence that one does see that p, provided no defeater or overrider intervenes.

of *epistemic* assessment, one more realistic and plausible than earlier views. That anyhow has been the objective.

Thus far we have explored a distinctive telic normativity, and a virtue epistemology that falls under that. One main new feature is the spandrel status of the epistemically prime sort of suspension—*deliberative* suspension—and how that fits hierarchically under the knowledge that functions as a main norm not only of judgment but also of such suspension.

Also of interest is a telic conception of degrees of confidence and the telic normativity that comes along with that. This conception enables us to improve on standard evidentialism by recognizing a basis for suspension in a proper epistemic psychology. Our degree of such confidence of <p> aims at reflecting one's balance of evidence for <p>, and has an important role to play in accounting for the full span of epistemic normativity, including the sort distinctive of knowledge.

Third, the notion and status of default assumptions also enable an enhanced conception of the competences and the aptness featured in the telic normativity of virtue epistemology.[15]

Once we give default assumptions their key role, however, we are bound to sustain them even in our assessment of reflective knowledge full well. Consider then the intuition that Barney does not know in fake

[15] Actually, telic normativity is particularly helpful for a *central part* of epistemology, namely the theory of *knowledge* (which for referential convenience we title "gnoseology").

Our main text has recently focused on the domain of ordinary, common-sense epistemology, along perhaps with domains of expertise, such as the legal, the medical, etc. But in fact our telic virtue epistemology seems quite naturally receptive to the admission of *ludic* epistemic domains. And with such admission of ludic epistemic assessment would come a kind of ambivalence in the assessment of whether one "knows" that one's opponent is about to hit a tennis lob, based on which one properly leans back toward one's baseline. One surely has no *ordinary* knowledge of any such thing if one knows that the lights are poised to fail with near-certainty. And yet if the lights do *not* fail, then, along with the tennis quality of one's leaning back and the relevant aptness, would come a corresponding tennis-epistemic quality of one's judgment that the opponent is about to lob, which could even amount to a sort of "tennis-knowledge" of that fact. So, along with the expert knowledge proper to the various domains of human expertise, we would now have various ludic domains of "knowledge" as well. And *these* ludic epistemic domains would seem to admit not only epistemic default assumptions unaffected by lack of safety, but also epistemic default assumptions unaffected by the agents' *knowledge* of such *lack* of safety. When one leaned back based on knowledge of the opponent's intention to lob, one could properly so judge, as one could see the intention in their approaching stance, and in so properly judging one would rely on a default assumption that the lights would not fail, *and* in making that judgment one could even rely on such a default assumption despite one's *knowledge* of the dire condition of the lights.

barn country. This can no longer be accommodated just as a denial that Barney can know *reflectively* (reflectively full well). And the same goes for many other Gettier cases. The following chapter considers why and how that may be so and advances an alternative account that does not appeal to reflective knowledge (full well). The alternative account appeals instead to a (Cartesian) category of *secure* knowledge, one explicated in what follows.

8
Grades of Knowledge

A. A Simple View Sketched

1. The following eye-exam example shows that animal knowledge need not even be credal.[1] Suppose I have been infallibly right for years in my eye-exam guesses at a row far down the chart. The statistics assembled over decades by technicians show that it has been no accident. *Somehow*, I can know the letters at that row even when I take myself to be guessing.

I am of course *trying* to get it right. That is what I am supposed to do in order to undergo the test properly so as to obtain a correct eye-glass prescription. So, why is it that I have been guessing? Because one can guess by affirming in the endeavor to get it right, as one does in a quiz show, and as one does when one takes the eye exam. What then prevents the guess from being a judgment? What is the missing ingredient? Recall our proposal: In a judgment, one must aim to get it right reliably enough, even aptly. If so, there is then a kind of animal knowledge that does not require judgment or judgmental belief, since it can be constituted by guessing.[2] The knowledge attained by our eye-exam subject is then a sub-credal knowledge constituted by no judgment or judgmental belief.

[1] The following first sketches the treatment of the problematic found in my *Judgment and Agency* (Oxford University Press, 2015), to be substantially improved in what follows here after that.

[2] As in our example, even if the guess is not a *sheer* guess. Thus our eye-exam subject is not just making a pure guess, as is the contestant of our example. Rather, he is trying to draw on his visual experience as he concentrates and squints, so as to make as competent and as apt an alethic affirmation as he can muster. But consider the fact that he is aiming to affirm as aptly as he can do so. That is still not enough to lift his alethic affirmation above a guess, a guess as educated as he can make it, but still a guess. When his performance rises above guessing as he moves up the rows, he changes in two ways that seem to make the relevant difference. He acquires steadily more confidence as he ascends, and, second, that confidence enables him to have a guiding thought that now he *would (or would very likely)* get it right if he did affirm alethically. Thus we will think of judgment as an alethic affirmation that is accompanied by those two factors of confidence and guidance.

Epistemic Explanations: A Theory of Telic Normativity, and What it Explains. Ernest Sosa, Oxford University Press (2021). © Ernest Sosa. DOI: 10.1093/oso/9780198856467.003.0008

Sub-credal animal knowledge requires apt alethic affirmation, but judgment aims not just at success but at apt success. To succeed with *this* aim, as one affirms, it is required that one be able to tell that one *would* then get it right aptly (or at least that one *would likely enough* get it right aptly). The judgmental knower must have a second-order grasp—an affirmative thought or presupposition—that her first-order affirmation would then be apt (or would very likely be apt, or some such thought that might enable enhanced guidance).

2. Suppose your gauge might just as easily be malfunctioning now as not. It is just random: *not* because *such gauges* suffer systematically from that deficiency, nor even because *this particular gauge* suffers generally from that deficiency; it is random only because a prankster happens to be in the vicinity and might as easily tamper with it as not. Indeed, the outcome is decided by a coin flip (and, although the presence of such a prankster anywhere on earth is most improbable, there he is anyhow). Can you then know the gauge reading to be correct? Can you know this, if in fact the prankster does not and will not intervene, and if the gauge is functioning perfectly well, as it normally does? Some of us would say that you *can* know, that you can know based on the gauge's reading.

Compare the three-point shot that is scored only because by luck there is *not* a power lapse and the lights do *not* dim at the very moment when the player shoots, spoiling the shot. Plausibly is then apt but not *fully* apt, since the likelihood of a power lapse makes it impossible for the player to know *that* her shot *would* then be apt. If so, her shot is apt without being aptly apt.[3]

B. Knowledge and Competence, Global versus Local

1. People know their surroundings through perception. How well does this thesis fare under skeptical scrutiny? How does it fare under telic epistemology?

[3] This was indeed our first approximation, but will be superseded in the present text through appeal to "default assumptions."

Barney is often thought to lose his relevant competence upon entering fake-barn country. He is thought to be in no position reliably to sort barns from the mere façades that he might so easily be viewing instead. Thus situated, he has no such competence, and hence cannot manifest any such in believing that he sees a real barn. If we agreed that Barney would lose his relevant competence because of the many nearby fakes, then our proposed analysis would save the apt belief account of knowledge. If Barney's belief is *not* apt, this saves the account, even for those who share the intuition that he does not really know.

2. In considering this reaction—that Barney falls short *both* of aptness *and* of knowledge—we need to consider competences, a special case of dispositions. These are dispositions to succeed if one tries, hosted therefore by goal-directed beings.

A competence, then, is a certain sort of disposition to succeed in a given domain. Consider the competences of an athlete, those of a performance artist, those of a surgeon, etc. These are all dispositions to succeed reliably enough. Athletic domains make it clear, however, that the required reliability can fall well below 50 percent. What is required is only that, upon trying, the agent would succeed reliably *enough*. The required rate of success is relativized, moreover, to parameters of situation and shape. How low the success rate falls for a drunk batter, or one who swings in dim twilight, is irrelevant to his possession of the relevant competence. What determines these parameters of appropriateness? For competences involved in conventional domains—performance arts, sports, games—it is social interest that does so. Here we may have a kind of quantifier restriction like that which determines that there is "nothing" in a box full of air. There is nothing *within the limits set by our interests*, which exclude air (at least normally, though exceptional situations are easily imaginable).

The *innermost* competence to hit baseballs, the skill, is an ability retained even when drunk and in the dark, so long as the batter's internal constitution would yield success reliably enough in the relevant conditions and situations, with the batter sober and the lights on. Given the required constitution, involving his brain and nervous system, his muscles, etc., the batter retains his *inner* competence in the dark, *provided* he is sober, and more generally in good enough shape. However, the *complete* distal competence of a batter requires not only the skill and the inner competence, but also an appropriate situation, with enough light, not too much wind, etc.[4]

3. That suggests the following difference between Norma, the normally situated perceiver, and Barney, who might so easily be fooled by a fake.

> Barney has animal knowledge only and falls short of reflective knowledge. In contrast, Norma has knowledge on both levels, both the animal and the reflective.

Why so? Is it because Norma *has*, while Barney *lacks*, the meta-competence required for reflective knowledge and for knowledge full well?

That is the answer we've been considering, but, despite its attraction, we shall find it to be unacceptable.

C. Grades of Knowledge

1. The foregoing invokes the animal–reflective distinction in a way that seems initially helpful (*seems* so, in enabling us to distinguish between Norma and Barney).

[4] The notion of an "innermost" disposition presupposes some nesting dimension. Thus, the complete SkShSi archery disposition may be said to "nest" the inner disposition (composed of skill + shape), which can remain even if the situational Si is lost, and the SkSh disposition may similarly be said to "nest" the innermost disposition (the skill), which can remain even if both the inner (SkSh) and the (SkShSi) disposition are lost. It remains to be seen whether that nesting dimension corresponds to a spatial dimension on which the brain is central, and the rest of the nervous system is less central, where the brain+nervous system is itself more central than is the brain+nervous-system+external-situation. Maybe we should think of it that way. I am myself inclined to do so, but it is not perfectly clear that we must or even that we should do so. This would seem to depend on how holistic the relevant action of the brain itself is, for one thing, and on what can go on in the space between the most relevant component items of the brain (at the most basic level? Neurons?). Can there be some substance in those spaces whose presence counts as part of the relevant "shape"? Here that will remain an open question.

For another speculative tack, perhaps our nesting dimension is not spatial at all; perhaps it is rather a dimension of causal power or explanatory importance, where even if there is that substance between the neurons (or the like) it plays a more adventitious role in explaining the pertinent behavior (hitting archery targets, as it might be) than do the items that more stably seat the archer's skill within their brain.

However, compare Norm and Abnor. Norm is again a normal perceiver who can know the layout of his environment through perception. Abnor, on the other hand, is in a mental ward where they have recently begun mental disability experiments. On any given day, when he awakens, he might have been deprived of any or all of his various epistemic competences. These come in two main sorts worth distinguishing as follows, with the first sort divided into three subcases:

a. *Non-global* competences to host experiences or seemings. These are all reliable enough dispositions to get it right with a certain propositional content.
   i. *Derived* competences. These are attained by the agent through more basic competences, as when one learns of the reliability of a fuel gauge either through testimony or through tests independent of that gauge's readings. One thus attains a competence to tell how full the tank is (by trusting the gauge).
   ii. Underived *modular* competences. These deliver experiences or seemings with propositional content, as when it perceptually seems as if one faces something shaped or colored a certain way. Unlike derived competences, however, *these modular competences* are not acquired through the use of more basic competences.
   iii. *Basic central-processing* competences. These competences reliably enough yield all-things-considered seemings, whether occurrent or implicit.
b. *Global* epistemic competence. By this I mean basic judgment- or belief-forming competence. This is the competence we exercise in determining how to judge, or what to judgmentally believe, *all things considered*, whether we do so through explicit pondering or just functionally and subconsciously. Almost anything could be relevant to any question we might consider, given proper stage-setting. Such holistic competence is global in that it is required in properly making *any* judgment or forming *any* belief.[5]

[5] It is no doubt an empirical issue whether there is a single such global judgment- and belief-forming human competence. Indeed, it seems an empirical question whether there are *any* such global competences.

2. Compare now two ways in which Abnor could be affected on any given morning as he wakes up in his mental ward.

a. He might be disabled with respect to one or another of his non-global competences, whether derived, modular, or basic central processing. And it might or might not be that he *would* have signs of such disability. How might this affect his cognitive position? Suppose Abnor might easily have been thus disabled, with *no tell-tale signs*. Is it not then in doubt that he really knows? Is it not doubtful that one can know by trusting the deliverances of a cognitive mechanism that might so easily have been *undetectably* faulty?
b. There is anyhow a second way in which Abnor might be affected that morning. His *global* epistemic competence could be totally disabled. Now there will be *no* way for him to take properly into account any tell-tale signs in his experience. By hypothesis, his competence to form such judgments has been disabled.[6]

3. Recall how Austin and Descartes try to deal with the dream scenario. Their strategy highlights a certain quality of dreaminess in our dreams, and a certain incoherence, which are signs that should prompt caution. However, totally dreaming precludes the thinker's proper use of any signs in his situation. So, how are we to deal with the possibility that one is disabled by dreaming, that one's current perceptual beliefs are inapt

Fortunately, the argument here does not depend essentially on any contrary assumption. The argument could be made regardless, at the cost of some complication. Even if there are no such global competences, we can still define a *minimal set of "fundamental" judgment-making or belief-forming competences* as follows. These would be the competences in a set such that *any* proper making of a judgment or forming of a belief would require one or more of the competences in the set, such that no proper subset of that set has that property. Call the members of such a set "fundamental" competences. Our argument in the main text can now proceed in terms of such fundamental competences, with no commitment to the existence of any global, basic ones.

[6] Suppose we wish to make our argument without assuming that there is any unique, basic, global judgment- and belief-forming competence. Then we can replace entry b with the following: "A second way in which Simon might be affected on a given morning is through the disabling of *all* his *fundamental* competences. Now the sort of defense used by Austin and Descartes seems unavailable. For, there is now *no* way for the subject competently to exploit any tell-tale signs that might be present in his experience. By hypothesis *all* of his fundamental competences have been disabled. Required in reaching any proper judgment or belief, however, is always the operation of at least one of these competences.

in *that* way? Shall we treat this "shape (inner condition)" component of our epistemic competence analogously to how we have treated its situational element? We would then need to require that if one were in bad shape that way, if one were so disabled, one would have signs of that fact. The mere danger of being ill situated need not deprive us of competent, apt belief that we are not ill situated. At least that is so *provided* we would have signs of our bad situation. Similarly, perhaps the mere danger of being in bad shape need not deprive us of competent, apt belief that we are not in bad shape, provided we would have signs of our being disabled that way.

Suppose there *would* be signs of our bad condition. Even so, if we were *globally* disabled, we would lose our ability to respond properly to those signs. That they would be there to be perceived is hence not enough. If too easily we might now be disabled so as to form our perceptual judgments *in*competently, that still puts in doubt our current perceptual knowledge.

4. Here is the upshot so far. Suppose we could too easily have been globally disabled (insane or totally dreaming, as Descartes imagines). Such disability would have prevented us from *properly* forming any judgment on whether we were thus disabled. It then helps little that if we were so disabled, there would be signs of our disability. Even if there were such signs, we would be in no position to exploit them. If we were liable enough to suffer any such disability, therefore, it looks like we could not save the reflective standing of our perceptual beliefs. We could not be confident that we retained our first-order competences. We could not properly guide our trust by relying on whether we perceived any tell-tale signs, those that would reveal the absence of the required competences.

Would we *fall short*, however, merely because we would be unable to discern such disability? Note well: No one could tell that he was thus, *globally*, disabled. To deplore our lack of such ability seems thus almost as bad as ruing our inability to find the barber who shaves all and only the non-self-shavers.[7]

[7] They are not *exactly* as bad, because of a *de re–de dicto* distinction that distinguishes them.

We humans can know things through our global epistemic good judgment. As we have seen, it cannot be required for this that we would be able to tell *that* we were globally disabled, *supposing* we were. Instead it may suffice that we simply *avoid* such disability, even if we do so through epistemic luck. Or perhaps we need at least to avoid it *safely*? We shall return to this.

5. Fortunately, the skeptic is in no position to *deny* that we enjoy such luck. The most he can say is that we *might* lack it, might-*metaphysically* lack it, and partly for that reason might-epistemically lack it. But, as we have seen, the fact that we might-metaphysically lack our good constitution does not imply that we fall short epistemically, that our relevant beliefs are inapt. Nor can it be required, not plausibly, that in order for us to perform up to epistemic standard we must fulfill a condition that we can easily see to be inevitably unfulfillable. Falling short of that obviously impossible standard is no real shortcoming.

6. We have distinguished between animal knowledge, or apt (alethic) affirmation, and reflective knowledge, or apt affirmation aptly noted. And our distinction yields the following result concerning our two characters: Norm, the normal perceiver; and Abnor, the mental ward patient. Whereas Norm has both animal and reflective perceptual knowledge, Abnor's knowledge, by contrast, may not rise above the animal level.

If Abnor's competence under threat is *non-global*, he then falls short of reflective knowledge *unless* he *would* be tipped off if that competence were absent, and would be in a position to make proper use of the tip. And this applies to both his epistemic *shape* and his epistemic *situation*. We can know through a certain competence only if we would be tipped off to our lack of the constitutive appropriate situation and also to our lack of the constitutive appropriate shape, while in a position to make use of the tip. (We shall return to this.)

7. What if it is our *global* competence that is under threat? Once the competence under threat is global, then we can attain reflective knowledge through that competence even when we'd have *no* exploitable signs of its absence. Global competence can give knowledge to someone

unable to exploit any signs of its absence *even if it could very easily have been absent*. You can still know even then, arguably, since you would not reasonably fall short by lacking the ability to tell that the competence was missing. You would obviously, necessarily, lack any such ability, since, being global, the competence in question would be *required* for you to be able to tell that it was *missing*.

Can we know such a competence to be present when it is present just by luck? Why not allow that we do "know" such a competence to be present simply by trusting that it is present, even if its absence could not possibly be discerned, and even if its presence is actual but *not* safe? Yet that is exactly what Descartes questions by seriously entertaining his third skeptical scenario, where we are creatures of a lesser creator, or even of a chance sequence of events. His considered response in the remainder of his *Meditations* is that we could not possibly have lacked the required global competence, given that we are children of the true, epistemically benevolent divinity.

However, if Descartes is wrong to require such *necessary security* for our knowledge, then we *might* indeed possess a basic competence by luck, without *this* sort of luck spoiling the epistemic efficacy of that competence.

And why not? Why not suppose that we could indeed know ourselves to be in possession of such a global competence, through essential reliance on the exercise of that very competence, even if we possess it only contingently, and might even *easily* have lacked it? This would seem rather like affirming that we can know ourselves to be conscious or alive despite our consciousness or survival being only contingent and even in grave danger. After all, if we were knocked unconscious or dead we could not then exploit any signs so as to know our sad fate.

True, when unconscious or dead we can form no judgments or beliefs whatsoever. And this is not necessarily so when we just lose a global competence. By losing such a competence we are perhaps deprived of the ability to form judgments or beliefs *properly*, but we do not necessarily lose the ability to form them at all. Despite this important difference, however, it remains plausible in all three cases that we cannot appropriately require for proper attainment something that is obviously, *necessarily* unattainable.

We are not deprived of knowledge by a mere danger to our global competence that we could not possibly be competent to ward against. On the contrary, if the danger is one that no rational being could possibly forestall, then it is through no fault or flaw that we lack the competence to do so. When we take ourselves to have the global competence, we do so with no flaw or shortfall, even if we would be powerless to respond properly to its absence. This means that we could after all believe competently that we have that global competence. We could do so even if inevitably unresponsive to its absence, and even when it might easily have been absent. (Compare: We can know ourselves to be conscious even if we would have been unable to tell that we were unconscious if that is how things had turned out. True, there is again this important difference: one could not have thought flawlessly that one was not conscious. But it still seems incorrect to fault a thinker for failing to attain competent awareness that his global competence was missing when it was indeed missing.)

8. Might this sort of solution to the problem of global disability be extensible to the case where the disability is local rather than global?

Do we really know that we are not very drunk only if *were we very drunk we would be able to exploit signs of our condition* so as to believe correctly? That seems doubtful. What shall we say about a non-global competence that requires sobriety? What shall we say when we depend essentially on such a competence although it might easily have been missing through heavy drinking?

A non-global epistemic competence can require a condition that we might easily have lacked or might easily lack. Sufficient sobriety is one such condition. We know we're not extremely drunk when we have tell-tale signs of sobriety while sober enough to take them properly into account. And this seems unaffected by how easily we might have been too drunk, *even* if *had* we been too drunk we *could not* have properly exploited any pertinent signs of our sad state. That inability seems no flaw or shortfall of ours, as things stand when we are quite sober. On this tack, we can extend our treatment of globally required competences to cover also local competences whose lack one could not possibly discern.

True, the impossibility of telling that we are extremely drunk, when that is our state, is not now logical or metaphysical. Someone could be extremely drunk while still able to tell that he is. Even if that is exceptional, it is not metaphysically impossible.

Still the following similarity remains. On one side of the similarity stand the cases where the impossibility is *logical or metaphysical*; on the other side are the cases where it is only *practically* impossible, or even just extremely difficult, to discern one's unfortunate condition. The cases might still be similar in the following respect: in none of them is there any epistemic fault or flaw that can be charged against the thinker for his failure to grasp the true nature of his condition. When extremely drunk one is deprived of full epistemic competence. So, if one might easily have been extremely drunk, then one might easily have been epistemically incompetent, including incompetence to discern one's own incompetence. But that one might easily have been incompetent does not entail that one is in fact incompetent, so long as one is perfectly sober.

9. There is however a further twist.

Is it not part of one's epistemic competence to avoid incompetence through excessive drink? If so, why not require for true knowledge that the believer get it right through deep enough competence, which would include the competence to avoid a disabling stupor. If too easily one might now have been forming one's belief while in that bad condition, *and if one would so easily have been in that condition through epistemic negligence*, then even at present one fails to get it right in a way that manifests sufficient epistemic competence. One could too easily have affirmed incorrectly, or at least inaptly, given how easily one could have been impaired unawares and indeed unknowably. Here again luck would enter in a way that blocks relevant competence, and in a way that blocks the attributability of that success to competence and not to luck.

This tack distinguishes two cases in which one falls into incompetence through lacking either the *condition* or the *constitution* required for complete competence.

In one case the loss lies beyond one's ability to control, or in some other way would *not* be due to negligence. Lack of global competence is an extreme case of that sort. But there are also less extreme cases. Falling asleep and entering a state of total dreaming is one. When one nightly enters such a state, this is not normally because of negligence.

A second way of losing one's relevant shape or constitution *might indeed* involve negligence on one's part, as when one is disabled through an excess of drink that one could easily enough have avoided.

10. So we have found ways in which one's competence might be in danger.

First, one might easily lose the appropriate *situation* required for a first-order competence. If one's situation is thus in danger, then one can know reflectively through that competence only if one has the second-order competence required for knowing that the first-order competence is present. Normally one will have that second-order competence only if one is so situated on the second order that one would have signs of the absence of the first-order competence, signs that one could then exploit competently in deciding whether one has that first-order competence.

Second, one might easily lose a *global* competence, one required for *any* epistemically proper judgment. Of course, one cannot possibly discern the loss of that competence. Accordingly, it cannot be required that one would be positioned to discern its loss. No one could be negligent simply because they would not be positioned to discern the loss of such a competence. And this remains so even if in fact one is in high danger of losing it. No matter how fragile that global competence might be, then, so long as it is in fact present, it can be properly manifest in the formation and in the accuracy of one's beliefs. This is akin to the fact that one can know oneself to be conscious even if one might very easily have been (undetectably) unconscious.

Third, one might easily lose a competence that is less than global. Some non-global competences depend on our being awake and alert, for example, and are subject to loss through falling asleep. But we need not be at all negligent by falling asleep (and in particular not epistemically negligent). Non-global competences that require being awake can thus be lost without negligence. These competences can therefore be manifest in apt success even if they might easily have been missing without negligence.

A further way to lose a nonglobal competence is through being negligently disabled, as by drugs or drink. If a belief and its correctness manifest a nonglobal competence, *and the deeper competence—the conscientiousness—involved in the avoidance of such negligence*, that belief can be apt, even if one *might* easily have succumbed thus to negligence. So long as one competently *does not* succumb, one can retain one's full relevant competence, which can then be manifest in the success of one's pertinent performances.

9
Reflection and Security

A. Default Assumptions

1. Human beings act in performance domains. It might be a sport, such as soccer, or a profession, such as medicine or the law. While domains normally carry risk of failure, they can vary radically in how risk affects assessment. A pure guess in a quiz show might quite properly win the prize. More often, though, we aim at *apt* success, through corresponding competence, not just by luck. An oncologist would not make a diagnosis just by guessing.

Even when we aim at aptness rather than luck, however, that may still allow or even require default assumptions that are unsafe and not known to be true. Thus, it is part of the competence of nighttime athletes to focus on their athletic performance, while ignoring whether the lights might fail. It is part of athletic competence to assume by default the satisfaction of background conditions like the stability of the lights.

An athlete can properly assume by default that the lights will stay on, as he considers whether to run for a fly ball, or to hit a crosscourt forehand, and he will attain *full credit* even if success is attained essentially by luck, since only by luck do the lights stay on. What is more, even while *knowing* the lights to be fragile, the athlete can still rely on the assumption that they will not fail. No matter how unsafe his performance may be, no matter how likely it may be that the lights will fail, the performance can be fully apt, even when the risk is *known* to the agent.

Compare what pilots can take for granted without negligence. Pilots must run through their check list prior to takeoff, but they need not kick the tires. They can trust others on the airline staff to have checked the tires. Still, it is not only what pilots know with safety that they can trust without negligence to be true. For example, they might trust without

Epistemic Explanations: A Theory of Telic Normativity, and What it Explains. Ernest Sosa, Oxford University Press (2021). © Ernest Sosa. DOI:10.1093/oso/9780198856467.003.0009

negligence that no terrorism is in the offing even when it is a near certainty. Even if the terrorist will miss the flight, so that disaster will be avoided, consider the high probability of a terrorist on that flight. That is still a dire danger faced by the pilot as he prepares to take off. But no such danger can lower the quality of that pilot's performance, nor reduce in the slightest the credit earned for piloting the plane to its destination. Not all risks of failure bear on quality of performance.

However, the pilot's performance would *not* have retained that high quality if the pilot had *known* of the highly credible threat of imminent terrorism, so that he should have aborted the flight.

An athlete can properly assume by default that the lights will stay on, as he considers whether to run for a fly ball, or to hit a crosscourt forehand, and he will attain *full credit* even if success is essentially by luck, since only by luck do the lights stay on. What is more, even while *knowing* the lights to be fragile, the athlete can still rely on the assumption that they will not fail. No matter how unsafe his performance may be, no matter how likely it may be that the lights will fail, the performance can be fully apt, even when the risk is known to the agent.

2. By contrast, walkers outside the stadium in a dangerous neighborhood cannot assume by default the truth of that same proposition, that the lights will not fail.

Yes, if they attempt to walk harmlessly, while assuming that the lights will stay on, and if this assumption turns out by luck to be true, walkers do attain the desired success of their walk. Unlike the fielder's catch, however, unlike the winning shot in nighttime tennis, such walker success is owed excessively to the luck that the lights stay on. When we walk at night in a neighborhood that turns unsafe in the dark, we cannot just assume by default that the lights will not fail. Here we do seem guilty of negligence or recklessness if we ignore that possibility, so that not even implicitly do we give it any weight. If we are credibly warned, we must heed the warning. Ignoring such warning will forfeit full credit for the walk's success.

In sharp contrast, the credit for a great catch is undiminished when the fielder ignores a warning about the fragile lights.

If the warning is ignored, the walker manifests *insufficient* competence of the sort required in order to own creditably the success of their walk. And once the safety of the walk manifests *insufficient* competence, its attainment cannot be apt (cannot manifest *sufficient* competence), and is hence not properly creditable to the agent.

3. In our telic framework, agents can assume by default the satisfaction of background conditions. Even when its satisfaction is required for the presence of a corresponding competence, a *background* condition can obtain *unsafely*, with no detriment to the domain-internal performance of an agent who assumes by default that it obtains, without knowing that it does. Agents sometimes risk the failure of a background condition, but running *that* sort of risk affects neither the quality of the agent's domain-internal performance, nor the credit earned for its success.

4. Epistemology's main domain is that of attempts to get it right aptly, along with proper storage of such beliefs. Thus, consider risk that one's epistemic competence may be diminished or lost *through failure of background conditions*. Such risk need not affect the epistemic quality of our attempts to get it right, nor the credit we earn for their success, and in particular need not affect whether we know. The risk that does affect quality and creditability of success is risk inversely proportional to degree of competence. *Such* high risk is tantamount to low competence, which surely does affect quality of performance. Creditable achievement requires success by competence, not by a fluke.

A similar conclusion may be drawn about radical skeptical scenarios. Conscientiously enough, without negligence or recklessness, we normally assume ourselves to be free of skeptical scenarios. And this assumption is proper even on the rare occasions when it is true but not known to be true and even quite unsafe.

5. Urgent, credible threats can still be harmless to quality of performance in domains *properly sealed* against external values.

What does such "proper sealing" amount to? Not that the domain just lays it down that one can properly disregard external threats *all things considered*. The point is *rather* the following.

Suppose one continues to make domain-internal attempts while dismissing all such threats and dangers, dismissing them by default assumption. One's continuing attempts may then be *unwise* in the extreme, while still attaining the heights of domain-internal quality, unaffected by the risks incurred.

B. Two Sorts of Performance Domains: the Ludic versus the Practical and Non-Ludic

1. Physical safety and well-being are basic, generally valued goods beyond any game or sport.[1] Ordinary domains of praxis within which we pursue such generally valued goods should be distinguished from domains with internal constitutive goods, many of them ludic, such as the many sports that obsess and delight contemporary culture.

However, a *non*-ludic domain ordered around some objective good can still be sealed off in the way of *ludic* domains such as baseball. Successful piloting of a plane to its destination is fully creditable even if based on a mere default assumption that the plane will not be blown up by a terrorist, an assumption that is *in fact* both unsafe and not known to be true.

Another example: the domains of farming, where people aim for good crops. Actions in these domains can be sealed off, so it is not *only* ludic domains that are properly sealed off for telic assessment. The performance of a farmer can also be assessed telically in abstraction from any pragmatic factors that may also bear on its *overall* assessment.

Knowledge is a valuable human commodity, as is food. Its production is of great interest to human communities, as is the production of food. And such pursuit is properly governed by practices relevant to corresponding telic assessment, whether what we harvest is food, or, alternatively, knowledge.

2. Consider a fielder's competence on a given occasion to perform well in the outfield by making catches. Such competence is determined by the athlete's pertinent Situation, Shape, and Skill. Each of these involves the satisfaction of certain conditions. One situational requirement in baseball, for example, is that the field remain sufficiently well lit.

[1] Ludic comes from the Latin; it and its cognates apply to play, as in games or sports.

In a night game, if the lights are nearly certain to fail imminently, a fielder's all-out running attempt is almost sure to fail. Yet the fielder's knowing this to be so has zero effect on the aptness and the full aptness of his great catch, provided he still acts with proper sensitivity to the factors that do matter, such as the trajectory of the ball above him, along with his tracking ability and foot speed. The fielder's taking such factors into account is crucial to the full aptness of his attempt. Factors like these he cannot neglect to consider at least quickly and implicitly. He would be negligent if he ignored them, and might be reckless if he assigned them improper weight.

By contrast, the fragility of the lights he can ignore or dismiss with no domain-internal negligence or recklessness. His great catch is equally admired and credited, as a baseball catch, despite the lights' being fragile, and even despite his knowing them to be fragile.

3. Take the risk recklessly dismissed by a basketball player who sinks a basket from the opposite end of the court when there was plenty of time to dribble or pass instead. That success (so bittersweet, certainly to the coach) will hardly earn full, unalloyed credit. The coach will not be pleased with the play selection. But does that affect the quality of the *shot*?

Well, the shot was poorly selected, too risky, dumb, *outrageous* really. The coach will be unhappy with the player, and specifically with those qualities of the shot itself. The shot is deplorable because poorly chosen, much worse than many easily available alternatives. *Its guiding intention is constitutive of the intentional action which is that shot itself.* And the quality of that intention is surely dependent on the agent's operative rationale. If the rationale is bad, that rubs off on the quality of that intention, and it rubs off in turn on the quality of the intentional action that is the shot itself, so that even if the shot succeeds, it will not be sufficiently through the quality of performance that guides the attempt, and it will have limited athletic worth creditable to the agent.

That player's rationale is *not* bad by being prudentially or morally or aesthetically bad. Nor is it even necessarily bad *all things considered.* All these respects of badness would be irrelevant to the *athletic* quality of that shot, and more specifically to its *basketball* athletic quality. As a basketball performance, the shot is poorly selected, too risky, dumb, even outrageous. The *basketball* rationale that motivates the choice and intention to so shoot is an awful rationale, and it is the quality of that basketball rationale that rubs off on the basketball choice and intention, and rubs off in turn on the basketball action essentially constituted by that basketball choice and intention.

4. A distinction should be drawn here, one that will prove helpful in epistemology. We should distinguish the *selection* quality of an attempt from its *execution* quality. Take that long shot so poorly selected given the far better available basketball alternatives. That shot itself has low quality in respect of its selection. But its execution may have been superb nonetheless, in that the degree of shooting competence exercised from that distance may have topped the scale, so that the shot's success manifested outstanding competence.

Compare a tiebreaker second serve with ad out in a tennis match tied at two sets each. Losing that service point will lose the match. Yet the server serves a flat serve at top speed, foolishly taking enormous risk. If that serve is a superb ace, its execution quality is then extremely high while its selection quality is extremely low.

Turning to epistemology, consider an insightful theoretician whose educated guess gets it right on a question that has defeated many others over many years. The guess may earn kudos for eventually paying off, and for being a guess that had not occurred to anyone, and would not have occurred to anyone else. So the guess attained excellence in its accuracy, even despite how risky it may have been, as the evidence was just not there in sufficient quantity and weight to make it a successful judgment by normal standards, nor by normal standards of the expertise proper to the pertinent domain of knowledge, whether it be one of a medical doctor, or an attorney, or a detective, or a theoretical scientist.

Of course, the thinker involved may not have been aiming for any such competence of expertise. And yet (by hypothesis) their alethic affirmation was not a sheer guess either. Their aim was to render an educated guess that might pay off with eventual demonstrated knowledge. So, their alethic affirmation was a "guess" by the pertinent standards of expertise, but it was not a sheer guess. The aim was not simply truth with an arbitrary or nearly arbitrary shot in the dark. The aim was rather to hit the mark with some degree of reliability, even the limited degree then available to that thinker, which may nonetheless have topped the scale for the relevant set of actual or potential inquirers. On that particular issue within its pertinent domain, the standards for admirable, creditable attainment may have been similar to the standards of skillful attainment with a difficult athletic shot. The pertinent degree of reliability for an excellent home run hitter in baseball or an outstanding striker in soccer or three-point shooter in basketball may lie far below 50 percent, and yet their successful shots are fully admirable and creditable to them.

This outcome is in some tension with our telic account of ordinary knowledge as apt judgment or belief. For, consider our insightful thinker, and the pertinent degree of competence that lies behind their getting it right on the difficult question to which they find the right answer. By hypothesis they fall far short of the standards required for knowledge, whether expert or even ordinary. So, they do not attain *that degree or sort of aptness.* And yet their alethic affirmation, as they offer an answer to the difficult question addressed, is not a sheer guess. Accordingly, they are aiming not *just* to get it right through an arbitrary guess, as it might be. They are aiming for some degree of aptness, some degree lying above the nil degree of a sheer guess, even if below the higher degree required for expert or even ordinary knowledge. We are now in the vicinity of the *educated, insightful "guess."*

The tension with our TVE account of knowledge may now be relieved by recognizing the standing of alethic affirmations backed by "enough" competence for storage, whether commonsense storage or expert storage. Information thus stored is worthy of sheer deference and of other special treatment that goes with accepted expert knowledge. The educated "guess" of the insightful thinker (detective, doctor, theoretician, etc.) certainly does not fully attain that sort of standing, even if it does attain an aptness of alethic affirmation of its own. This is the aptness of the educated guess that can properly guide inquiry, the sort of inquiry that may eventually enable the elevation from educated guess to real knowledge.

5. Unlike the basketball shot so poorly selected from across the whole court when there was no time pressure, many other athletic attempts involve both high risk and great creditable accomplishment. In

basketball, there's the three-point score from near mid-court by the pure shooter under pressure from the clock and from defenders. In tennis there's a player running to make a nearly impossible return of a lob over their head at the net. Despite how high the risk of failure is, they properly run that risk given the circumstances and the great importance of that point.[2]

That player takes account of two sorts of risk. There is the salient risk of not returning the ball because of the extremely high probability that the topspin lob will elude them. And there is the background risk that the lights will go out, as they are extremely likely to do. The first sort of risk is taken into account, as the player knows that they are taking that risk, while proper tennis competence requires the player to run in any case. What about the lights? Isn't the player again just acting despite knowledge of a certain risk, where his competence requires that he dismiss the risk. Why say that the first risk concerns a salient condition whereas the second risk concerns a *mere* background condition?

Salient conditions are those that agents must feed into their cost–benefit analysis, as they calculate which of the options before them is to be opted for. That is how it is for the basketball shooter under time pressure near the end of a game. That is how it is for the tennis player who must scramble back despite how unlikely success may be given the heavy topspin on that low lob overhead.[3]

[2] A better example, for those who know baseball, is that of the runner on third base who must run for home when an easy fly ball is hit to an awaiting fielder for an extremely probable easy out. The runner must run even if his chance of scoring is nearly nil, since the out is so easy. The point is that if the fielder somehow muffs the play, then the runner will score the winning run. So, the runner must run for home plate despite awareness that his risk of failure in that attempt to score is extremely high.

That runner takes account of two sorts of risk. There is the salient risk of not scoring because of the extremely high probability that the easy fly ball will be caught. And there is the background risk that the lights will go out, as they are extremely likely to do. The first sort of risk is taken into account, as the player knows that they are taking that risk, while proper baseball competence requires running in any case. What about the lights? Isn't the player again just acting despite knowledge of a certain risk, where his competence requires that he dismiss the risk. Why say that the first risk concerns a salient condition whereas the second risk concerns a background condition? We next take this up in the main text.

[3] And that is how it is for a baseball runner on third as the easy fly ball is hit right to an opposing fielder, even if here cost–benefit analysis yields the result that no change in the risk will affect the choice of whether to run for the score or not.

Is it like that for the condition of the lights and the role of this in the assessment of athletic performance? The condition of the lights *is* a condition that can enter into the conscious cost–benefit analysis of *whether to continue playing the sport on that occasion*. It is properly a part of cost–benefit analysis of whether to continue playing. And that decision can be properly assessed on the basis of the various factors relevant to it. However, the quality of that decision and of the players' continuing play may vary enormously, while that variation has zero bearing on the quality of the various domain-internal plays by the players.

6. Two further distinctions should be drawn as we turn our focus more fully to epistemology. First is one that derives from the bearing of the diachronic and the social for epistemology. It is these factors—the diachronic and the social—that explain the need for a threshold of competence above which we have competence *enough*. Enough for what? Enough, I submit, for storage. We properly need not store the evidential support enjoyed by our beliefs when they are initially acquired, nor any other features that may bear on such initial acquisition and its attendant degree of reliability. Soon after the belief's addition to our background knowledge, what we have may be just the belief itself, absent the factors that supported its initial acquisition. Such beliefs might later, over time, have bearing on a huge variety of potential decisions and actions, individual or collective. Others, and also our later selves, will need to presuppose that some minimal level of reliability will be attained by taking at face value the deliverances of memory and the testimony of others. This makes it proper for human communities to impose norms for belief storage, such that adherence to those norms would provide such reliability. And this works best if the requirement has the force of deontology and is not just one more factor subject to tradeoffs. So, the competence intrinsic to the epistemic domain is not just the competence to judge on normative tradeoffs generally, or to conduct cost–benefit analysis on all values that pertain in any way to the performance under consideration. Rather, in the epistemic domain we are to bracket non-epistemic considerations, and even consequentialist calculation pertaining to epistemic outcomes downstream from our judgment under consideration. The epistemic competence pertinent to knowledge is thus

a very specific competence sensitive only to how likely our judgment (belief) is to be correct (true), given the competences that we rely on in that instance.

7. An additional distinction should be drawn as we turn to epistemology. Consider a baseball fielder's competence at a given time. This requires conditions of two sorts: salient conditions and background conditions. We already took note of these briefly; let us now consider them more expansively. This will lead us to a distinctive category of "ludic knowledge," and a corresponding "ludic epistemology."

Salient conditions include the ball's trajectory and spatial relation to the fielder, along with his tracking ability and foot speed. Such *salient* conditions must fall within certain parameters and Fielder must consider all this at least quickly and implicitly. He would be negligent if he ignored it all, and might be reckless for not giving it all proper weight. This is how it matters that attempts be not just apt but fully apt, reflectively apt full well.

By contrast, lights known to be fragile can be properly ignored in assessing domain-internal credit for athletic success. Success remains about as creditable even when an athletic attempt is made in the knowledge of such risk. The condition of the lights is thus a *background* condition, one the agent can assume to hold good, even without knowing that it does, and no matter the degree of risk.

There is, however, a notable difference between domains that are ludic and those that are practical (and non-ludic).

8. Practical domains concern the pursuit of non-ludic desiderata, including objective human goods, such as the production of food and of knowledge. Like domains that are ludic, practical domains allow default assumptions. The fact that a farmer failed to grasp the extremely high danger of a massive tornado or earthquake or tsunami need not reduce the credit earned for a great crop aptly produced through lengthy exercise of farming competence. A main point here again is that the quality of the farming performance can be *unaffected* by potential disasters that never materialize, no matter how probable a threat they may have posed.

Such practical domains still differ from the ludic in one important respect. A ludic performer's performance is not affected even if they *know* of the highly probable disasters. No increase in the known probability of a relevant disaster affects the quality of a ludic performance, so long as the agent *in fact* opts to ignore the possibility of such disasters.

Not so for agents in a domain aimed at securing some objective human desideratum, such as food, or knowledge. (And physical safety, such as that required for a satisfactory walk in a bad neighborhood, belongs of course with such objective human desiderata.) Consider such an agent heedless of some danger that they in fact confront unawares. They may not be called upon to investigate and might just properly assume by default that the danger will not be realized. In this respect ludic and practical performers are alike. However, any practical performer who *knows* about the danger must take this information into account and cannot just continue to act within that domain on a default assumption that the danger will not be realized.

That is how it is for our farmers, and for other agents in pursuit of objective human goods, such as doctors, engineers, mechanics, accountants, and so on. And it now seems that way for the ordinary knower as well. Our ordinary default assumptions in epistemology seem to differ importantly from their correlates in ludic domains. Default assumptions seem less powerful in the epistemology of ordinary judgments and beliefs, and in practical domains generally. In ludic domains one can still assume by default that even *known* risks to success will not be realized. In practical domains, by contrast, such default assumptions can be proper *only if* one has no good reason to put them in doubt. No such default assumption is allowed once one knows of the pertinent risk and its severity.

9. Here we focus on the domain of ordinary, commonsense epistemology, along with domains of expertise, such as the legal, the medical, etc. But our telic virtue epistemology is *also* quite naturally receptive to the admission of *ludic* epistemic domains. And with ludic epistemic assessment would come a kind of ambivalence in the assessment of whether one "knows" that one's opponent is about to hit a tennis lob, for example, based on which one properly leans back towards one's baseline. One surely has no *ordinary* knowledge of any such thing if one knows that the lights are poised to fail with near-certainty. And yet if the lights do *not* fail, then, along with the tennis quality of one's leaning back and its

aptness, would seem to come a corresponding tennis-epistemic quality of one's judgment that the opponent is about to lob, which could even amount to a sort of knowledge of that fact.

Along with the expert knowledge proper to the various domains of human expertise, we would now have various ludic domains of knowledge as well. And *these* ludic epistemic domains would admit not only epistemic default assumptions unaffected by lack of safety, but also epistemic default assumptions unaffected by the agents' *ordinary* knowledge of such *lack* of safety. When I position myself based on knowledge of my opponent's intention to lob, I can properly so judge if I can see the intention in their approaching stance, and in so properly judging I rely on a default assumption that the lights will not fail, *and* in making that judgment one might even rely properly on such a default assumption despite one's *ordinary knowledge* of the dire condition of the lights. Ludically, the fact of this dire condition is *properly* bracketed in the heat of the game, so as to allow ludic knowledge of the opponent's intentions.

10. How could we credit a tennis player with an apt angled winning volley without also crediting them with knowledge of the position and mobility of the opponent? But then, if the shot is apt despite the known likelihood that the lights will fail, then the knowledgeable judgment or representation must surely be apt as well given its role in the aptness of that winning shot; and all this despite the fragility of the lights.

11. The plausibility of such ludic varieties of knowledge is a surprise, and the role of default assumptions in epistemology turns out to have additional surprising implications for virtue epistemology specifically. That is next on our agenda.

C. Grades of Knowledge

1. Here is a familiar sort of case, which will soon raise some unfamiliar questions:

> Simone is an ace fighter pilot with many years of experience. What she does not know is that she is now routinely subject to

> testing under simulation. While in the dark about that, she now takes herself to sit in her genuine cockpit up aloft, seeing targets down below, and she is entirely right. But most often now she is only in a simulation cockpit that she cannot distinguish from its genuine twin. Can Simone really know to be true what she correctly and justifiedly takes to be true? Many answer emphatically in the negative.

Here true beliefs seem justified while short of knowledge. Most of us would take Simone to fall short that way, as supposedly does Barney (of fake-barn lore). But there is also considerable dissent, so we may wish to take into account not only the majority's reaction but also the minority view.

My own attempt has in the past distinguished two sorts of knowledge: the animal versus the reflective. Simone can then be said to have the former without the latter. We might thus hope to maximize explanation by having it both ways. But what exactly is the difference between these two sorts of knowledge?

Animal knowledge requires that one get it right through competence rather than just luck. Reflective knowledge goes beyond that by requiring not only apt attainment of truth but also apt attainment of *aptness*. Reflective knowledge (full well) is belief whose aptness manifests the believer's *meta*-competence to attain aptness not just by luck but through competence.

Plausibly, Simone enjoys animal knowledge while falling short of reflective knowledge (full well). She has *merely* apt alethic success but lacks the higher-grade *full* aptness. Since she cannot tell whether she is in a genuine cockpit or only in the fake simulation, she seems to lack the competence to ensure that she would reliably enough get it right by trusting her perceptual input.

In retrospect that turns out to have been only a first approximation, however, as should become clear once we recognize more fully the role of default assumptions in epistemology.

2. If knowledge can be based on default assumptions, we can no longer so plausibly understand the case of Simone by distinguishing two forms of ordinary knowledge, the animal from the reflective. We can no longer

argue that she has animal knowledge about the scene below *while lacking reflective knowledge.*

In order to attain reflective knowledge, all Simone needs is apt awareness that her alethic representations about that scene below will be not just true but also apt. But what could deny her such awareness?

Our default assumptions now come to the fore. Once they are admitted, we *cannot* after all explain how it is that Simone and Barney fall short of ordinary knowledge, not in the way we had supposed. We cannot just say that what they lack is reflective knowledge (full well). Aided by default assumptions, they can attain reflective knowledge after all. Simone, for example, can no longer be said to lack knowledge that she is in the genuine cockpit, not if she has a right to default assume that if it appears to her that she is in a real cockpit, then that is where she is. What she still lacks is pertinent competence *secured* against simulation. Because of how easily she might be under simulation, the epistemic competence provided to her by the genuine cockpit is not secure; she is not securely so located, since she might so easily have been in the simulation cockpit instead.

That is why we now need to appeal, beyond reflective knowledge, to *secure* knowledge full well.

D. Security Explained

1. What is it for a belief to be thus "secure"? Is safe possession of the pertinent SSS competence required?[4] No, one can surely know even when one's competence and even one's life are in great danger. A pilot could have perfectly secure knowledge even while in great danger of being knocked out or shot to death. The sort of safety that security requires is rather the following.

> Secure Knowledge
>
> A given judgment of yours constitutes secure knowledge only if you are safe from the following fate: *losing* your pertinent

[4] My grateful thanks to John Greco for pressing this question.

> complete SSS competence to so judge while at the same time *retaining* a disposition to make or suspend judgments when you "inquire" into that question *even absent any such competence* (on a broad notion of inquiry requiring only that you take up that question, at least implicitly and representationally, if not through intentional conscious questioning or affirmation).

So, the key issue is whether too easily you might have asked yourself the very same question and even delivered the same judgment in response, *without* manifesting any SSS competence (like the one manifest in the alethic answer that you now actually give, and manifest also in the *success* of that judgment). This is a sort of safety lacked by Simone but retained by our knowledgeable pilot in dire danger of being shot dead. She lacks it because she could so easily have lacked the relevant competence to gain apt true belief through perceptual competence, since she could so easily have been under simulation.

2. And we can now admit *grades* of knowledge. *Securely knowing full well* can be recognized as a higher grade than even *reflectively knowing full well.*

Although we rarely recognize and require that higher grade in ordinary epistemic assessments, it can still affect our intuitive responses to thought experiments, as it affects Descartes's intuitive response to his third skeptical scenario, where we are creatures of a lesser creator, or of a random sequence of causes. This seems thus a higher knowledge involved in our intuitive *denial* that Simone can "really know," as she might so easily have been in the simulation cockpit rather than where she is up aloft. The higher knowledge then lacked by Simone is one that requires security, beyond aptness full well.

Take then any remaining intuition according to which the threat of simulation blocks her from *really* knowing as she views the scene below her cockpit. How is any such remaining intuition to be accommodated? No longer by denying that Simone reflectively knows full well. Perhaps rather by recognizing that what she lacks is *secure* knowledge, even when her judgment is apt (her alethic affirmation *fully* apt), so that she knows reflectively.

E. A Closer Look

1. What now distinguishes the following two Simones? And let's suppose them both to be veteran pilots whose training decades ago included simulation, but always knowingly, and never repeated until now.

> First is Simone-, who is *now* unbeknownst to her *much* more likely to be in a simulation than in a real cockpit, since unbeknownst to her she is now regularly tested under simulation.
>
> Second is Simone+, who is even now in no danger of being under simulation, having been a fully functioning fighter pilot for many years, completely safe from simulation, as she still is now, when for one thing she is not remotely a candidate for such testing.

If we are still pulled intuitively to think that Simone+ is epistemically better off than Simone-, if we still think that Simone- falls short and does not know, or does not know as well as does Simone+, it is tempting to explain that difference through the difference in security. The two differ in that Simone- might far more easily be misled by simulation, which lowers the epistemic quality of her pertinent beliefs (even if she suspects no epistemic danger, and has no reason for suspicion).

If a belief is to constitute *secure* knowledge, more is required than just that it be a belief whose correctness (truth) manifests the thinker's competence, while its aptness does so as well. Security goes beyond aptness and even beyond reflective knowledge full well.

2. But is this too facile?[5]

It does seem facile to just declare Simone to lack a sort of "knowledge," namely "secure" knowledge full well. After all, we could with equal facility declare that there is a sort of "sensitive" knowledge lacked when one believes that one's lottery ticket will lose.

[5] My grateful thanks to Chris Kelp for pressing this question.

And similarly for a "safe" knowledge that p, one requiring, of a true belief that p, just that not easily would one then believe that p without it being so that p.

We might thus try to explain both of the conflicting intuitions as to whether one knows that one's lottery ticket will lose (knows based just on the statistical facts). We would explain the pull to say that one *does not* know by appeal to "sensitive" knowledge, and the pull to say that one *does* know by appeal to "safe" knowledge. Presto!

In fact, we could even propose, on a similar basis, a notion of JTB knowledge. This is a distinctive sort of knowledge that one has, of the fact that p, when one believes that p with both truth and justification. There was a lot of intuitive support for this until its ostensible refutation by Edmund Gettier. Why not say here again that the best way to account for that intuitive support is to grant that there is a distinctive sort of knowledge, JTB knowledge, and that supporters of JTB were just responding to that?

Such facile methodology explains intuitions, and the clash of intuitions, by alleging that intuiters just focus on different real varieties of knowledge, and then voice their intuitions in ways understandable through linguistic explanations.

If these latter moves seem so facile for supposed special varieties of "sensitive" or "safe" knowledge, or even JTB knowledge, why is it less facile to propose a sort of "secure" knowledge full well.

F. What Unifies the Hierarchy?

1. Does security belong with aptness and full aptness among the metaphysical categories pertinent to epistemology? *More generally*, does security belong with aptness and full aptness among the metaphysical categories pertinent to the assessment of human performance in the many domains where humans perform telically. At the core of such assessment are questions of credit and blame, and of responsibility even of the sort that involves only *attributability* and not necessarily *accountability*.

2. Security has been given a place in our metaphysics of epistemology, so as to explain why it is that our Simone would not really know if she might so easily have been under simulation. What she would lack is a demanding sort of knowledge, *secure* knowledge full well.

But wait. Wasn't the domain of ordinary judgment and belief supposedly sealed off from external dangers in ways familiar from human performance domains generally, be they athletic, artistic, professional, etc.? How can we now be told that the dimension of security *does* affect epistemic quality of domain-internal performance, that in epistemology a belief is somehow epistemically more creditable when it is not only fully apt but also secure.

Security requires not only the *actuality* of ostensible background conditions but also their *safety*. But this clashes with the idea that a domain is sealed off from external dangers if agents can perform *flawlessly* in that domain based on a default assumption that the relevant conditions are satisfied, even when this is *far from being known* and even *far from being safe*. That's how it is for the baseball fielder with respect to the fragility of the lights. This is why in that domain the condition of the lights is a *mere background* condition.

But now we're told that it's different for our Simone, as concerns the fragility of her situation. The epistemic quality of the perceptual judgments made by Simone when aloft *is* now supposedly affected by their security, and not just by their aptness or full aptness. And isn't this to say that the domain of ordinary epistemology is not sealed off after all? Isn't it to say that the safety of Simone's situation does after all affect the epistemic quality of her domain-internal ordinary judgments and beliefs?

3. What to say? First of all: Good point! This requires attention; and here now is a start. Consider first *domain-defining* conditions: that is, any condition constitutive of performing in a given domain, in such a way that performing in that domain requires satisfying that condition. Thus, a condition for playing a given sport at night may require that one play in a lighted field. Once the lights go out and the field is *too* dark, participants are no longer in conditions where they can really play that sport. The domain of baseball, for example, requires a lighted field, one *well-enough* lit, either through natural daytime light or through artificial lighting.

When agents in a domain are ready for performance in it, they must assume that the conditions for so performing obtain. Even when they do not check to make sure, they can still assume by default that those conditions do hold; they *can properly* assume this by default in the following sense. If they do assume it by default and the conditions do hold (no matter how unsafely) then the quality of their domain-internal performances is not at all affected by any lack of safety in those conditions. Nor is the quality of their performance affected by their failing to know that those conditions hold.

Up to now, by hypothesis, our Simone has been well into a long career as an ace fighter pilot. Simulations have been entirely in her remote past as a pilot trainee. Nevertheless, if now pilots are subjected to extensive and surreptitious simulation testing, her SSS competence becomes insecure. In particular her situational S becomes highly insecure. But might she not *assume by default* that her competence is secure? Why would she be subject to a charge of negligence or recklessness, if athletes in a night game with fragile lights escape any such charge?

Yet the quality of epistemic performance by Simone does very plausibly seem to suffer. Intuitively she does not know as well as when she is safe from simulation. So, the pertinent epistemic domain seems not sealed off after all. It is not sealed off from the influence of insecurity on the quality of domain-internal performance.

Let us have a closer look.

4. Let us compare Fielder (a baseball fielder in a night game, under fragile lights) and Simone (the veteran fighter pilot who is now more often in the simulation than in the genuine cockpit). What threatens Fielder's competence also threatens his ability to perform in a proper baseball domain. His performance marred by darkness would no longer belong in a proper baseball domain. *By contrast*, whether in the simulation or up aloft, Simone *would* still issue judgments, still make affirmations aimed at aptness, even if they would be defective. Even under surreptitious simulation, she would of course still make genuine judgments.

Distinguishing that way between Fielder and Simone is in line with our account of secure knowledge. Now the *ordinary* epistemic domain is not after all sealed off from failures of security, in the way of ludic domains. In the case of epistemology, agents can fail a requirement of the sort of security explained above in our account (see “Secure Knowledge” in section D1 of this chapter). Thinkers can continue to make judgments even having lost their pertinent epistemic SSS competence. And, in respect of epistemic quality, insecure judgments fall short of those that are secure.

By contrast, the baseball fielder’s attempted catch is not downgraded because of the loss of security consequent on the fragility of the lights, nor does it even matter if the fielder knows of the fragility. Fielder and Simone differ, moreover, in a way that helps explain that distinction: Fielder loses the ability to engage in his domain when the lights go out, but Simone does not lose her corresponding ability when her danger materializes, and she is under simulation. When the lights go out, Fielder can no longer engage in baseball—in that organized athletic practice—through attempted catches, having lost the preconditions for a proper game, as does a chess player whose chess board is whisked away or painted black. By contrast, Simone can still engage in epistemic practice through genuine judgments, even when she is under simulation.

5. What of familiar skeptical scenarios like the evil demon, the brain in a vat, or the Matrix. These are radical by comparison with Simone’s simulation, which raises the question of whether the victims retain the capacity to make genuine judgments. My own preference is to answer in the negative: radical victims are unable to make genuine judgments. To me this seems plausibly connected to the metaphysical detachment from society that comes along with their detachment from their surrounding world. Human beings and human knowledge plausibly require the metaphysical connection with human community and an external world that radical scenarios would tear away from them.

Once someone is envatted, we can speak of their doings in the past tense but no longer in the present tense (not strictly). If we say that they are still there, that’s like saying that someone is being buried, at “their” burial, or that “they” did certain things in their life. Those can be proper and true things to say, while having no real existential import, in the sense of referring to someone still in existence. By hypothesis, there *was* someone so-and-so, who *did* various things, but strictly no one still in existence did those things.

In the case of a live brain in a vat of nutrients, a BIV, there is still a brain in existence, and it was formerly someone's brain, when there was someone in existence whose brain this was. But now no one has that brain, and there's no one who has mental properties through the doings of that brain. The brain has various properties, but none is or determines a property of a person, since there is no longer any person whose brain that is, so that they can be determined to have any properties through the properties of the brain.

Why not? Well, in part because there's no entity that owns the brain while playing the social and causal roles required for the constitution of a person. Advanced technology might give such a detached brain the chance eventually to underlie the existence of a person. Maybe technology would provide new ways for a brain to relate to a wider world so as to play the roles of intercommunication and collective action proper to a fully-fledged person. And that might even count as the resurrection of the dead. But, until that happens, there is no longer any person constituted by such a BIV, nor are there any doings of a person that are constituted by the doings of that BIV.

But why not? Why not rather say that the person remains so long as there is an entity that retains a unified complex set of *potentials* whose realization would ensue upon its being properly "reconnected" by surgery, by some advanced technology. All we would need for the constitution of a person is that there be such an entity.

Yes, we *could* try to think of it that way. But consider a collection of minuscule entities that constitutes that brain. Is it not true of that collection as well that it has such potentials, even when those particles are scattered? All it would take is the construction of that brain by bringing about the proper interrelation of those particles, etc.

Suppose our intuitive response is that the set of particles is just too remote from a full human being and person. Consider its potential to gain the proper connections with the external world and with external communities (actual or potential) that would enable it to acquire the causal and social roles required for the constitution of a real person. We are told that this potential is too remote for the collection of scattered particles but not too remote for the BIV.

Is that supposed to be obvious? What then is the difference that makes so crucial the supposedly greater remoteness of the scattered collection of particles, its greater remoteness from full personhood, by comparison with the lesser remoteness of the coherent BIV? Something must account for why the BIV *can* and does but the collection *cannot* constitute a person, not while scattered. There is supposedly a difference in the sorts of potentials retained by the brain once detached from the human body and the sorts of potentials retained by the collection once its member particles are scattered. But we've been offered no clue as to what sort of difference that could be.

Is it supposed that we can directly intuit that the BIV *would* metaphysically underlie a person, whereas the collection of particles would not? Why couldn't the collection underlie a person in a condition analogous to being totally asleep or otherwise unconscious?

Alternatively, why couldn't the collection of scattered particles simply no longer underlie a person, no longer constitute a human being or a person, nor even a thinker, not an actual thinker of thoughts nor even a potential one? And once we say that of the collection, why not say it of the BIV as well?

Compatibly, we could grant that there are things quasi-mental that go on in the BIV and in any higher-order being that might be constituted by the BIV. That might be like saying that there are quasi-assertoric things that go on in the performance of a play. There are many complex sayings complexly arrayed with other sayings by other players, with all the players in complex sequential interaction. Still there may be not a single assertion in the whole two-hour performance.

Similarly, there might be lots of quasi-thoughts by the BIV (or by any higher-order entity constituted by that BIV), without a single real assertoric thought in the whole lot. But why? Well, first: why not? Is such metaphysical truth supposed to be open to the bare eye of the mind just straightforwardly as is the presence of hands to competent visual perception?

And what do we lose, really, if we take another path, if we say that to us it seems no less obvious, or no more unobvious, that a BIV is no real thinker? What if we find it plausible that real thinking requires proper insertion into a larger social world involving insertion in an external world with channels through which we gain access not only to hands and fires but also to other minds, for interaction and collective action?[6]

What do we lose, really, if we deny that a BIV can be a proper, real thinker? Well, one thing we seem to lose is radical skeptical scenarios, such as that of the BIV, and, by similar reasoning, others as well, such as that of the Evil Demon, and that of the Matrix. But are these things we really want? Or is their loss part of the therapy that might give us proper intellectual peace?[7]

6. All of that being so, should we conclude that the commonsense, ordinary epistemic domain is a ludic domain? Is that how we can properly ignore radical skeptical scenarios? Is our default dismissal of such scenarios quite like the fielder's dismissal of the possibility that the lights might fail? True, these dismissals *are* similar, and have been argued to have a similar basis. The basis in each case is that if the truth that we assume by default to be true were false instead, that would deprive us of the ability to perform in the relevant domain. Thus, the failure of the lights in the night game would block us from being able to make baseball plays, such as attempted catches. Similarly, our being envatted, or Matrixed, or victimized by an Evil Demon, would block us from making proper judgments, or so they would by the suggestion floated above.

That being so, the ordinary epistemic domain is then strikingly similar to ludic domains, as we have seen. But the respects of similarity do not suffice to entail that the ordinary epistemic domain *is* itself just a ludic domain. Epistemic domains *can* indeed be ludic, as is the epistemic subdomain of crossword puzzles. But when the successful pursuit of

[6] True, we need to distinguish the isolation of the BIV from that of Robinson Crusoe. How that might best be done will here remain an open question. (Notably, the *sort* of isolation suffered by R. C. differs just in degree from that suffered regularly by a normal city dweller. Humans are detached routinely from others, but brains are not.)

[7] This response to radical skepticism is notably similar to the approach to dream skepticism in "Dreams and Philosophy," published in the *APA Proceedings* as my Presidential Address of 2004, which also figures as the first chapter of *A Virtue Epistemology* (Oxford University Press, 2007). Both responses dispute the claim of the skeptic that in their adduced scenario we would be misled into false judgments. What is disputed is that in the respective scenarios we would so much as make judgments. However, neither of these is a universal all-purpose response to all forms of skepticism. My *Reflective Knowledge* (Oxford University Press, 2009) has broader scope.

truth amounts to knowledge there is no apparent reason why we should always consider that to be success in a game, even if there are shared elements. There is no apparent reason to think that the pursuit of truth and its apt attainment must always amount to the playing of a game, any more than to think that the successful production of a good crop is success in a game.

7. Consider categories pertinent to degree of attributability/responsibility, and opposed to metaphysical luck. In this regard, the category of security (of secure fully apt attempt) stands in stark contrast to any alleged categories of sensitive attempt or safe attempt.

Sensitivity and safety, as applied to attempts, are more general versions of sensitivity and safety of beliefs.

A *sensitive attempt* is *one that the agent would not have made if it would have failed*. But this does not properly connect the success of the attempt to the agent as a source of that success. After all, compatibly with the sensitivity of their attempt, perhaps an agent would have omitted that attempt *regardless*, i.e., even if it would have succeeded. Why they *would have omitted* that attempt regardless is perhaps because they are *unable* to make *any* such attempt, disabled as they are by some injury.

Something similar applies to safe attempts. A *safe attempt* is *one that the agent would have made only if it would have succeeded*. But this again fails to properly connect the success of the attempt to the agent as a source of that success. After all, it may be that the success would have come forth *regardless*, i.e., that the success was bound to happen, and that the source of its happening had nothing to do with the agent's effort. An agent might thus attempt to stay awake throughout a lecture, and might do so safely, in that he would have made that attempt only if it would have succeeded: that is, only if he would have stayed awake throughout the lecture. But what if he stayed awake for reasons that had nothing to do with his effort? Rather, it was just the highly caffeinated cup of coffee he drank (while believing it to be decaffeinated), where a huge conspiracy has arranged several layers of backup protection to keep him awake for that important lecture.

Nor is either of *sensitivity* or *safety* plausibly constitutive of any of the categories on the higher levels of our hierarchy, the way *success* and *competence* are so constitutive.

All of that being so, neither the sensitivity nor the safety of our attempts plausibly belongs in a metaphysical hierarchy designed to reveal levels or degrees of attributability/responsibility, or (in the opposite order) levels of telically pertinent *luck*.

Secure knowledge does seem properly to occupy a higher level of our epistemic/metaphysical hierarchy. Secure knowledge (full well) rules out additional luck that is plausibly credit-reducing (credit-reducing in the sense of attributability-reducing, with no further axiological or deontic implication, so that a perfect murder could still be fully "creditable" to the agent).

8. That is still compatible, however, with our frequent focus in ordinary human affairs on levels of attributability that do not require security. Despite this focus and how it affects ordinary epistemic and other performance assessments, a clear failure of security in a thought experiment can still bear on our intuitive responses to the question of whether the protagonist *really* knows, whether they are fully responsible, whether their action is fully attributable to them. An outcome can be sufficiently attributable for all practical purposes of ordinary human life, even if it is not sufficiently attributable for purposes of full Cartesian assessment. Similarly, a box might be empty for all practical human purposes, even if it might still be full of air.

Moreover, a Cartesian-light attributability/responsibility requires, not the *radical Cartesian* security of one's pertinent SSS competence, but only the sort of ordinary security that one has when not easily would one have lacked one's pertinent triple-S competence. Even if we do not share an interest in full Cartesian assessment, we can still recognize that when our Simone fails even the Cartesian-light requirement is when she so plausibly fails to *really* know, by failing to earn sufficient credit for her alethic successes. Simone falls short not only of radical Cartesian security; she falls short even of ordinary security, so that she lacks even *ordinary secure knowledge* about her surroundings, including the targets down below. So, there seems a clear and intuitive enough sense in which she does not *really* know.

9. *The role of default assumptions.*

And yet. Put yourself in the cockpits of nearby flyers in formation next to Simone on a genuine mission. The maneuvers that you all make as you fly that dangerous mission over enemy territory will require constant fast assessments of Simone's state of mind and what she is likely to do. How would you conceptualize this if not by adverting to what she sees and hears, what she knows accordingly, and how you can trust her to perform in the light of that assessment of her mind? Within the subdomain of your joint mission, you make default assumptions like the assumptions made by a tennis player who "knows" what an opponent is likely to do (despite the acknowledged extreme fragility of the lights). The knowledge that fellow pilots attribute to Simone during that mission is of course no mere "ludic" knowledge. You are not just playing a game or engaged in a sport. Your mission is deadly serious.

Yet there seems a close analogy between the ludic knowledge of a tennis player about the opponent's actions and the "mission-relative" knowledge that you must rely on as fellow pilots. In both cases there are domain-defining default assumptions relative to which a kind of domain-internal knowledge is properly possessed and attributed even despite its clash with domain-external *ignorance* on the part of the same agent (Simone as it might be) about the very same propositions. Simone does not have *secure* knowledge on which to base her maneuvers and you, her fellow pilots on the mission, need not attribute such knowledge to her as the mission unfolds successfully and creditably. It suffices that you attribute knowledge on a lower level to her—thus animal knowledge or reflective knowledge—so that, based on such attribution you can jointly successfully conduct your mission.

And that is tantamount to your assuming by default that no spoilers are at work (such as the surreptitious deception that Simone might now so easily suffer). Let us have a closer look.

Simone and her fellow pilots act collectively, and the propriety and creditability of those actions depend on their shared ability to take into account the intentions of the others, so as to adjust mutually as the mission unfolds. Such joint action would seem to suffer to the extent that those required judgments fall short of knowledge. But what sort of knowledge is required? Does it allow default assumptions? Suppose secure knowledge is required, even if the security required is just ordinary and not Cartesian. If so, then the pilots on that joint mission all fall short, and whatever success the mission may attain will not be attributably creditable to them.

Can that really be so? Recall the epistemic plight of our Simone when she is now subject most often to simulation, and consider the implied plight of the fighter group as they enter their mission. Ostensibly Simone no longer knows what she is about. She no longer really knows what goes on in her surroundings, so as to respond to that properly. Worse yet, her fellow pilots can then no longer properly predict what she will do, since they can no longer tell what she knows about her surroundings, so as to be able to predict what she will do on that basis, and so as to attain proper joint action.

If we focus on the topmost knowledge that requires security, that is what we have to say about those pilots as they enter their mission. Is there an alternative that more forgivingly allows us to credit them all properly for the great "success" of their mission? Well, if we focus on a metaphysically less demanding level of "knowledge full well," this permits them all to rely on proper default assumptions.

Recall how Fielder deserves credit for a great catch despite the fragility of the lights. This is because he can properly assume by default that the lights will be stable. And now, similarly, our pilots on their mission deserve credit for destroying the enemy targets, and returning safely to their home base. But, given the lack of security in their pertinent knowledge, we cannot require secure knowledge of them.

Compatibly, though, they can host all the relevant knowledge full well required for creditable action. However, for Simone to have such knowledge, she needs to rely on a default assumption that her situation is as it seems, that she is in a genuine cockpit, flying a real plane, jointly with her fellow pilots. And her knowledge full well requires only that this assumption be true, even if she does not *securely* know it to be true, nor need it even be *safely* true.

10. *Hinges again.*

That opens up a further interpretative option concerning Wittgenstein's hinges. Some at least of these, some important ones pertaining to radical skepticism, can now be viewed as default assumptions properly shared by humanity in our joint life and action. We are fellow pilots leading lives that are intricately interrelated. Our success can then be individually and collectively creditable even in the absence of security. So, it can be based just on default assumptions that need only be true, that need not be known to be true, nor even safe.

Default assumptions have an important role, however, well beyond the radical reaches of philosophical speculation. The pilots in formation entering enemy territory are not involved in philosophical reflection, nor is their pertinent knowledge like the sort involved in Cartesian meditation, and assessable by such high standards. The secure knowledge lacked by Simone (when she is now highly subject to simulation) is not just the sort of knowledge that requires defense against the recondite possibilities posed by deep skeptics. No, the relevant possibilities are of a sort that might affect any of us much more ordinarily than by being envatted. Yet, even when such a possibility is actually realized, as with Simone, fellow pilots do not let it affect their reliance on her as they all engage in proper joint action. Nor need Simone herself let it affect her action and belief, whether animal or reflective. And if she does not, if she plunges ahead with her life as if normal, then she can attain much success and highly creditable success, both animal success and success full well, despite her lack of security. In this respect at least, Fielder provides a proper model for our assessment of Simone.

11. Finally, there is now the prospect of a further significant twist. Earlier we had likened the ordinary perceiver, Normal, to Fielder, in our view that just as Fielder would be alienated from baseball altogether by the failure of the lights, so Normal would be alienated altogether from the domain of human perceptual judgment through envatment. So, we surmised that a BIV would be alienated from the domain of judgment, since there would be no real thinker to be making any judgments through any doings of the envatted brain.

That, however, is not open to us in defending Simone's ability to properly default-assume that she is in a normal cockpit. There is zero plausibility to the notion that simulation would take away Simone's ability to make judgments, perceptual or other.

Although we can still retain our limited defense against radical skepticism by arguing that the BIV is no more able to make real judgments than can the dreamer, this will not suffice to explain the status of the default assumptions made by Simone and her fellow pilots that they are not then under simulation.

What then makes those default assumptions proper assumptions for them to make?

The domain of those pilots in their dangerous mission as they fly in formation is clearly not a ludic domain. And yet, it might be that they are *all* mostly subject to simulation around that time, and that only monumental "luck" accounts for their all flying that perfectly genuine and dangerous mission on that occasion.

Compare the warning to Fielder that the lights are nearly certain to fail and the warning to Simone that she (and her fellow pilots) are nearly certain to be under simulation. And suppose both Fielder and Simone can appropriately assume that their respective situations will be normal in all relevant respects.

Assume indeed that Simone would be both epistemically and practically negligent or even reckless to suppose otherwise (given how much turns on her contribution to the dangerous joint mission). That will then enable us to assess their respective performances (as a baseball fielder or as a fighter pilot) in the normal way, so that they can attain full credit for their apt and fully apt performances.

And will it not also be appropriate to assess their intellectual, epistemic performances likewise? Included prominently here will of course be those epistemic performances that essentially underlie their important domain-internal actions, whether they be the ludic actions of baseball, or the practical (non-ludic) actions of a fighter pilot in formation on a dangerous mission.

Whether to continue performing in a certain domain is thus subject to normal cost-benefit reasoning, where every consequential consideration must be considered. Once the agent does commit to domain-internal performance, however, some external considerations will be bracketed as irrelevant to the assessment of domain-internal choices and actions. Now only salient considerations will have such relevance, whereas background considerations are presumed by default to be satisfied. A sort of deontology will now have full sway, with some important consequentialist factors bracketed away into irrelevance.

12. In sum, what distinguishes belief that rises to the level of knowledge in our epistemic/metaphysical hierarchy is that it is belief whose *success* is significantly *creditable* (*attributable*) to the believer, one for which the believer is attributably responsible as their own doing, and not just something that comes about by (agent-external) *luck*. However, there are distinct ways of attaining such creditable success, ways that form a metaphysical hierarchy. And what *orders* that hierarchy? What orders the hierarchy, I submit, is the level to which the success is creditable to the agent.

At the lowest level the *merely* apt alethic affirmation is found, whose success (truth) is due to the first-order competence of the thinker. That is the level of animal knowledge. (This can be a *sub-credal* sort of "knowledge," as is the knowledge of eye-exam subjects who "guess" right with supreme reliability even when they reach the bottom of their eye chart, where the letters are extremely small.)

Above that lowest level of creditability to agents for their success is the *fully* apt alethic affirmation, the apt *judgment*, whose aptness is due to the meta-competence of that thinker, the meta-competence sensitive to when their alethic affirmations would be not just true but also apt. This is the level of *reflective knowledge full well*.[8] Here we have a significant increment of credit to the thinker, one aligned with a reduction of the pertinent luck in the thinker's attainment of success.

Finally, we have found a third level of knowledge, above reflective knowledge full well. Here the thinker does attain reflective knowledge full well, and *in addition* this attainment derives from competences retained safely, not just through luck. This is the level of *secure knowledge*.

What unifies these three levels of our hierarchy, as distinct levels of *human knowledge*, is that on these levels the thinker attains an epistemic success (truth, or aptness) attributable to them, as really their own doing. Coordinately, such success corresponds decreasingly to adventitious external luck. This holds good all along the ascent of attitudes from the animal level of the merely apt, to the reflective-full-well level of the fully apt, to the *securely* reflective-full-well level attained through

[8] The British Empiricist faculty of "reflection" included both the mind's reference to itself and also the aspect of being a *conscious* operation. We here abstract from that, to a reflection that needs to be mental but need not be conscious. This is in line with the now recognized subconscious depths of the mind. Our proposed abstraction makes room for a subconscious "reflection" constituted by *mental* (though not necessarily conscious) reference of the mind to itself.

competences retained safely and not just by luck: i.e., competences that would not too easily have been missing.[9]

That rounds out the sketch of our telic normativity, and of the special instance of such normativity found in virtue epistemology. In earlier chapters this account has been put to work in offering epistemic explanations.

Now our next chapter will aim to illuminate a further epistemic obscurity, that of what is involved in distinctively epistemic justification.

[9] Note, finally, that the whole structure has two quite distinct incarnations. One of these is constituted by consciously deliberative judgmental knowledge. And this is the incarnation prominent in the history of epistemology, where philosophical skepticism concerns the possibility of judgmental knowledge. The whole structure then unfolds at that level. But there is also a second incarnation, more recently prominent, which involves knowledge that is not judgmental, but is rather functional, whose main element is that of *representation*, which can be subconscious (rather than consciously intentional affirmation).

Against this latter, the accusation of over-intellectualization is misplaced. Two components unify the two incarnations: both the *conscious exercises of conscious agency that constitute judgment* and are at the heart of the judgmental metaphysical structure, and also the *subconscious representational exercises of functional competence* at the heart of functional knowledge. The first of these unifying metaphysical components is the phenomenon of *aiming*, which encompasses both the conscious and free exercises of competence in judgment, and *also* the merely functional teleology of aimed representations that remain subconscious. In *each* incarnation one can *also* distinguish aptness, full aptness, and secure full aptness, and in each case what unifies these is how each involves levels of credit for success, or attributability.

10
Competence and Justification

Critics have argued repeatedly that no externalist epistemology can account for epistemic justification.[1] Their main argument repurposes the celebrated Cartesian evil demon thought experiment. The conclusion is now that the beliefs of the demon's victim can be about as well justified as are many of our perceptual and other beliefs, although it is hard to see how any externalist epistemology could account for this fact. What follows seeks a way out for the externalist virtue epistemologist.

What is it for a belief to be epistemically justified? This is our main question.

Consider a *good case*, in which Normal knows perceptually that p. A *bad case*, the case of Victim, is identical to that good case except only that <p> is false.[2] The following plausible theses are in line with that extreme case.

Consider first:

Phenomenal Parity If they are *appeared to* exactly the same, Victim and Normal are *equally well justified* in perceptually believing that p, if they both do perceptually believe that p.

Alternatively, we might stipulate not just that they are *appeared to* the same but that they are the same in all *internal respects*, or that *internally and mentally* they are the same. This is a stronger, broader supposition

[1] This chapter will develop a response to the "New Evil Demon Problem," the problem posed for any externalist epistemology by the question of whether victims of radical skeptical scenarios can be so much as epistemically justified in the judgments that they make. But here we will not presuppose the position reached in the preceding chapter: that such victims cannot so much as make judgments.

[2] And except also, of course, for whatever else the introduction of this falsehood may entail.

Epistemic Explanations: A Theory of Telic Normativity, and What it Explains. Ernest Sosa, Oxford University Press (2021). © Ernest Sosa. DOI:10.1093/oso/9780198856467.003.0010

than that *they are appeared to the same*, since there can be internal respects that are not just a matter of how things appear. And this favors the following, second, principle.

> *Mental Parity* If they are *internally and mentally* the same, Victim and Normal are *equally well justified* in perceptually believing that p, if they both do perceptually believe that p.

How should we understand epistemic justification so as to assess such claims of epistemic parity?

How intuitively plausible it surely is that the New Evil Demon victim is no less well epistemically justified than is a normal and normally situated counterpart. Somewhat surprisingly, a *virtue-theoretic* externalism can agree with that intuition, while distinguishing varieties of justification, as will soon emerge.

First let's replace Descartes's theologically inspired example with a contemporary counterpart, a case of brain envatment, an instance of our Victim–Normal contrast.

A. Competence, Safety, and Reliability

1. How reliably one succeeds is irrelevant to how skilled one is. Skill *requires* reliable enough success, not for one's attempts in general, but only *for one's attempts in the conditions of special interest within the domain of one's performance.*[3]

2. A wizard may come along, determined to correct the trajectory of our archer's shots when they are (otherwise) off target. The archer might then be said (with some semantic stretch) to have a "disposition" to succeed. Still, even so, this wizard-dependent disposition cannot plausibly amount to a true competence.

[3] Thus, despite their awful situation and shape, evil demon victims may still exercise epistemic skill of a very high order, which clues us into a "justification" they might still enjoy.

The archer has a skill, when she does, by being disposed to succeed reliably enough *when in appropriate shape and situation*. Wizard-aided success is irrelevant, as the wizard is an ad hoc external factor outside the relevant situational dimension.

Archery skill must dispose one to succeed reliably enough with one's shots in *certain appropriate, preselected conditions* of shape and situation. Wizards have no role in the situations of interest for archery, those relevant to true archery skill.

3. A performance domain determines what are the "appropriate" Shape and Situation dimensions of a competence in that domain. In the practice of a community, various domains of performance are determined conventionally, by explicit or implicit agreement. Athletic and artistic domains are examples.

As for *basic* human competences, these are not just conventionally set.[4] Rather, they are required for human flourishing regardless of cultural overlay. They are determined by the species, not by any particular culture or group. They are in play already even in the earliest stages of humanity, since they include the competences involved in the nutrition, movement, reproduction, nurturing, and basic collaboration essential to a social species. Already in the Paleolithic Age we were no doubt crediting each other for aptly good performances and blaming each other for those inapt or worse.

4. The success of a performance is properly credited to a skill only if the following two conditions are met. First, the skill needs to be one that would yield success reliably enough *within* the preselected shape/situation conditions of interest in the domain of that performance. Second, the success of the particular performance must *manifest* the skill. Thus, it cannot be owed to a wizard's intervention. If the skill is to be thus *manifest* in a particular *success*, moreover, it must be reliable enough *in specific shape/situation conditions* wherein its exercise explains that success.

[4] Much human competence is not thus "basic," of course, but manifests rather our higher, more sophisticated human powers. That this includes some of our most important epistemic competence is argued in my *Judgment and Agency* (Oxford University Press, 2015).

Let's pretend for simplicity that there is just *one situational dimension* (incorporating all situational factors that matter relevantly, which in archery would involve wind, light, distance to target, and more), and that there is just *one shape dimension* (incorporating all shape factors that matter: sobriety, wakeful alertness, and so on). These then will be the shape and situation dimensions preselected in the domain of performance. And there would be thresholds of good enough shape and good enough situation, beyond which the agent *must* succeed reliably enough in order to be relevantly skilled *full stop*. Even higher degrees of skill would of course be found in any agent who would *still* succeed reliably enough as the shape or situation worsened.[5]

Two things can be determined once the relevant dimensions are preselected by the community in the relevant domain. Given our simplifying assumption, once the situational dimension has been preselected, and once the shape dimension has been preselected, the community can set what is required for skill in that domain. In order to be skilled in that domain, an agent *must* be disposed to succeed *reliably enough* within *certain ranges* of shape/situation conditions within those respective dimensions. That is how the agent would possess a relevant competence to succeed in those conditions.

However, an agent can be highly enough skilled and competent beyond those shape/situation ranges. He can be superlatively skilled by being competent well beyond the ranges where you *need* to be competent to count as outright competent (*period*) in that domain. Someone's success could manifest such superlative skill even in a situation far *beyond* the normal range, in an abnormal situation, where *merely competent* performers would *not* be reliable enough.

Finally, despite manifesting high skill, an archery shot can still fail, as when a spoiler gust takes it off course. As we turn now to epistemology, this will give us a model for how a belief can be justified while false.

[5] But a fuller account would need to accommodate those who are admirably skilled even if they would lose interest and regularly fail through boredom when the conditions were *too* good. Moreover, a better shape could compensate for a worse situation, and the other way around.

B. Epistemic Competence

1. Epistemology provides a special case of competent performance, starting with perception. Our ability to detect objective sweetness, for example, is affected by our relevant shape at the time, as is our ability to detect objective temperature.[6]

2. Suppose Victim has recently placed much sugar on his tongue, or his hand in ice water, which has degraded his ability to discern objective sweetness or warmth. Victim's epistemic competence to judge on those matters is then degraded below Normal's, even if things "appear" the same to them both.[7] However, their innermost competence or skill can *still* be the same, since this requires only that they be equally reliable *when both are appropriately shaped and situated.*[8]

Victim's ability to perceive objective taste or warmth is then lowered, with a loss of competence. What is degraded is Victim's temporary *shape* for perception of the objective qualities of taste or of warmth. This is what is spoiled by the sugar or ice water.

3. Our two subjects might still be appeared-to the same (either because of sameness of relevant sensory qualia, or because of sameness of seemings or attractions to assent, or both). What is more, they might also be equally skilled, by being equally able to discern the relevant objective qualities, *if in the same shape/situation condition.* However, only Normal is actually in good condition. Victim is not. Although they are appeared to exactly the same, and believe with equal epistemic *skill*, Victim's belief does not then manifest *complete* competence. He is too poorly situated, and in bad epistemic shape.

Thus, we can distinguish complete (SkShSi) competence from inner (SkSh) competence, and the latter in turn from innermost (Sk)

[6] Here I assume that there are objective properties of *sweetness* and *temperature*, even if they have the nature of response-dependent secondary qualities.

[7] Here and in what follows 'things appear the same to two subjects' is meant to convey no more than 'two subjects are appeared-to the same.'

[8] Of course, we can alternatively suppose that the two cases vary in respect of such competence, which means that we must distinguish between *appearance* duplicates and *mental* duplicates.

competence. This may help explain some of the "disagreement" in the literature as to whether the bad-case subject is "justified." On our threefold account, we can see how "it depends." Although he fails to judge with *complete* competence, the bad-case subject *does* judge *skillfully*, perhaps even in good shape.

That is like the "disagreement" as to whether a good driver in good shape is or is not competent to drive on a certain road, one that is then unsafe. The driver might still have the inner competence to drive on that road. But the road's bad condition deprives him of the *complete* competence to do so at that time.

Similarly, the archer in a windy environment might still retain his *inner* archery competence. But he may seem to lack the complete competence at that time, because spoiler wind is too likely. I say "may seem" to lack complete competence, because of the subtlety of this case.

Thus, suppose that, although the wind is *very likely* to intervene, in fact no gust intervenes and the arrow goes straight to the bullseye, just as it would normally do, given its orientation and speed off the bow.

Does the success of that shot manifest skill and competence? Or does the archer fall short? Does he fail to succeed *reliably enough*, despite his good shape and great skill? Does the high likelihood of spoiler gusts put the archer in an *in*appropriate *situation*, denying him the complete competence required for apt success? We earlier concluded that a shot is apt and to the archer's credit so long as the arrow is *in fact* unaffected by wind on the way to the target, *no matter how likely a spoiler gust may have been.*

That being so, it emerges that the *relevant situation is not simply a modal property of the spatiotemporal volume involved*: namely, how likely success would be in that volume (by someone skilled and in good shape). Consider our shot's pertinent spatiotemporal volume from the moment when the arrow is released to the moment when it strikes the target. Success in that volume would be quite unlikely despite our archer's excellent skill and shape. What makes success so unlikely is the very high risk (by hypothesis) of a spoiler gust. However, so long as no spoiler gust *in fact* comes along, our archer enjoys the complete competence required for creditable, apt success.

Aptness depends, not on a modally safe situation, but rather on the situation's *in fact* occupying the appropriate preselected *situational dimension*, no matter how accidentally so. Beyond this, the situation need only combine with the agent's skill and shape for a threefold combination likely enough to yield success. Such an SSS combination is what amounts to complete competence.[9]

C. *How* Is a Skill Manifest in a Skillful Performance?

1. An archer's shot can be skillful (adroit) even if it is not apt. The shot is skillful if and only if it manifests skill. When the shot is also apt its *success* manifests skill. But a *shot* can manifest skill even when its success fails to do so, and even in the absence of success. The arrow might leave the bow headed straight to the bullseye, absent spoiler gusts. Even with the skill that *the shot* manifests because of that initial orientation, its *success* might still fail to manifest skill, because of the spoiler gusts that turn up, even when those gusts are mutually compensating so as to yield success anyhow, though only by luck. So, a shot can manifest a skill because some good quality of that shot manifests that skill, whether the shot succeeds or not.

2. With our BIV example in mind, consider this: Could you manifest archery skill, could you *exercise* such skill, if deprived of limbs?

[9] This is our first approximation. A fuller account would include the role of competent default assumptions detailed in Chapter 7, and the place of security in the full metaphysical hierarchy relevant to the telic assessment of human performance.

In addition, a fuller development would distinguish more sharply the sort of competence that is required for attributable aptness of attempt. When you perform at a given moment, what matters is your SSS profile indexed to that particular moment and act). An archery example brings out why we need this distinction. Thus, you might at some moment be such that, even for tightly time-encompassing spans that include that moment, here's what is relevantly true: *if we were to consider the totality of your possible attempts to hit the target at times within such spans that include that moment, you would extremely probably fail miserably*. This is because of the very heavy winds that are so likely to come across the relevant volume of space as you attempt your shot. Nevertheless, it just might be that for the very narrow channels of space that your arrow will traverse if you shoot at exactly that moment the wind *will* be perfectly calm. And it is this *actual* calm in that narrow channel that matters to your possession of the relevant situational S as you ponder whether to shoot just then. (And precisely similar points apply to the skill S and to the shape S. So, what matters at any such given moment of decision on whether to ø, is what your pertinent SSS condition *will* be, and *not what it would be*.)

Take an archer who not only wishes or hopes but *decides* to release her arrow *here and now* and implements that decision by actually *trying*. The trying might either be constituted by, or directly yield, a certain brain state with the following property. If the subject were in good shape, that state *would* reliably enough eventuate in the arrow's leaving the bow with good orientation and speed. However, something accidental (gust-like) intervenes in the causal chain *within the efferent nerves*, which affects the outcome at the limbs, so that the shot fails. That subject manifests her skill in the relevant quality of her attempt, despite the unfortunate lapse in her inner shape.

3. Compare a brain in a vat who wishes or hopes to raise an arm here and now, and even *decides* to do so forthwith, yet akratically fails to try. Of *two* BIVs, if one tries, while the other does not, that can surely matter to responsibility and proper blame.

For a *naturalist*, an attempt might be constituted just by a brain's entering a certain complex state, whereas a *dualist* might require a purely mental, nonphysical happening that directly causes the brain to be in that state. *Either way*, when an agent performs a physical act by intentional design, there will be an initial physical state (however complex) constituted (at least in part) by that brain's having the specified property. And that will be something the agent brings about. He does not bring it about intentionally as such, *by design*. He is unlikely to be able to specify that particular brain state. But an agent can bring about something attributable to them under a certain description *as their doing* even without bringing it about as such, under that description, *by intentional design*. Because it is thus attributable, that doing is a *deed*. For something to be a "deed," its constitutive doing must be attributable to the agent as their own doing.

For example, I may need to bear down at a government office so as to sign in one doing carbon copies of a certain form. I do not know that I sign the third copy, since I think there are only two. So, I may think that I do *not* sign a third copy, and yet may do so anyhow, as my own doing, attributable to me. I sign that third copy even if I do so unintentionally (*not* by design), unaccompanied by any corresponding intention, either concurrent or aforethought. Despite being unintentional (*not* by design), that doing of mine is an attributable doing. It is not a *mere* "doing," as is my squashing a rabbit by falling on it when I am pushed unconscious off a cliff.[10]

4. Perhaps then I can bring about a relevant brain state, one normally sufficient for the rising of my arm, even if I do not bring it about intentionally, not by intentional design, either concurrent or aforethought. What is more, my doing so may be a deed, an exercise of competence and of skill, despite not being a consciously intentional doing (by design).[11]

Exercise of skill requires only that one manifest a disposition to succeed through deeds, even if these are not consciously intentional (not *by consciously intentional design*). At a certain point, a pianist in performance may press a certain key with the third finger of her right hand. She does not then pick out that particular action as such for that very instant. So, she does not press that key with that finger at that moment *by consciously intentional design*, either concurrent or aforethought. And yet it is something she does, the doing of which is attributable to her as her doing. Moreover, that deed of hers manifests her skill as a great pianist.[12]

[10] We need not even commit to the idea that it is really a *doing* at all, nor even to the idea that English would happily abide our saying that it is something the agent "does." We can leave it open that strictly speaking doings are *all of them* attributable.

However, you might well ask about a ball held at the top of an incline: "What would it do if released?" And here's an answer in proper English: "If it is glued to the top, it will just stay there, but if it is not glued then here's what it will do: it will roll down the incline." What a ball can "do" when released, a human being can "do" when pushed unconscious off a cliff. So, it looks like we *can* "do" things unattributably.

[11] But the skill exercised need not be the skill to bring about that particular brain state. We need not commit at all on that. The skill exercised may be an ordinary physical skill: the pianistic skill to play a certain concerto, say, or the skill to tie a knot, etc.

[12] The case of the pianist and that of the brain performance reveal a distinction between intentional and ontological "by" relations. Once the pianist knows that in the playing of a certain phrase she will be hitting a certain key with a certain finger, she can intentionally, by design, bring it about that she does hit that key with that finger. She can do so by intentionally playing the relevant phrase. But *ontology* reverses the "by" direction. It is ontologically by hitting that key with that finger that the pianist brings about her intentional playing of that phrase. This seems also relevant to the "X first" controversy. X could be "first" in ways that do not affect the ontological order of the relevant domain, and so do not affect proper *metaphysical* explanation in that domain. Here we have several dimensions, respectively involving: first, agential priority, second, metaphysical priority, and, third, conceptual priority, which seem severally independent, pairwise and otherwise.

Similarly, then, we might manifest our competence to raise our arm, and indeed our pertinent skill, when we try to do so through a certain brain state, whereby one normally brings about the rising of one's arm. And that is then a way in which a BIV might manifest the skill of a great pianist, even if it falls dramatically short of exercising any fuller competence, in the ways in which it very obviously must fall short.[13]

The analogy to the believer who manifests virtuosity in her perceptual judgments should now be obvious. In one clearly specifiable and plausibly acceptable sense, that believer is then "justified" in so believing, even if her belief is false.

D. Do We Really *Disagree*?

1. Is "justification" worth a fight? Is it any more worth a fight than is "competence"? Both terms are polysemous, at least in the usage of theorists.[14] Better to distinguish and agree to "disagree." We can plausibly enough identify the category of justification with that of epistemic competence, while still drawing our threefold distinction among competences: the innermost, the inner, and the complete.

"Justification" is too fraught with technical disputes and associations, while insufficiently nailed down by ordinary usage, to be the safe property of any one epistemic faction.

2. Consider a passionate dispute as to whether astronauts lose weight when they rocket into outer space. One side contends that they lose *not one ounce* in their brief ascent. But the other side rejoins that they are weightless once they float in their cabin, and that to go from weighing many pounds to being weightless is certainly to weigh less, and to come to weigh less that way is certainly to lose weight.

[13] Why do I say "it"? Well, one can think of "the BIV" as the *person* whose brain is envatted. And the *sex* and *gender* of that person may become uncertain when the brain is excised and survives in a vat, while the rest of the body is cremated.

[14] But we need not insist on polysemy, since the semantic variability can be contextual instead.

That dispute resembles the "disagreement" noted by William James as to whether a man goes "around" a squirrel if she scurries so as to keep a tree trunk between them, while the man traverses a perimeter enclosing the squirrel full circle.

Both of these are pseudo-disputes. What each side alleges is compatible with what is alleged by the other, as they talk past each other.

3. On the virtue-theoretic account of justification as competence, the dispute over *Parity* that we met at the outset (whether Phenomenal or Mental) is like those two disputes. The radically deceived subject lacks complete SSS-competence and perhaps even inner SS-competence. He thus lacks one sort of "justification" while still retaining cognitive, epistemic S-skill, and thus another kind of "justification" for his relevant beliefs. That is how those *skillful* beliefs can be "justified" *despite* the bad shape or situation that accounts for why they are still false.

4. Moreover, there is a further respect in which disputants on this set of issues might talk past each other. We have seen how to distinguish *skill*-competence from *skill+shape*-competence, and this in turn from *skill+shape+situation*-competence. Compare what it takes for a driver to have the competence required for driving on a certain highway. Does he still have it when drunk? Well, yes (the innermost driving skill), and no (the complete competence that requires sobriety). What is required for a belief to be "epistemically justified" is that it manifest a corresponding level of competence (innermost, inner, or complete).

What if Victim were to lack not only one or another of the relevant levels of competence *in his specific conditions at that particular time*? What if, instead, the Sk, Sh, and Si conditions that constitute relevant competences *in the actual world* do not likewise constitute competences *in that other possible world w where Victim is now placed*?

Suppose Victim then manifests an *actual-world* skill Sk, in judging that p, or in a corresponding judgmental belief. Should we say that he is then skill-justified in so judging or believing? This seems akin to the question about James's squirrel example. About Victim, we might well say, speaking and thinking as we do *in the actual world*, that he *would* be skill-justified (with a skill-justification indexed to the actual world), but would *not* be skill-justified(w), with a skill-justification indexed to the world w in which we imaginatively place him.[15]

SSS profiles that make for competence in one world need not do so in another. Consider whether Victim, in some postulated possible world, is competent, *when we raise that question in the actual world.* We can then naturally index the question either to the world of the thinker or to the world of Victim, and we will get different correct answers. And this seems just like the question whether the man goes "around" the squirrel.[16]

E. Epistemic Justification and Agential Competence

As we look back over the foregoing proposals, a question lingers: *Why think of epistemic justification on the model of agential competence?* And here is an answer within virtue theory: *Because knowledge (of a basic, animal sort) is best understood as a form of apt agency* (while more sophisticated sorts of knowledge build on that basic sort).

It might be thought that Barney, the fake-barns unfortunate, refutes that thesis, since his apt belief is too unsafe to be knowledge. That supposed refutation is put in doubt, however, by surprising x-phi results.[17]

Indeed, one might even allow that those who agree in saying that Barney does "know" may speak metaphorically, as do those who say an

[15] Suppose heating systems will have changed many years from now so that the devices that are presently excellent thermostats will be useless relics, since relative to that world they are deprived of the situational conditions that would enable them to function well (with complete "competence" or functionality) as thermostats. We can surely imagine that future buffs of ancient devices might dig up a couple of those relics and run simulations that show one but not the other to be still functioning with fine *innermost* functionality (analogous to skill). We can thus imagine from our temporal perspective, in the actual world, that some such device could still be a perfectly functional thermostat as shown by how well it functions in a simulation. Of course, in doing so we would be making implicit reference to our own heating situational conditions with furnaces, etc., conditions receptive to the installation of such a device that enables it to regulate ambient temperature.

[16] Consider Victim's wondering in world w whether he is justified in judging that p. True enough, *that* would have to be a wondering whether he is justified (w), and not whether he is justified (α), since from world w no-one would be able to pick out our specific actual world α.

[17] See "Epistemic Intuitions in Fake-barn Thought Experiments," by David Colaço, Wesley Buckwalter, Stephen Stich, and Edouard Machery, *Episteme*, 11(2) (2014) 199–212.

electric-eye door "knows" when someone approaches. After all, if what we are studying is not the semantics of ordinary language, then it is unclear why or how it should matter whether the usage through which we agree is *metaphorical* or *literal*. Either way we may be picking out an objective phenomenon well worth considering in the domain of epistemology. Moreover, we then see how impressively that phenomenon aligns with the aptness found in domains of human performance *generally*, not just in epistemology. And this suggests the hypothesis that aptness of belief might thus be just a special case of achievement, an *epistemic* accomplishment, and a plausible candidate for being some sort of "knowledge."

Even granting all of that, however, how does it matter for our main question: *What is epistemic justification*?

The foregoing discussion matters because, *first*, the sort of justification that is of interest in epistemology must be distinguished from pragmatic justification; while, *second*, such *epistemic* justification is best understood as "the (or at least *a*) particular normative status importantly involved in *knowledge* (as opposed to moral or prudential action)."[18] It is a normative status that a belief can attain, one that would be distinctively and importantly involved in the subject's *thereby* attaining knowledge, but one that can be fully present even if the subject falls short of knowledge.

Given those specifications, we are naturally led to the idea, within telic epistemology, that epistemic justification is a form of the epistemic competence of a judgment or belief. And once competence slots into place that way, we have our three varieties of more specific status: the complete competence, the inner competence, and the innermost competence or *epistemic skill*. Finally, beliefs can then be justified—or competent—in three corresponding ways. The beliefs of our BIV Victims

[18] More strictly, this is a sort of epistemic justification *constitutive* of knowledge ("gnoseological" justification). It is a sort of epistemic justification *directly* constitutive of knowledge, while knowledge *itself* may be constitutive of a proper moral or prudential status of an action; which is not to deny that there are forms of justification properly termed "epistemic" though different from our *telic* epistemic normativity constitutive of knowledge. There *is* surely a realm of intellectual ethics beyond the theory of knowledge, one that concerns proper inquiry, including wise choice of intellectual pursuits given one's own capabilities, one's context and potential collaborators, and so on. What is defended here is that the normativity of *theory of knowledge* is telic. Compatibly, the normativity of a broader intellectual ethics may be telic in some ways and non-telic in other ways.

can thus be plausibly competent, and hence "epistemically, *gnoseologically*, justified" or at least "rationally justified" (with the rationality distinctive of *gnoseological* skill), even if they fall short not only of knowledge but also of the more inclusive forms of gnoseological competence, the inner and the complete. Our victims act in ways that are plausibly gnoseologically "faultless." Their pertinent judgments manifest their skill just as well as if they had been apt judgments, since any failure to attain their distinctive gnoseological objectives (truth and aptness) is attributable to inadequacies of shape or situation, and not of skill.

Just how might skill be manifest when both inner and complete competence are ruled out by the agent's bad shape or poor situation? Skill might then be manifest in the performance by the agent of some deed *by performing which* the agent *would* reliably enough attain pertinent success provided she were in proper shape and properly situated. Such a deed might constitute an attempt by that agent, even one that fails. And that is why, despite its massive failures, the BIV can perform with skill so as to be thereby epistemically, gnoseologically, justified.

PART IV
A HISTORICAL ANTECEDENT

11
The Relevance of Moore and Wittgenstein

A. Moore and Common Sense

1. Prominent among the beliefs defended by Moore in his "Defense of Common Sense" are those voiced as follows, all of which he takes to constitute certain knowledge:

> I now have an existing, living body that has existed continuously since its birth some time ago. During that time it has been in contact with or some distance from many other bodies with shape and size. These include living human bodies that had been born some time earlier and had existed continuously since then. I have perceived things and observed facts about them, and have also been aware of unobserved facts, such as that my body existed yesterday. And the like is true of many other people. Finally, many other people also know corresponding things about themselves.

That is lifted or paraphrased from the beginning paragraphs of his celebrated paper.[1] We might well consider such beliefs "core components of common sense." In "Proof of an External World," Moore then argues that the physical bodies accepted by common sense are "external," i.e., metaphysically independent from all human minds. It is on this basis that he offers his proof that there is an *anthropically* "external" world. (It may come as a shock that Moore does not in that paper so much as address the traditional skeptical concern, for which it does not matter

[1] My reference is to Moore's paper "A Defence of Common Sense," where he defends a robust common sense realism against the idealism then dominant in British philosophy.

Epistemic Explanations: A Theory of Telic Normativity, and What it Explains. Ernest Sosa, Oxford University Press (2021). © Ernest Sosa. DOI:10.1093/oso/9780198856467.003.0011

whether the world external to the subject is (a) anthropically constructed or (b) "external" even relative to humanity at large. Regardless of whether such a world is of sort (a) or sort (b), the traditional skeptic will worry equally whether he can justify belief in its existence on a basis provided by what is given to *his own subjective experience*. In his article, Moore is hence *obviously* not directly concerned with traditional skepticism!)

2. Contained in basic common sense are hence general propositions like the following:

> M1. There are and have been physical, spatially related bodies.
> M2. Some of these are living bodies.
> M3. Among these are people.
> M4. People perceive things and observe facts.
> M5. People are also aware of unobserved facts.
> M6. People know these things.

Having postulated such known truisms definitory of common sense and beyond reasonable doubt, Moore leaves room aplenty for philosophical action. For one thing, the analytic philosopher can provide an analysis of these known facts, of how they are metaphysically constituted. That is a task for analytic metaphysics. For a second thing, we can try to understand just *how* we know these things that we take ourselves so obviously to know. This is a task for epistemology. And the two tasks may intertwine.

In the course of his long career, Moore tries to carry out the epistemological task, in repeated attempts that culminate in his papers "Certainty" and "Four Forms of Skepticism." These adopt a form of indirect realism, according to which we know about external, mind-independent objects through inductive or analogical inference from what we know immediately. As far as contingent reality goes, what we know immediately seems limited to knowledge restrictedly about ourselves, including knowledge of our own sense experiences. Knowledge of perceived physical objects and of other minds is inferential, based on a hierarchy of reasons that bottoms out in what we know immediately. Even the knowledge that one is awake and not just dreaming is based on reasons constituted by our concurrent and recent experiences; for Moore, these reasons can be *conclusive* even if *we cannot list them fully*, which would be required for a *proof* effective against the skeptic. (A "proof" for Moore has to be something you could "give" to someone, at least to yourself, which would require a listing of the premises.)

3. What about our "core components of Common Sense," the propositions that according to Moore constitute basic theses of our ordinary view concerning the world and our place in it?

> Would the core certainties of common sense also acquire their status on a foundation of reasons known immediately?

They would indeed, or so we can plausibly infer from the concluding paragraphs of "Four Forms of Skepticism."

Much earlier, in "Hume's Philosophy," Moore already tackles our above question directly, and concludes with a related question:

> Must we admit a class of propositions that assert "matters of fact" and are known to be true "...neither by direct observation nor by memory, nor yet as a result of previous observations"?

In that 1909 paper he remains agnostic. He says only that there "may" be such propositions.

By the time of his "Defence of Common Sense" in 1925, Moore is ready to say more. About his core components of Common Sense, he now asserts that

> in the case of most of them, I do not know them *directly*: that is to say, I know them only because, in the past, I have known to be true *other* propositions which were evidence for them.

This appears to be his final view on the epistemic status of core components of common sense. No deviation from it is discernible in his later work.

4. That sums up Moore's Common Sense philosophy, as laid out in a paper thought by Wittgenstein to be Moore's best, one that stimulated his own *On Certainty*. In that book Wittgenstein repudiates Moore's epistemology and offers a radically different alternative. I will here present the gist of that alternative, and invite the reader to compare this gist with supportive passages gathered in the Appendix to this chapter.

B. Wittgenstein's *On Certainty*

1. Wittgenstein juggles many issues in *On Certainty*. He is concerned with language games, with pragmatics of language use, with dialectical interplay, with what it is proper to *say* to someone, with the effects of context on all this. Whether we agree with his pre-Gricean take on such issues, much in his text is detachable from that. Much concerns just belief, knowledge, and certainty, regardless of how this may or may not relate to language use and dialectical context. Moore, for his part, in his relevant epistemology is largely unconcerned with such dialectical, linguistic, and contextual issues (whatever may be true of his thoughts on Moore's paradox). In what follows I too will abstract almost wholly from them, while remaining neutral on their substance and on their relation to our more purely epistemological issues. Here then is how I see the position that Wittgenstein lays out in opposition to Moore. It contains four theses.

W1. We do not learn the core components of common sense through ratiocination or evidence. Rather we "acquire" them as part of a coherent system: "light dawns gradually on the whole."

W2. We do not strictly *know* these components. Rather they "stand fast" for us, and it is upon such a riverbed that our retail beliefs flow; it is by turning on such hinges that doors open to our retail knowledge.

W3. Core beliefs of common sense generally require no conscious assent. Many are manifest rather in how we act.

W4. We can grasp the core propositions that give content to such beliefs only through believing enough of them (along with other related propositions with which they form one's individual system of beliefs). We might doubt any one of them, but we could not possibly doubt them all (and retain our grasp).

Wittgenstein thus rejects Moore's view that we know core components of common sense on the rational basis of other things we know or have known. In fact we *know* no such components, nor of course do we learn them based on evidence grasped through other beliefs already in place.

2. Wittgenstein seems misled by his focus on language games and dialectical linguistic interplay into affirming that we *do believe* but *do not know* core components of common sense.[2] Even if he were right about that, moreover, the following question would still remain: If a set of core commitments "stand fast" for a community in a way similar to the way our set of common-sense core commitments stand fast for us, is that enough to render the beliefs of that community epistemically proper, and indeed to make them knowledge (at least modulo Gettier issues)? Does the community's sheer adherence suffice to make it true that their interlocking system of beliefs has core components that "stand fast" while the rest constitute knowledge?

3. Wittgenstein notoriously took a dim view of philosophical "theorizing." So, in keeping with that attitude he may simply have rejected the search for a philosophical explanation of how our common-sense knowledge might come about. If so, his project would diverge fundamentally from ours in this book. But we may still be able to draw insight from his reflections.

Among the things that philosophy ponders are some I would put as follows:

> What sort of thing *is* such knowledge, and how *might* it come about? Can we answer this question so as to enable understanding of how we *might* have as much of it as we do? Might we even explain with philosophical generality how we *do* have as much of it as we do?

[2] Indeed, Moore makes some of the relevant points in a letter to Norman Malcolm just prior to the conversations between Malcolm and Wittgenstein that led to *On Certainty*. See T. Baldwin (ed.), *G. E. Moore: Selected Writings* (Routledge, 1993), pp. 213–16. The letter is dated June 28, 1949. Wittgenstein visited Malcolm from July to October of that year, and their conversations inspired Wittgenstein's work until his death some two years later.

Even if it is as obvious as it is to Moore that we do enjoy such knowledge, the question remains as to just how in general it comes about. Moore's answer to this philosophical question is his foundationalist indirect realism in terms of immediate knowledge, inferential knowledge, and so on.[3]

4. Wittgenstein may think he can avoid our philosophical question by denying that we really know all the things that Moore thinks we know. Some things we know are said to be based not on things we know but rather on things that "stand fast" for us. The thought seems to be that if we are to grasp the relevant propositions, then enough of the things that stand fast for us must so stand. Given their understanding-endowing status, such propositions "stand fast" for us rather than being things we "know."

In fact Wittgenstein *seems* to adopt a wildly implausible stance. Does everything that "stands fast" for us do so justifiably, with proper epistemic standing, so that, for example, it can serve as a proper basis for *knowledge*, for the knowledge that, according to Wittgenstein himself, does gain proper support from such fast-standing beliefs?

Also implausibly, Wittgenstein appears to reject Moore's realism, the view that there is an "external" world of facts independent of human minds, including facts accepted at the core of common sense.

Possibly Wittgenstein adopts the anti-modal animus that long infected broad swaths of analytic philosophy, including not just the radical positivists but also the descendants led by Quine and his many followers. With the rejection of modality would come a rejection of any such thing as an "external" world knowing which might be a philosophical worry. On this approach Moore is just wasting his time with his painstaking (and painsgiving) intuition-based minute detailing of what "externality" might involve, which leads him to conclude that "externality is independence." Without modality it is unclear what any such independence might amount to, and so Wittgenstein may be led to reject any such metaphysical framework for philosophical explanation.

[3] That is the *sort* of answer that according to Sellars is to be found in perennial philosophy's treatment of the manifest image.

C. What Alternative Might Be Available?

1. If we find no plausibility in *such* positivism, if we have moved beyond that desert landscape, we might explore rather a response that agrees with Moore both that we do *know* the core components of common sense, and that these, along with much of what any of us knows, pertain to an *objective reality* independent of the mind of any one thinker, and even of human minds altogether.

Given this twofold stance, we must still face with Moore the question of how we manage to know the core components of common sense that we seem so obviously to know, indeed with certainty, just as Moore asserts.

2. The best answer that might then be extractable from *On Certainty*, even with some strain, is relativistic, either to one's culture or to one's humanity. But consider again our questions:

> How do we know the core components of common sense? Why are such beliefs so much as rationally, epistemically justified?

Cultural consensus is insufficient for knowledge, since, for one thing, it is compatible with falsity. And even *truths* consensually accepted within a whole culture need not constitute knowledge, if the way these truths attract agreement is no better than the way falsehoods get consensually installed. That would make the culture's access to such truths a matter of epistemic luck incompatible with true knowledge.

3. Relativism seems thus uninviting, at least initially. Alternatively, shall we invoke evolutionary or other genetic theory? Can we thus support the view that human consensual agreement upgrades to knowledge through our genesis, which guarantees reliable human faculties? Not clearly, for more than one reason.

For one thing, it is not clear to what extent and with what scope evolution can be seen to ensure epistemic success. Even if it does yield considerable success, it would seem guaranteed only within limits set by what our species needs for its fitness and survival as a species.

4. We have ostensibly learned a lesson in two parts.

Part 1. Moore is right to defend his Common Sense, including its core component beliefs, but he is wrong to force our knowledge into the foundationalist framework of the tradition, with its immediate evidence epistemically supporting our body of beliefs.[4]

Part 2. Wittgenstein is right to reject the Moorean epistemology of indirect realism, and to offer an alternative picture of how our body of beliefs comes to be and hangs together.

What is wrong with traditional foundationalism is the myth of the given, of presentational mental states that supposedly yield justification *just* through their intrinsic character. There are two problems for this: first, the Speckled Hen problem; second, the apparent fact that we do not infer or base all the core components of our common-sense picture on such states. Our belief system falls into place as a whole in such a way that the epistemic standing of its core components does not derive wholly through "ratiocination" (rational basing), from some foundation of such self-presenting, given states.

Compatibly, the child's evolving system is visibly interlocking already as light dawns gradually on it. The system contains general as well as particular beliefs, present observational beliefs included, as well as beliefs once observational and now stored in memory. Vast systems of folk physics and folk psychology are also included. And there is of course much mutual support, including much that crosses the generality lines. However, the epistemic standing of the whole cannot possibly derive *merely* from such mutual support. Nor does it plausibly derive from such interlocking coherence *together with* the external, animal

[4] How is this traditional epistemology related to a Platonic–Cartesian dualism, for which we are embodied souls? On that view we are pilots in a ship that must be steered from within based just on the deliverances of certain screens or loudspeakers (or the like, if we think metaphorically of the "screens" and the "loudspeakers"), where we have no reason to take these deliverances at face value, but must work out the extent to which they deserve our trust. We must hence rely on our reason to infer from our auditory and visual data to the reality outside the ship. Once we see ourselves as essentially embodied human beings, this may free us more plausibly to include in our basic endowment the innate knowledge constitutive of our ability to act on our environment. Souls too, after all, need inbuilt knowledge constitutive of their intuitive and deductive reason, of their ability to act intellectually. (Descartes does of course explicitly deny that his soul's embodiment fits the model of a pilot in his ship; but it is quite a mystery how he avoids this, and indeed how causal interaction can take place between two *substances* across his seemingly bridgeless metaphysical chasm.)

competence of the *particular* beliefs, the present observational ones and those stored in memory from earlier observation. When one first believes that *here is something red and round*, that belief derives from the exercise of competence to discern colors and shapes. Such competence is tantamount to implicit beliefs (or commitments) of the form: *if it looks red (round) then it is (likely) red (round)*. And these must themselves have proper standing if they are to play their justifying role. But this standing cannot have derived merely through blatantly bootstrapping induction from corresponding particular beliefs. A human developmental competence is thus plausibly involved in the acquisition of such perceptual abilities that come paired with corresponding implicit general beliefs (or commitments).[5]

5. Wittgenstein seems alive to such insights. Unfortunately, he does not so much as address the sort of philosophical question that drives Moore to his traditional, foundationalist stance.

D. Exploring an Alternative

1. The foregoing yields the following desiderata:

   a. Joining Moore in defending realist common sense.
   b. Joining Wittgenstein in rejecting Moore's traditional epistemology of indirect, foundationalist realism.
   c. Seeking to explain how we can possibly know the things that according to plain common sense we do know, including the core components listed by Moore.
   d. Rejecting the sort of answer to that very general philosophical question that we have tentatively attributed to Wittgenstein's *On Certainty*.

[5] The general standing belief might plausibly have as its content that if things seem perceptually to be thus and so, they *tend to be* or *habitually are* thus and so. This belief might be either innate or installed through subpersonal mechanisms in the normal development of the child. Once installed, moreover, it would then be applied through a kind of logical reasoning to specific situations again and again. If we view the matter thus, then the specific commitments (that here now, for example, if things look thus and so then they are thus and so) would be reason-based after all, with the general-tendency-belief furnishing the reason applied to the specific instances.

e. Rejecting also any appeal to the actual origins of humans, with our cultures and belief systems, as essential to the current epistemic status of the beliefs in such systems. Believers could conceivably have come into being accidentally, eventually becoming rational believers and indeed sophisticated knowers nonetheless.

2. Wittgenstein observes that the developing child "acquires" his belief system without the explicit instruction that would make such acquisition a case of *learning*. Few if any children are ever explicitly told that "there is a world of physical bodies in three dimensions, etc." Nor is the system plausibly learned through inference from particular observations. The child learns rather to interact effectively with such a world, and his "beliefs" are just manifest in his behavior the way deep prejudice is so often manifest in behavior towards people perceived as members of a target group. In neither case need there be conscious formulation of belief contents. Such beliefs can remain implicit, and might even be denied if brought to consciousness.

3. What sort of competence is manifest in the child's development of that evolving system of common-sense belief? One sort of competence is the holist reasoning competence that keeps things coherent. But is only that sort of competence required? Beliefs could develop for years through the rare and imaginatively coherent thinking of an obsessive paranoid. Shall we then say that, in addition to his competent rational coherence, the evolving thinker needs also perceptual and mnemonic competences, along with the social competence that enables sensitive reception of good testimony? Yes, surely, but now we must ask: Is this a sequential process, temporally or at least logically, whereby the thinker first acquires lots of specific data, from which eventually he generalizes to his common-sense general principles? It is unclear how we could even understand coherence without principles already in place, and unclear how particular beliefs could have proper standing without the benefit of even minimal coherence.

That being so, it remains to be seen how the competence that leads to the general principles can be constituted by pure perception, memory, reception of testimony, or introspection, individually or in any combination, if *unaided by general beliefs*. General beliefs (or commitments) are needed from the start. And in order for them to play their proper epistemic role, they must have been competently acquired. But *this* competence, involved in the initial acquisition of those beliefs, cannot be explained *just* in terms of inference from specific, particular data already in place.

Some such general beliefs must hence have a source beyond inference from antecedent data. The operation of that source is hence not just a matter of rational basing. Nor is it a matter of sensory experience directly supporting principle after principle seriatim. As Wittgenstein suggests, such a body of core beliefs is more plausibly *illuminated as a whole by the dawning light*. True, such core beliefs are acquired together with many specific details about the particulars of the young thinker's life, and together with the many sense experiences that help constitute that thinker's perception of his environment, and with the effects of such experiences through perception or memory.

Such clusters of belief are plausibly required for understanding of the propositions believed, just as Wittgenstein suggests. True, any one of them is dispensable without loss of understanding. But some critical mass must remain if the understanding is also to remain.

So far I have tried to sketch one sort of concern that may have detained Wittgenstein about Moore's foundationalist view. The key metaphor is that of the dawning light, which illuminates how the child's view gradually develops, a view connected by Wittgenstein functionally with the child's evolving conduct.

Nevertheless, I see in none of this any sufficient reason to deny that understanding-constitutive beliefs can amount to knowledge. Nor do I see why we should deny that the propositions understood can correspond to a world of facts metaphysically independent of the thinker who understands, and even of human thinkers altogether.

4. We could perhaps see Moorean beliefs constitutive of common sense as understanding-related in two ways. First, none requires a *reason* that surpasses the sheer understanding of its content. Their epistemology need not be rational in *that* way. Second, each may be part of a cluster, understanding of whose members requires belief in a critical mass of them. Thus, understanding is in each case internally connected with a tendency towards acceptance.

Perhaps then their epistemic standing does not require "ratiocination," to put it as does Wittgenstein. But what then *does* it require? What accounts for the epistemic standing of any such Moorean cluster?

5. Even given all of the above, we thus still face our unresolved issue. How do such general core components of common sense become knowledge? Suppose that, unlike Wittgenstein, we take up this question without commitment to relativism, while, unlike Moore, we eschew traditional foundationalist indirect realism, but still hold to an objective realism of common sense. How then do we so much as sketch an answer to our general philosophical question?

We must first recognize a source that goes (or sources that go) beyond perception, introspection, testimony, and inference, whether deductive or inductive, and indeed beyond rational basing generally. Some things we know are not known in any of those ways. Simple arithmetic, geometry, and logic provide examples aplenty. In such cases, we know something that we believe or are inclined to believe with no rational basis beyond our understanding of the question.

As we have seen, however, irrational biases and superstitions can share that feature with our simple beliefs of math or logic. So, not all intuitive beliefs are acceptable as ipso facto rationally competent. Only by deriving from a competence does such a belief or seeming constitute a rationally competent intuition. Simple beliefs of math or logic qualify. These are rationally competent even independently of any rational basis that they may have. Biases and superstitions imbibed arationally do not qualify. These are not only arational but also irrational. An intuition is rationally competent only when it manifests competence.

6. The sort of indirect realism favored by Moore, a kind of traditional foundationalism of the given, was said near the outset to be defensible as an account of a positive epistemic status that the beliefs of knowers can share with the beliefs of victims in skeptical scenarios. But that status was said to fall short of the fuller epistemic competence involved in our knowledge of contingent facts, particular and general. We are now, I believe, in a position to pose a more serious problem for such internalism.

Suppose Moore is right that we know with certainty the propositions constitutive of our general picture of our contingent world. And suppose Wittgenstein is right that we neither acquire nor sustain that picture through ratiocinative learning. The epistemology of given evidence plus inductive inference does not explain our basic, general commonsense knowledge. Where do we turn for a better alternative?

E. A Better Alternative

1. We have drawn from Moore and Wittgenstein some hints for understanding our epistemic justification: What for example distinguishes intuitions that are epistemically justified from those that are not? The answer, we reasoned, may not be far to seek once we recall that even the presentational given can provide justification only through the subject's relevant competence. Perhaps we need only invoke a competence that is not reason-based, one that sub-personally enables reliable discernment of the true from the false in the relevant class of beliefs. This competence would yield seemings, attractions to assent, even those that prove illusory as in the sorites paradox. Paradox-enmeshed seemings might still be competent so long as they derive from a normal human competence. In this regard they might be analogous to the perceptual seemings of the child who first encounters a Müller–Lyer setup. But what is it that distinguishes seemings that are competent from those that are not?

Why not posit the epistemic efficacy of *all* seemings, adopting thereby a latitudinarianism of seemings even beyond the intuitive? In my view this is plausible only through confusion of sensory experiences with perceptual seemings. Once having confused these, one might then extend to all seemings an epistemic standing that plausibly belongs only to sensory experiences and not to perceptual seemings. Even with my eyes closed, deprived of visual experience, it just might seem to me (intellectually) that I face something red and round. I might just feel that to be so "in my bones." Is such a seeming still ipso facto justified? Does it even prima facie justify the corresponding belief? Not plausibly. But the same would then seemingly apply to seemings generally. It is not their sheer existence that renders them justified, foundationally so. It is rather something about them, even if it remains to be seen what this might be.

Take the case of a perceptual seeming. What renders such a seeming justified, foundationally so? Its reflecting a concurrent experience with the same content, it might be thought, at least in part. That is part *at most* of the explanation, however; in addition, as we have seen, the subject must not exceed subitizing limits. What figures more importantly at the basis of foundational justification is, hence, I submit, competence, the sort of competence involved in the subject's ability to subitize.

It might be argued to the contrary that what is important is the *involuntary* character of seemings. Is it not rather this that puts them beyond relevant rational justification and unjustification? Not so: plenty of beliefs are similarly involuntary without being insulated from rational assessment. Seemings, attractions to *assent*, are concept-involving, just as are beliefs. One cannot be thus attracted to what one does not understand, but understanding requires concepts. Why should seemings be exempt from rational assessment, if beliefs are never so exempt?

The bottom line is that internalists have no good recourse to mere seemings in order to explain how it is that we are internally justified epistemically in the component beliefs of our common-sense picture, beliefs acquired and sustained without ratiocination.

2. "Too bad," some might say, some *do* say. Skepticism is then the upshot. What *would* be required for knowledge of our common-sense picture? For the skeptic what would be required *is* still that it be soundly inferred from the given, from the particular self-presenting experiences undergone by the subject. To the extent that Wittgenstein and others make it plausible that this is not what happens in human life, to that extent must we then grant that humans just do not know what they take themselves perhaps too readily to know.

But why? Why insist that the only way to know is through inductive inference from the presentational given? "For one thing," it might be replied, "only thus could we hope to *understand* how we do know what we know. What other explanation could there be?" We find ourselves believing in a world of physical objects, some of them live human bodies, etc., and believing that we ourselves have been alive in such a world for a long time, and so on, for a vast set of propositions constitutive of one's common-sense picture. How can we possibly understand our knowledge of those things if not in the terms of "inference from the given"?

Well, hold on: Given our need to appeal to competence, to subitizing competence, and given the place of competence in understanding basic knowledge of logic, arithmetic, and geometry, our understanding of how we know seems limited *in any case*. How well do we really understand the variation among humans in their subitizing abilities, or the theoretical basis for such abilities? Besides, we also vary vastly in our powers of mathematical intuition. As far as I know, we have no good account of how it is that Ramanujan was able to excel so far beyond the rest of humanity. None of this, however, holds us back from attributing to ourselves the knowledge that we enjoy either foundationally through such intuition (within the bounds of one's individual endowment) or inferentially based on such foundations.

At several crucial junctures, then, the vaunted explanation of our knowledge, on the basis of inference from the given, is limited by our need to attribute a competence of which we have only slim understanding. Once again, it is the appeal to competence that seems crucial, even while we still hope to gain fuller understanding of the workings of such postulated competence.

3. Note, finally, that *epistemic competences can be of use in epistemology even in the absence of a detailed theory of their nature and operation.* We can appeal to such competences in epistemology even with limited understanding of their modus operandi.[6] This in fact applies not only to rational intuition but also to introspection and even to perception and memory. Up to a point, people could surely know how they knew things even before we gained our fuller understanding of how perception actually works, in its various modalities. Our knowledge through various perceptual sources is of course enhanced with our improved understanding of their nature and operation, but this boost of meta-sophistication is not essentially required. It is not required for animal

[6] This is defended in my "Minimal Intuition," in *Rethinking Intuition: The Psychology of Intuition and Its Role in Philosophical Inquiry*, ed. Michael R. DePaul and William Ramsey (Rowman & Littlefield, 1999).

knowledge through such competences. Nor is it required for some measure of reflective knowledge, even through limited understanding of the operative competences.

F. Why We Need to Go beyond *both* Moore *and* Wittgenstein

1. Let's go back to the Matrixing intergalactic interlopers of Chapter 7, and their lottery to determine whether Earthians are all to be Matrixed. To me it remains plausible that if we are lucky enough to win their lottery, whereupon they move on to remote galaxies never to be near us again, then their visit is *epistemically inconsequential for humanity at large*. This despite the fact that post-lottery we would be getting it right just by luck, and despite the fact that just prior to the lottery all of our predictions and even our specious-present beliefs and judgments would run monumental risk, and would be nearly certain to be false.

2. But if that is correct, then even the enhanced view of *On Certainty* is unable to explain how it is that we can still be as unaffected as we seem to be by the interlopers' fleeting visit. Not even the world view of *On Certainty*, with its fast-standing beliefs will give us the desired explanation. None of that can explain how it is that we can still predict knowledgeably at the moment of the lottery, nor how it is that we can retain our background knowledge once we luck out so monumentally and carry on with our lives undisturbed epistemically.

3. We must go beyond beliefs for the desired account. No matter how steadfastly our framework beliefs may stand through the occasion of the lottery, that will not give us the desired explanation. Why not? Because *beliefs* do not acquire the required status by just standing fast, if their likelihood of being true drops precipitously to approach zero, as their likelihood of being false approaches infinity. That is why the desired explanation requires not background beliefs but background assumptions, and that is why we should welcome the route provided by virtue epistemology to the plausibility of such assumptions.[7] Our normal human epistemic flourishing requires not just fast-standing human belief systems acquired sans ratiocination. It requires also fast-standing *assumptions* that incur no relevant epistemic negligence or recklessness, as they block inappropriate skeptical concerns.

[7] Consider entry 411 of *On Certainty* (reproduced in this chapter's Appendix), which may suggest some awareness that *assumption* has an epistemic role to play. But such possible awareness, if it is there at all, is not given its proper development and scope. (Compare our section on barn-spotting—Chapter 7—for what would seem to be required.)

APPENDIX

Moore and Wittgenstein on Knowledge and Common Sense

This appendix consists of selections from Moore's "Defense of Common Sense" and Wittgenstein's *On Certainty.*

1. At the outset of his paper Moore writes:

> (1) I begin, then, with my list of truisms, every one of which (in my own opinion) I know, with certainty, to be true. The propositions to be included in this list are the following:
>
> There exists at present a living human body, which is my body. This body was born at a certain time in the past, and has existed continuously ever since...; and, at every moment since it was born, there have also existed many other things, having shape and size .... Among the things which have, in this sense, formed part of its environment (i.e. have been either in contact with it, or at some distance from it, however great) there have, at every moment since its birth, been... other living human bodies, each of which has, like it, (a) at some time been born, (b) continued to exist from some time after birth, ... Finally (to come to a different class of propositions), I am a human being, and I have, at different times since my body was born, had many different experiences, of each of many different kinds: e.g. I have often perceived both my own body and other things which formed part of its environment, including other human bodies; I have not only perceived things of this kind, but have also observed facts about them...; I have been aware of other facts, which I was not at the time observing, such as, for instance, the fact, of which I am now aware, that my body existed yesterday...; I have had expectations with regard to the future, and many beliefs of other kinds, both true and false; I have thought of imaginary things and persons and incidents, in the reality of which I did not believe; I have had dreams; and I have had feelings of many different kinds. And, just as my body has been the body of a human being, namely myself, who has, during his lifetime, had many experiences of each of these (and other) different kinds; so, in the case of very many of the other human bodies which have lived upon the earth, each has been the body of a different human being, who has, during the lifetime of that body, had many different experiences of each of these (and other) different kinds.

And he adds the following, as a second important sort of proposition, also part of common sense, (2) that he also knows with certainty: that many other people have known about themselves and their bodies propositions corresponding to the ones that according to (1) above Moore knows with certainty about himself and his own body.

2. Wittgenstein's book is an extended reply to Moore, and includes the following:

> 94.... I did not get my picture of the world by satisfying myself of its correctness; nor do I have it because I am satisfied of its correctness. No: it is the inherited background against which I distinguish between true and false.
> [...]
> 100. The truths which Moore says he knows, are such as, roughly speaking, all of us know, if he knows them.
> 101. Such a proposition might be e.g. "My body has never disappeared and reappeared again after an interval."
> [...]
> 116. Instead of "I know...", couldn't Moore have said: "It stands fast for me that..."? And further: "It stands fast for me and many others..."
> [...]
> 136. When Moore says he knows such and such, he is really enumerating a lot of empirical propositions which we affirm without special testing; propositions, that is, which have a peculiar logical role in the system of our empirical propositions.
> [...]
> 138. We don't, for example, arrive at any of them as a result of investigation...
> [...]
> 141. When we first begin to believe anything, what we believe is not a single proposition, it is a whole system of propositions. (Light dawns gradually over the whole.)
> 142. It is not single axioms that strike me as obvious, it is a system in which consequences and premises give one another mutual support.
> [...]
> 144. The child learns to believe a host of things. I.e. it learns to act according to these beliefs. Bit by bit there forms a system of what is believed, and in that system some things stand unshakeably fast and some are more or less liable to shift. What stands fast does so, not because it is intrinsically obvious or convincing; it is rather held fast by what lies around

it.

[...]

151. I should like to say: Moore does not know what he asserts he knows, but it stands fast for him, as also for me; regarding it as absolutely solid is part of our method of doubt and enquiry.

[...]

192. To be sure there is justification; but justification comes to an end.

[...]

225. What I hold fast to is not one proposition but a nest of propositions.

[...]

232. "We could doubt every single one of these facts, but we could not doubt them all." Wouldn't it be more correct to say: "we do not doubt them all". Our not doubting them all is simply our manner of judging, and therefore of acting.

[...].

253. At the foundation of well-founded belief lies belief that is not founded.

[...]

273. ... There are countless general empirical propositions that count as certain for us.

274. ... Experience can be said to teach us these propositions. However, it does not teach us them in isolation: rather, it teaches us a host of interdependent propositions. If they were isolated I might perhaps doubt them, for I have no experience relating to them.

275. If experience is the ground of our certainty, then naturally it is past experience. And it isn't for example just my experience, but other people's, that I get knowledge from.

[...]

279. ... This system is something that a human being acquires by means of observation and instruction. I intentionally do not say "learns".

[...]

287. The squirrel does not infer by induction that it is going to need stores next winter as well. And no more do we need a law of induction to justify our actions or our predictions.

[...]

358. Now I would like to regard this certainty, not as something akin to hastiness or superficiality, but as a form of life... .

359. But that means I want to conceive it as something that lies beyond being justified or unjustified; as it were, as something animal.

[...]

401. I want to say: propositions of the form of empirical propositions, and not only propositions of logic, form the foundation of all operating with thoughts (with language)... .

[...]

410. Our knowledge forms an enormous system. And only within this system has a particular bit the value we give it.

411. If I say "we assume that the earth has existed for many years past" (or something similar), then of course it sounds strange that we should assume such a thing. But in the entire system of our language-games it belongs to the foundations. The assumption, one might say, forms the basis of action, and therefore, naturally, of thought.

[...]

475. I want to regard man here as an animal; as a primitive being to which one grants instinct but not ratiocination. As a creature in a primitive state. Any logic good enough for a primitive means of communication needs no apology from us. Language did not emerge from some kind of ratiocination...

[...]

538. The child... Learns to react in such-and-such a way; and in so reacting it doesn't so far know anything. Knowing only begins at a later level.

Bibliography

Burge, T. (2003). "Perceptual Entitlement." *Philosophy and Phenomenological Research*, 67 (3): 503–548.

Casullo, A., and J. Thurow (2013). *The A Priori in Philosophy*. Oxford: Oxford University Press.

Clifford, W. K. (1877). "The Ethics of Belief," *Contemporary Review*. Reprinted in Madigan (1999).

Colaço, D., W. Buckwalter, S. Stich, and E. Machery (2014). "Epistemic Intuitions in Fake-barn Thought Experiments." *Episteme*, 11 (2): 199–212.

Conee, E., and R. Feldman (2004). *Evidentialism: Essays in Epistemology*. Oxford: Oxford University Press.

Dretske, F. (2000). "Entitlement: Epistemic Rights without Epistemic Duties?" *Philosophy and Phenomenological Research*, 60 (3): 591–606.

Friedman, J. (2017). "Why Suspend Judging." *Nous*, 51 (2): 302–326.

Friedman, J. (2019). "Inquiry and Belief." *Nous*, 53 (2): 296–315.

Graham, P.J. (2012). "Epistemic Entitlement," *Nous*, 46 (3): 449–482.

Greco, J. (2010). *Achieving Knowledge*. Cambridge, UK: Cambridge University Press.

McGrath, M. (forthcoming). "Being Neutral: Agnosticism, Inquiry and the Suspension of Judgment," *Nous*.

McCain, K. (2014). *Evidentialism and Epistemic Justification*. New York: Routledge.

Madigan, T. ed., (1999). *The Ethics of Belief and Other Essays*. Amherst, MA: Prometheus Books.

Moore, G. E. (1925). "A Defence of Common Sense," in J.H. Muirhead (ed.), *Contemporary British Philosophy* (2nd series), Allen and Unwin, London, 193–223.

Peacocke, C. (2004). *The Realm of Reason*. Oxford: Oxford University Press.

Sosa, E. (2007). *A Virtue Epistemology*. Oxford: Oxford University Press.

Sosa, E. (2009). *Reflective Knowledge*. Oxford: Oxford University Press.

Sosa, E. (2013). "Intuitions and Foundations: The Relevance of Moore and Wittgenstein," in Casullo A. and J. C. Thurow (eds.) *The A Priori in Philosophy*. Oxford: Oxford University Press, 186–205.

Sosa, E. (2015). *Judgment and Agency*. Oxford: Oxford University Press.

Sosa, E. (2017). *Epistemology*. Princeton, NJ: Princeton University Press.

Steup, M., and J. J. Ichikawa (2018). "The Analysis of Knowledge," *Stanford Encyclopedia of Philosophy*, <https://plato.stanford.edu/archives/sum2018/entries/knowledge-analysis/>.

Willard-Kyle, C. (forthcoming). "Being in a Position to Know Is the Norm of Assertion," *Pacific Philosophical Quarterly*.

Wright, C. (2004). "Warrant for Nothing (and Foundations for Free)?" *Aristotelian Society Supplementary Volume*, 78 (1):167–212.

Index

For the benefit of digital users, indexed terms that span two pages (e.g., 52–53) may, on occasion, appear on only one of those pages.

Printed and bound by CPI Group (UK) Ltd, Croydon, CR0 4YY

01/10/2024

01039752-0002